You
Don't
Need
a
Budget

You Don't Need a Budget

Stop Worrying about Debt,
Spend without Shame, and
Manage Money with Ease

Dana Miranda

LITTLE, BROWN **SPARK**

NEW YORK BOSTON LONDON

Little, Brown Spark
Hachette Book Group
1290 Avenue of the Americas, New York, NY 10104
littlebrownspark.com

First Edition: December 2024

Little, Brown Spark is an imprint of Little, Brown and Company, a division of Hachette Book Group, Inc. The Little, Brown Spark name and logo are trademarks of Hachette Book Group, Inc.

The publisher is not responsible for websites (or their content) that are not owned by the publisher.

The Hachette Speakers Bureau provides a wide range of authors for speaking events. To find out more, go to hachettespeakersbureau.com or email HachetteSpeakers@hbgusa.com.

Little, Brown and Company books may be purchased in bulk for business, educational, or promotional use. For information, please contact your local bookseller or the Hachette Book Group Special Markets Department at special.markets@hbgusa.com.

ISBN 978-0-316-56893-7

Library of Congress Control Number: 2024936048

Printing 1, 2024

LSC-C

Printed in the United States of America

For Emily

Contents

Contents

You
Don't
Need
a
Budget

I Was Sure I'd Hate
Personal Finance

In 2015 I was hired for my first professional job: a staff-writer position with a fast-growing digital media start-up. I was stunned at the opportunity. I'd been toiling away for almost five years as sort of a freelance writer, rarely securing stable work and barely cracking $12,000 a year in income from writing and occasional stints in food service. I'd stumbled into being positioned as an "expert" in making money writing, because I blogged about my experiences as a freelancer, a creative writer, and a self-publisher. But I never liked the role; it was pretty damning that I barely earned money doing the work I taught others to do. So I never fully embraced a niche, the way I learned from seemingly more successful writers I was supposed to do. After winding along a path of building something of a career, I applied for a full-time job that would take me away from my identity as a nomadic freelance writer. And to my surprise, they wanted me. I found myself entrusted with a bona fide job, offered a salary of $42,000 a year just to write.

The only drawback, I thought, was that I'd be writing about personal finance.

In all my twenty-nine years of life to that point, I'd avoided thinking or even caring about money. I was annoyed at how much of the advice about freelance writing centered on money when I was just trying to express my creativity. I couldn't be bothered to think about debt I'd accrued going to college or figure out the ratio of my income to my rent in cities like Madison, Wisconsin; Berkeley, California; and Seattle. I'd broached the idea of a spreadsheet budget in my early twenties, but it didn't stick, and I decided thinking about money was beneath my inflated sense of myself. My friends and I mocked our peers who found salaried jobs with big companies, calling them sellouts the way we imagined the 1960s hippies we admired would have done. I was a creative soul. Of all the jobs my writing path could have led me to, why did I have to end up in finance?

But I adored the editor who'd hired me, a former journalist whose blog about writing and solopreneurship I'd been following for five years, and the rest of the team she'd hired, many of whom were also bloggers in our orbit. The site's schtick was making personal finance fun and accessible for regular people, a growing trend it'd hopped on early in 2010. My voice was a fit for the site precisely because I knew nothing about money going into it, which would help me tell sympathetic stories and speak on the level with our readers in the lunch-with-your-best-friend tone popular with my fellow millennials (the target market du jour for digital media at the time). I committed, in my mind, to doing the job for a year even if I hated it, so I could get my feet under me in my career and maybe stand a chance of making a comfortable living.

I stayed for four years.

In that time, I did get my feet under me—and more. As employee number eight of what would balloon to more than a hundred by 2019, I morphed and grew as quickly as our media start-up, learning how to work with, and eventually manage, a team. I came to enjoy collaboration and to appreciate taking assignments, compared with the haphazard, muse-driven approach I'd always had in the past. I got a master class in my own personal finances, learning about our financial systems and best practices one assignment at a time. To my utter surprise, I came to love writing about money.

Before that job, I'd assumed, like many people I've met, that I was Bad with Money. I was raised in rural Wisconsin with a midwestern work ethic and little talk about money except the admonition to work hard, spend little, and avoid debt. Discipline was next to godliness in our conservative, white, working-class small-town culture, and that seemed to be the only approach to money management accessible to those of us who, as my parents said, "weren't born rich." My options were to embrace discipline or reject it; no middle way seemed to present itself. Comparing the culture around me to the freewheeling artists and thinkers I admired in books and movies, I deduced discipline was no fun.

My parents were among the cohort of baby boomers who'd graduated from high school in the late 1970s and early '80s and missed the booming economy we generally imagine their generation to have been gifted at birth. Culture writer Anne Helen Petersen mentions this group in *Can't Even: How Millennials Became the Burnout Generation*: "They were the first boomers to enter into the workplace after the 'miracle economy,' and understood, in some way, that they'd have to chart a different route than their parents toward middle-class security."[1]

Being part of the rural white working class, my parents were never yuppies, the college-educated coastal elites of the 1980s. But they still adopted their generation's approach to money: working hard, earning money, and gaining upward mobility. As Petersen writes, "Navigating a baseline nervousness about your class position, and struggling to find a job that will allow you to try and maintain it—that was the boomer's iteration of what we now know as burnout."

Like many millennial children of boomer parents, I absorbed my parents' anxiety about money, even if it was never spoken. I learned implicitly that my job as a kid was to work hard in school so I could go on to work hard in college and then get a job where I would work hard to earn a living. It wasn't greed; it was reality. I was never taught to imagine myself rich, but if I were responsible and hardworking enough, I could be a little more comfortable than my parents had been. I might prefer to lose myself in my journal all day, but that simply wasn't practical. I'd need a job, and with my potential, it ought to be a job that paid well. This was what being Good with Money looked like to me as I entered adulthood—and it didn't appeal to me. I rejected discipline and any notion of financial security in favor of that oft-disdained millennial pursuit: following my passion. I chose to enjoy my life, promptly dropping any notions of financial well-being I might have held.

In my early twenties as an aspiring iconoclast, I went in and out of college and accumulated student loans. I worked in fun coffee shops for hourly wages and tips, instead of committing to a full-time job that would deplete my soul in exchange for a salary and a 401(k). I lived paycheck to paycheck, splurging when I had money and restricting when I didn't. I was thrifty and minimalist in general but spent every free dollar on drink deals. I paid 11 percent interest (that's high) on a seven-year loan (that's long) for an $8,000 used car. I paid the maximum security deposit to move into new apartments. My disciplined roots could only keep me away from credit card debt for a few years. By the time I turned twenty-five, I was living in my first real city, and finally gave in to the urge to fill my youth with concerts, drinks, restaurants, trips, and socializing. I maxed out a $6,000 credit limit before closing the card. I believed being Good with Money meant settling for a boring job and forgoing all luxury or excitement until retirement, and I didn't want that experience. The other option seemed to be to throw it all out the window, bury my head in the sand, and hope for the best. For years, I chose option B (Broke).

When you're "not born rich," you accept the narrative that financial products and services aren't made for you. Neither my parents nor anyone we knew watched CNBC or talked about mutual funds. They contributed a sensible amount to the company 401(k), if it was offered, or counted on a union pension. They might use a favorite store credit card for the points but otherwise avoided non-mortgage debt. A local CPA did everyone's taxes for a small fee, but she wasn't advising on "tax efficiency" strategies for moving wealth around. I never even heard the term *financial planner* until I was in my twenties. I got student loans to pay for college because the FAFSA was one of the steps included in the college prep that high school guidance counselors led us through. I don't remember anyone asking how I intended to pay for college; borrowing money was just the way we did it. And I'm certain no one ever talked about repaying the loans; few of the adults in my life had gone to college, so I imagine it didn't occur to anyone what it would look like for our generation to shoulder monthly loan payments in adulthood.

I had to calculate hourly wages and paychecks to make sure I could pay my portion of rent each month, but otherwise I didn't do any kind of personal financial planning or money management until I was twenty-eight, almost four years after I'd left college for the last time. A kind woman from my alma mater's financial aid office called to let me know my student loans were in default (i.e., very overdue) and to walk me through my options for repayment. She helped me apply for a Direct Consolidation Loan and then income-driven repayment, so I could pull my loans out of default status without the burden of a monthly payment that was out of whack with my resources. I was relieved to know my loans were on the up-and-up, but I still didn't consider the rest of my financial situation. I was ignoring calls from unknown numbers, presuming they were debt collectors. I didn't know my credit score, how to find it, or why it mattered. I didn't have a credit card anymore, but I'd learned how to use debit cards strategically to float by with a tight cash flow on my sporadic and sparse income (this was when those transactions would take a few days to settle with the bank, so you'd have a little wiggle room around purchases).

Getting that full-time job with the personal finance site immediately changed my relationship with money. I was earning a solid living—with a salary! And benefits!—and yet I was doing creative work I loved for scrappy and passionate bosses. This wasn't the life-draining work I'd believed I'd have to settle for if I wanted financial stability. Plus, we wrote about personal finance in a way that was about more than discipline. This wasn't boring and stodgy; it was . . . interesting. I was fascinated with the ins and outs of financial products like bank accounts, student loans, and rewards credit cards. I wasn't excited because they presented me with the prospect of becoming (or at least feeling) rich, which was the implicit promise of so much competing personal finance advice. But I was excited to understand these products that had been so opaque, that had never been presented as *for me* before. Suddenly, it seemed, I could be Good with Money—without relying on discipline.

When I entered the personal finance industry in 2015, I was a veritable poster child for the millennial in need of an injection of *adulting*, the cute word my cohorts coined for coping with the crushing reality of coming of age into an historic economic recession. I quickly became comfortable being the dumbest person in the room, and I wasn't shy about asking stupid questions—all in the name of serving readers facing similar circumstances.

Around six months into the job, I joined our nascent editorial team for our daily stand-up to pitch stories. Someone had found a *Washington Post* article about a study out of the University of Michigan about "why poor people pay more for toilet paper," and we pondered covering the study ourselves.[2]

For the study, Professor Yesim Orhun and PhD student Mike Palazzolo analyzed panel data from more than a hundred thousand American households to track purchases of toilet paper over seven years. They chose this sundry because it's a reliable measure for spending across economic circumstances: toilet paper is nonperishable, and we consume it pretty consistently. We don't go without it just because we're strapped for cash, like we might go without new clothes or haircuts. And we don't buy more when we have extra money, like we might with food or entertainment.

The study found that people with less money pay more for toilet paper, because it's technically cheaper in bulk. When you have a cushion of money (i.e., your expenses won't drain your account before next payday), you buy the twenty-four-roll pack. But the twenty-four-pack costs more in the moment than the four-pack. When you have only enough in your pocket for the four-pack, and your bathroom needs toilet paper, you're not going to wait just because the math says the twenty-four-pack is the smarter choice. "Having more money gives people the luxury of paying less for things," as the *Washington Post* puts it.

I was excited to cover this study. We didn't talk about this phenomenon in personal finance, and I was delighted to see science behind the experience I'd had for years. I'd bought the four-roll pack. Honestly? Sometimes I'd bought single rolls of toilet paper at a corner store because I didn't have a car to get to the grocery store where I could buy the four-pack. And in my city apartment, I hadn't exactly had the ample storage space bulk buying requires. I wanted to plant a flag in the personal finance space for those of us who weren't doing all the right money things all the time.

My coworkers wanted a different tack, though. They thought the story should be about how to avoid spending more on toilet paper, even when you're broke. That's what we did in the personal finance industry.

"We could suggest using a credit card to buy in bulk, then paying off the balance with your next paycheck," one writer suggested.

"We can explain how to figure out when it's worth it to pay a little interest if it'll save you money in the long run."

"But what if you can't get a credit card?" I asked.

"What do you mean?"

I wasn't sure how to respond. What was missing from my question? I reworded it. "What if you don't qualify for a credit card, so you have to buy everything with cash?" Then, considering my own 520-something credit score, I added more bluntly, "People who can't afford twenty-five bucks for bulk toilet paper probably don't have a great credit score."

"Oh," she replied, with empathy but genuinely surprised. "You really think so?"

I scanned the circle for others to back me up, but their faces all registered surprise, too. No one else had thought of this possibility.

My coworkers weren't stupid or unsympathetic. They were brilliant thinkers who shared knowledge generously and made me smarter with gentle prodding and an eye for the questions readers would want answered. They were college-educated and experienced. They'd traveled to far reaches of the world and met diverse communities of people. They volunteered more than I did, donated to causes they cared about, got out the vote, and made fair-trade, eco-conscious choices whenever possible. We were the same in so many ways: ambitious women in our thirties obsessed with the written word and concerned with equality and the environment and other social causes. Until that day's stand-up, I hadn't noticed that I was different from all of them in one stark way: they'd all been raised in middle-class families.

What did it mean for our readers that the bulk of our advice came from a middle-class perspective? For that matter, what did it mean for the readers of almost every publication that a vast majority of journalists are white men from the middle class? The industry, I realized, isn't serving most people well.

How's Your Relationship with Money?

For most of our readers in personal finance media, the answer to the above question is, at best, complicated. Far too few Americans have access to enough resources to feel secure in their options for food or housing. Others have more than enough but hoard it without a plan because of scarcity anxiety. Still others live a spendthrift life and get by fine, but are constantly nagged by a worry that there's something they should be doing differently. Or their tenuous financial plans crumble at the slightest suggestion of trouble.

I used to tell people I was grateful to work in personal finance because what I've learned has helped me get my own money under control. Throughout my time as a staffer and freelancer in financial media, I grew a small IRA, built a comfortable $20,000 savings cushion, set up automatic bill payment, finally got a credit card, and raised my credit score to above 750. But I've stopped giving financial literacy the credit, because I know the real reason my finances got "healthier" after I got that first job: I had more money. I took a job with a salary that quadrupled my income, and voilà—I became a lot more "responsible" with money.

I didn't conquer budgeting or eliminate debt with extra fervor. I opened a secured credit card because I had the $200 to spare for a deposit, and my credit score shot up 100 points, opening a ton of doors. My income kept rising, tipping over $100,000 after I returned to freelancing, and the financial anxiety I'd experienced throughout my twenties miraculously vanished.

My colleagues in financial media and education often talk about the paradox that the people who need financial education most are the least likely to have access to it. But there's an inherent condescension to that idea. It's based on an assumption that poor people have a greater need for financial education, feeding a narrative that knowing the right set of rules unlocks the key to wealth. That assumption isn't borne out in the data, though. Increased access to financial education doesn't necessarily mean improved financial circumstances later in life. Racial and class disparities in financial knowledge and wealth persist even among adults who had equal requirements for financial education in high school,[3] and parental income remains the greatest predictor of a child's income mobility later in life.[4] Financial education can't overcome the systems and policies that create and maintain disparities—especially when that education is created *within* those systems.

The reality is that wealth begets wealth, and we exist in a system that perpetuates that truth.

The Endless Pursuit of One Right Way

As I earned enough income as a personal finance journalist to experience financial security and learned enough to recognize my agency with money, my relationship with money shifted from choosing between discipline and recklessness toward a more mindful approach. Despite the tactics I learned and taught through my work, I wasn't optimizing for wealth building; instead, every decision I made was toward worrying less about money and using it to bring ease and joy into my life. Yet at my day job, I was still sharing at-home coffee and avocado recipes as if they could solve my generation's financial insecurity.

That single moment with the toilet paper story didn't push me out of personal finance media; I still had a lot to discover before I would turn a more critical eye on the industry. But it poked the first hole in everything I was learning, even as I was still learning it. It showed me the gaping chasm between the experiences of the people doling out financial advice and those of the people consuming it as they search for the secret to that upward mobility our parents (and culture) promise us.

An abundance of personal finance advice would have readers believe prosperity is just on the other side of a Google search: learn the right answers, do the right things, be rich (however you define it). The You Need a Budget (YNAB) app promises no less than "life-changing" results if you adopt its "four simple rules," which creator Jesse Mecham admits in his book are all versions of "make a budget." It promises the system will let you break the paycheck-to-paycheck cycle, get out of debt, and "live the life you want." Dave Ramsey's Financial Peace University course and *Total Money Makeover* book offer a seven-step plan to help you pay off all debt, build your savings, and change not just your life but "your family tree . . . regardless of income or age." David Bach infamously suggested his readers could become "automatic millionaires" by giving up their daily lattes (or any small luxuries they often "waste" money on)—resting the promise on fudged math and unrealistic economic circumstances.[5] Countless others peddle similar advice, preaching restriction and promising a singular path to a good life—defined, mainly, by wealth.

This promise is the crux of what I call budget culture: the prevailing set of beliefs around money that relies on restriction, shame, and greed. Budget culture encourages deprivation and promotes an unhealthy and fantastical ideal of success with money. Worrying about money isn't unusual; money has long been a top cause of stress among Americans. Rising prices, stagnant wages, a nonexistent childcare system, and a volatile national and global economy have exacerbated that stress since the start of the COVID-19 pandemic, but the issues that plague us now are the same that have plagued us, in some way, for ages. Financial experts across the industry have watched our mounting stress and uncertainty for years as education has been defunded, domestic labor has been undervalued, and employers have legally discriminated on the basis of gender, race, and ability. They've universally come up with one flaccid solution they say can soothe your financial woes regardless of your age, resources, education, or relationship with money: make a budget.

The budget culture that pervades personal finance media and education offers up broad strokes and binaries, a one-size-fits-all approach that doesn't leave room for the diversity of our relationships with money. In reality, the impact of making a budget is too low for any rational expert to consider this an effective strategy for financial wellness.

This dearth of diversity and compassion in the space inspired me to stop relying on traditional personal finance media and create my independent financial education newsletter, *Healthy Rich*. Through this newsletter, I examine how our financial systems and culture impact the ways we think, teach, and talk about money, and I make space for those voices I've always found minimized and underappreciated in personal finance media, including women and BIPOC, LGBTQ+, rural, working-class, and disabled people. Through their stories I've learned to critique conventional advice like "You need a budget" and seek new perspectives on money. In my work, for example, I've heard stories from:

- Raniah, a Black Haitian immigrant navigating the career expectations imposed by her family and trying to keep up with the lifestyles of her affluent white peers.
- Carmen, who grew to resent the condescending white people who celebrated her "surviving the streets" without pausing to ask why it was so common for people like her—Black and Latina—to grow up in poverty.
- Megan, who experienced severe financial anxiety about the fee she paid a therapist to treat her hyperorganization and other autistic traits as "symptoms" without realizing they were the exact strengths that could help her spend consciously and reduce her anxiety around money.
- Aaron, a formerly incarcerated entrepreneur who learned it's impossible to maintain a healthy credit score or finances while incarcerated and cut off from our financial systems, making conventional financial education moot when it's time to rebuild.
- Gary, who spent money "like there was no tomorrow" because he grew up watching gay men like him die from

HIV, suicide, and hate crimes before they had a chance to accumulate wealth or worry about credit scores.

Folks like these aren't the exception. They represent the majority of Americans, whose relationships with money are far more complex than the picture our financial media and education have painted.

Through this growing industry, financial experts, educators, journalists, social media influencers, advisors, and gurus have mucked up our relationship with money by perpetuating budget culture. My work is about breaking free from that paradigm to make money better, for everyone. Whether you earn a six-figure salary or get by gig to gig, work for tips, pay bills with unemployment or Social Security checks, are saddled with unpaid caretaking or domestic work, run a small business, or manage a nonprofit, we all breathe the air of budget culture. An approach to personal finance that rejects this culture can give us the tools to change our individual and societal relationships with money.

This book is an exploration of what I've learned so far through this work and a comprehensive introduction to the antidote to budget culture: a *budget-free* approach to thinking, teaching, and talking about money. As you'll learn throughout these pages, "budget-free" is more than a way to manage household finances; it's a new perspective to transform your personal relationship with money and shift your expectations for how we treat money as a society.

The cacophony of competing prescriptive budgets, debt-payoff plans, and so-called expert investment strategies in the personal finance industry overcomplicate money and make you feel like you're failing and falling behind no matter what you do. Money doesn't have to be so hard! With this book, I give you permission to shut it all out. We'll examine the major tenets of budget culture, see why they don't make sense for most people, and look for ways you can thrive without them.

A New Way to Think about Money

Throughout this book, we'll search for an answer to the inevitable question that follows a critique of budget culture: If not budgeting, then what?

Doing away with the budget and giving yourself free rein to use money sounds radical and scary to a lot of people. That's because all we've learned about money is through a budget culture lens. We're convinced we don't know how to manage money without applying a set of guardrails. So, once you've rejected the premise of budgeting and the paradigm of budget culture, how do you learn to trust yourself to manage money without risking your sanity and security?

Nearly every personal finance book I've picked up aims to tell you how to fix yourself. That's not the aim of this book. I know there's nothing wrong with you. I want to assure you this book isn't about finding the flaws in yourself that keep you from achieving financial . . . success? Independence? Freedom? Whatever name you give to the elusive fantasy budget culture wants you to pursue. This book is about the ways our financial system is designed to keep you from that goal—and how you can live a life of ease and joy in spite of it.

I'm not going to offer you an alternative budget, savings plan, debt-payoff method, or get-rich-quick scheme. I'm not here to replace one set of rigid rules with another. We're here for a conversation that helps you see money in a new light. You'll see the mutability of money and value, and realize no set of rigid rules could ever encompass the vastness of our collective and individual relationships with money. You'll learn to question and let go of the rules and expectations budget culture thrusts on you. You'll discover the strength of your own perspective and skills to find ease in money management and joy in life. By adopting a new approach to money, you can find freedom from the tyranny of budget culture and learn to trust yourself to choose your next money move.

My goal as a financial educator is *not* to do what financial institutions have done for centuries: keep information gated to the wealthiest and most privileged. It's *not* to do what financial media have attempted to do for decades: help less privileged people act like those with more privilege. And it's *not* to do what the latest crop of socially conscious financial influencers have attempted to do: condescendingly bestow (underprivileged) populations with the guarded rules of personal finance.

My goal is to help you see the brokenness of the system, care for yourself within it, and help us all get out of it. This book is a critique of budget culture as a system of oppression, but also a survival guide for life in this system and a call to action to change it.

The first part of the book diagnoses and examines budget culture so you understand exactly what it is, where it came from, and how it impacts your relationship with money. Naming this paradigm gives you a language and lens through which to recognize how financial education and advice fail you personally and systemically. But I won't leave you hanging with this downer of a revelation. Next, I break down nine core maxims of budget culture and give you permission to let them go—and together we construct a new way to think about money that works for you. Each chapter includes reflections and practical tools to help you manage money with ease and joy without giving in to budget culture.

In the final chapter I zoom back out to the bigger picture to help you apply a budget-free philosophy to our broader society. Divesting from budget culture can improve your individual relationship with money, but your individual actions alone can never overcome an entire cultural paradigm (nor should you expect them to!). We have to do that in community. This final chapter covers ways to share the budget-free approach through the language you use, the behaviors you model, the ways you vote, and how you use power and influence in your community.

I sum up my perspective on money as a "budget-free approach"— this isn't a method or prescription, like so many one-size-fits-all solutions peddled in this industry. I don't attempt to prescribe an alternative "right" way to manage money, because I know no way will ever be right for everyone. Instead, I explore how our financial systems work, pose questions to encourage self-reflection, and make space for diverse perspectives so you can discover what makes sense for you. I trust the value of your wisdom to choose your next move; I'll make space to help you listen to it.

A Word about Your "Money Mindset"

I'll talk a lot in this book about how you think and feel about money; that is, indeed, what the personal finance and self-help industries call your "money mindset." Looking beyond the numbers is important for stepping out of the rigidity of budget culture and gaining a deeper understanding of the nuances of money in your life. But I prefer to frame the idea as your *relationship with money* and avoid using money mindset, because of the implied agency and blame the self-help world often connects to the word *mindset*.

Capitalism Is Our Reality

Remember as you read: I can't give you a series of steps to climb out of your financial circumstances and toward the shiny fantasy of being rich. Budget culture gurus like to make this promise—and many of them even believe it. But no one can give you the right formula to change your financial situation, because your circumstances are the result of something much bigger than your individual choices.

No matter who you are or what you've experienced, your financial circumstances are, ultimately, that you live in a society controlled by a capitalist economy. The systems of that society are designed to take drastic, subtle, traumatizing, brutal, genocidal, oppressive measures to keep you from enjoying stability, prosperity, and power. The degree of those measures varies depending on the privilege and dominance tied to your identity, background, and experience, but make no mistake: this is everyone's reality. Even the most privileged among us live with the reality that this system is poised to pull the rug out from under anyone at the slightest whiff of deviance.

Plenty of brilliant thinkers have brought a critique of capitalism as an economic system, so don't worry; I won't waste this book rehashing those arguments. But we *are* going to talk about capitalism throughout this book, because it's impossible to talk honestly about our individual financial circumstances without mentioning the system that governs them.

Given this reality, no money management method will change your circumstances, short of dismantling capitalism (and I won't make that your job). I won't contribute to budget culture's gaslighting by convincing you it's your responsibility alone to change and improve your situation. Following budget culture's pursuit of discipline and wealth won't change the reality that every system you encounter is designed to pry them away from you. But that doesn't mean you have to relent and suffer. Until now, you've probably been responding to your circumstances through the lens budget culture holds up to them: accepting blame for your lot and seeking a set of answers to change it. It's no wonder, with that perspective, that you'd try to better yourself by budget culture standards—more restriction, more discipline, more wealth. This book will help you see your circumstances for what they are: the inevitable result of a system designed to keep you small. With that new lens, you can respond to your reality, instead of to the picture budget culture has painted for you. You can stop responding to systemic oppression by buying fewer lattes and start experiencing ease and joy while the systems exhaust themselves trying to deprive you of them.

The ideas we'll explore in the following chapters will help you investigate, understand, and survive the reality of your circumstances. Systems of oppression—which capitalism is—thrive by withholding knowledge from those they're designed to oppress. As the feminist activist Audre Lorde writes, "So long as we are divided because of our particular identities we cannot join together in effective political action."[6] Budget culture supports capitalism's project of divisive oppression by blaming you for your circumstances, othering those whose circumstances are different, convincing you to feel ashamed, and offering restriction and greed as solutions. By leaning on individual responsibility, it discourages you from investigating the inner workings of our systems. By offering restriction and greed couched in maxims about responsibility and wellness, it pushes you to skim over your innate understanding of your needs and your place in community. We'll question the most common maxims, demystify the systems, and discover strategies to reclaim power in spite of them.

At no point in this book will I suggest that, if you learn everything I have to teach, you'll be rich or debt-free. The point of a budget-free approach is not to give you a new way to pursue the goals budget culture idealizes. It's to help you experience ease and joy by releasing those goals rooted in restriction, shame, and greed.

YDNAB TOOLS TO HELP YOU GO DEEPER

Reflection Exercises

Each chapter of the book includes questions to help you reflect on what you're learning. Grab a notebook or a friend, and write or talk through these questions as you go to dig deeper into your relationship with money.

This process might be uncomfortable. Digging in and getting to know parts of yourself you haven't explored before is almost certain to conjure up difficult memories and feelings (as well as pleasant ones!). Take care to recognize when that's happening and give yourself a break.

Your Money Map

Alongside the unlearning and rethinking you'll do throughout this book, I offer practical steps you can take to deal with the practical challenges capitalism thrusts upon you. Often, simply seeing your situation through a different lens can significantly reduce the stress you're feeling. But our society attaches very real-world consequences to money, as well, and a shift in your relationship to money and social justice actions might not be the salve you need to get through this day, this week, or this month. I can't offer you individualized advice to face your circumstances, but I can guide you in untangling the information you need to make the decisions that are right for you. A money map is the foundational tool that lets you see all aspects of your financial situation laid out in one place, so you have a clear starting point from which to make those decisions. You'll build your own money map at the end of the book.

YDNAB Online

To complete the reflections and exercises throughout the book, you can always keep a notebook nearby as you read. But I know some readers prefer reusable digital worksheets, so I've made some of those, too. Also, financial technology and products change and disappear quickly, so I won't recommend a lot of third-party tools in the book. To give you all the resources you need to practice a budget-free approach in your life, I've gathered the book's exercises and up-to-date tool recommendations online at youdontneedabudget.com.

CHAPTER 1

Budget Culture Has Ruined
Our Relationship with Money

In the mid-1990s I was a young tween, and my fully adult dad was a fan of the quirkiest of my generation's pop music. He independently enjoyed the Offspring and learned the words to Hanson's "MMMBop" to hang with my sister and me. He went through a stint of loving "If I Had $1,000,000" by Barenaked Ladies, and we listened to the song on repeat in his truck's CD player.

The song is a fun and silly exploration of what people "not born rich" might do with a million dollars. Build a tree fort (with a mini fridge). Buy a (faux) fur coat. Hire a limousine. Enjoy expensive ketchup. Buy a monkey. The song ends with a twist on the chorus: *"If I had a million dollars . . . I'd be rich."*

After the last line, my dad would always call out, "Hey! My dad's rich!"

It was a Dad Joke Classic. His dad, my grandpa, was named Richard. (So really he was saying, "My dad's Rich!")

I loved this dad joke for its cleverness at the time, but none of us ever questioned the nuance that made the joke work. It was more than a silly pun (though it nailed that genre on the head, too). Beneath the puniness of "rich" in the joke was a dark layer of the self-deprecating humility bred into us as working-class midwesterners. The joke worked because it was so obvious that my dad was never suggesting his dad was lowercase-*r* rich. Of course he wasn't, because real people weren't rich. We didn't know anyone who was rich. Rich people didn't live in our town. They existed on TV and in big cities far away, where we couldn't afford to live and might only someday, rarely, visit.

To my mind, when I was growing up, rich wasn't a thing you were. And, unlike the coastal yuppie boomers and the hipsters they were raising in those faraway cities and suburbs, rich wasn't a thing we strove to become, either. We would never have—imagine it!—a million dollars. The only way we could be rich was to be called Richard.

The fantasies embodied in this song steer toward the absurd—monkeys and Dijon ketchups—because working-class culture trained us to believe the very idea of having that kind of money was absurd.

The disciplined, working-class folks I knew rarely strayed into get-rich fantasies like the ones Barenaked Ladies entertained. We never talked about putting a windfall away for college, opening an investment account, or starting a business, either. Those luxuries and wealth-building activities weren't even on our radar; they seemed reserved for rich people.

But that posture was changing as personal finance gurus gained popularity throughout the late 1990s and early 2000s. Books like

Dave Ramsey's *Financial Peace*, Robert Kiyosaki's *Rich Dad Poor Dad*, and David Bach's *Smart Women Finish Rich* promised to bring the secrets of the rich to the rest of us. A new generation of financial gurus, led by Ramsey's domineering radio personality, told us we could in fact become rich, regardless of where we'd come from. That life was within our grasp; we just had to get the money right. For the first time in generations, working-class southern and midwestern folks who'd been conditioned not to pursue wealth could indulge in what middle-class Americans had been devouring for decades: the fantasy of being rich.

The personal finance industry that emerged as I and my fellow millennials came of age, the first to meaningfully sink its tendrils into communities like mine, was ostensibly no longer interested in stock picks and trust fund strategies to help the rich get richer. These new gurus wanted to bring the magic of the financial industry to those of us it had previously ignored—to those of us who, also, had previously ignored the financial industry. They weren't selling a small boost, a leg up out of poverty, a buoy for the shrinking middle class. They were promising that everyone had the potential to be lowercase-*r* rich.

This became the unabashed goal as personal finance reached the masses in a meaningful way for the first time at the turn of the century through airport bestsellers, talk radio, and cable TV. Money management advice for individuals and families was no longer limited to the sensible household budgeting tips peddled in women's magazines throughout the first half of the twentieth century. If you followed the rules, everything you did with your money was aimed at a single goal: becoming rich. By this time, Reaganomics of the

1980s and the welfare reform of the 1990s had made it clear that the system wasn't going to give an inch to most of us, and it only seemed fair to find ways to take it for ourselves. Striving for riches no longer seemed greedy; it was about reclaiming what the culture—whether that meant coastal elites, big government, working immigrants, or some other bogeyman—had taken away.

The Dave Ramseyfication of Money

Kel Schulze and their spouse didn't quite resonate with Dave Ramsey's teachings when they discovered him, but his popular "7 Baby Steps" system offered an approachable way to tackle their otherwise overwhelming debt.

The couple closed on a house in 2018, and that "changed our relationship with money [by] changing our values," Kel says. "Which things meant more to us at that moment versus the long-term goals we wanted to reach? Did things that we spent money on align with that?"[1]

Kel had a nascent interest in personal finance after receiving Ramsey's *Total Money Makeover* from a friend a few years earlier. When in 2019 another couple invited them to join a Financial Peace University course being taught at a nearby church, Kel and their spouse thought it would be a good place to talk through feelings about money and debt openly.

"It was," they say. "But [also], another friend in our group said, 'This feels like a cult.' Oh, did he pin that right."

Like a lot of past students, readers, and listeners, Kel thought Ramsey's teachings, which the licensed course is built around, were "a mixed bag." The Baby Steps include (and have been a blueprint for) many of the same types of advice you can find from any modern personal finance guru. The first few steps are seemingly innocuous: build an emergency fund, pay off debt, invest for retirement. But as you get deeper into the advice, later steps quickly become over-zealous, inaccessible for many, and in at least one case, shamelessly self-serving and unethical: Baby Step 7 encourages wealth building through investing—then directs followers to work with Ramsey's SmartVestor network of affiliate investment advisors, who put your money in pricey managed funds that most experts have advised against for decades. Ramsey's cultlike customs, spread through church networks and social media, have gained mass appeal in part because they can make followers feel less alone on the difficult path his teachings pave for your relationship with money.

"The needs for identity, purpose, and belonging have existed for a very long time, and cultish groups have always sprung up during cultural limbos when these needs have gone sorely unmet," writes language scholar Amanda Montell in her book *Cultish: The Language of Fanaticism*. "What's new is that in the internet-ruled age, when a guru can be godless, when the barrier to entry is as low as a double-tap, and when folks who hold alternative beliefs are able to find one another more easily than ever, it only makes sense that secular cults—from obsessed workout studios to start-ups that put the 'cult' in 'company culture'—would start sprouting like dandelions."

"Secular cults," as Montell calls them, show up as audiences and communities following self-anointed gurus like Ramsey, as well as Jesse Mecham, creator of You Need a Budget (YNAB); Ramit Sethi, creator of I Will Teach You to Be Rich; David Bach, creator of the Finish Rich Brand; and many others.

This is the state of the personal finance industry we see today: the likes of Ramsey, Mecham, Sethi, and Bach—and the thousands of social media mini gurus they've spawned—have shaped an industry that promises a rich life to cultish followers struggling with money and looking for the one right route to so-called financial freedom. Eliminating debt, tracking your spending, or forgoing small indulgences are presented as accessible solutions to massive money problems. These (mostly) white, middle-class men make blanket statements without consideration for their position within the system. They don't often address how their advice might land on the single Black mother, the queer couple, the person with a chronic illness, or the multitude of others in their audiences who face daily discrimination and restraints on their ability to access resources and navigate our financial systems.

Modern cultishness shows up as budget culture on a broader scale, a homogenous way of thinking about money that lends itself to rules we can follow to feel in control, in the know, and—more to the point—in the "in" group. "Modern cultish groups feel comforting in part because they help alleviate the anxious mayhem of living in a world that presents almost too many possibilities for who to be (or at least the illusion of such)," writes Montell.

Despite that feeling of being in control, though, modern cultish groups and modes of thought are ways of *being controlled*. Throughout history, normative social organization has always been enforced in some way, but the mode has changed over time. Philosophers considered preindustrial societies to be "societies of sovereignty," where control was top-down. Social norms were set and enforced by a single ruler, like a king. In the 1700s and 1800s, as society was reorganized around industrial institutions like the factory, school, church, and military service, the culture became what the twentieth-century philosopher Michel Foucault dubbed "societies of discipline."[2] In these societies, the institution set and enforced norms; for example, you could be punished at work or school for deviating from a set of explicit or implicit rules.

In his 1990 essay "Postscript on the Societies of Control," the philosopher Gilles Deleuze described a shift toward our current mode of control. He recognized the boundaries between institutions blurring. The typical American was no longer living a linear life going from family to school to service to factory, as Foucault described; we're no longer contained within a set of places, but instead operate among vague institutions like the corporation and capitalism. We now operate as what Deleuze calls "societies of control."[3]

In this culture, "we've completely internalized the standards of conduct," author Tara McMullin writes in her analysis of Deleuze's essay. "We police ourselves and others. We're constantly under surveillance, whether through anxious self-monitoring, the gaze of our neighbors and coworkers, or the bits of code that follow us around wherever we take our devices. We don't need punishment because we punish ourselves."[4]

This shaming and cultish self-control are foundational to the way we teach personal finance in budget culture. As Kel notes of their Dave Ramsey experience, "The shame and the shame tactics [Ramsey] uses on his show and within the class can further worsen how people feel about their relationship to money. Having a worse relationship with money after paying for a course defeats the purpose of that course."

To his credit, Dave Ramsey ushered in an approach to money that made it okay for regular folks to talk about it in a way that used to be reserved for rich people. Before Ramsey's call-in talk show *The Dave Ramsey Show* and his 1992 book *Financial Peace*, prevailing financial advice was largely for people who were already rich. It went straight to stock picks and skipped what to do if you relied on credit card debt or lived precariously from paycheck to paycheck. Financial advice assumed people were in those situations because they didn't care about financial education. Those of us in those situations, in turn, *didn't* care much about financial education, because stock picks aren't useful if you don't have disposable funds to purchase stocks. Ramsey began speaking to the people traditional advice ignored.

Ramsey's signature strategies, like saving just $1,000 to start an emergency fund and the "debt snowball method," are popular targets for criticism from savvy financial experts for their lack of optimization. These strategies encourage people to reach for financial goals that provide small, quick, frequent wins that improve their motivation. They're not the most fiscally efficient options, but they feel more accessible to many people than the perfectly optimized alternatives. I'll talk in later chapters about why I don't advocate for Ramsey's strategies *or* the alternatives, but it's worth noting why Ramsey's are so popular: they represent the first time in modern history that nonrich folks were told they could be in control of their money.

Other budding financial experts saw the hunger for this kind of advice following its ascendance in the 1990s. They recognized the need to drop Ramsey's religious-conservative tone and Bach's and Kiyosaki's preoccupation with the already rich, and a new "commonfolk" niche in personal finance emerged around the turn of the century. Millennials entered adulthood into an economy shaken first by the dot-com bubble and then the housing crisis, primed for financial advice by and for people like us. The personal finance industry ballooned with the popularity of personal blogs, where so-called everyday millionaires could chronicle their journeys out of debt and into the middle class, continuing the narrative that it could be done if we just followed the right rules and worked hard enough. In this new age of personal finance, success is no longer about stock picks and IRA tax strategies. Ramsey and his successors put the "personal" into finance so—they say—anyone can find success through a new set of rules made just for us, like paying down debt, starting a side hustle, and, above all, making a budget.

What Is Budget Culture?

Budget culture is the prevailing set of beliefs around money that relies on restriction, shame, and greed. Financial advice and education for the supposedly common person all boils down to these basic tactics:

- **Restrict** how you use money, whether by spending less, saving more, or buying different things.
- **Shame** yourself for financial moves, including spending and accumulating debt, and lack of investment or savings.
- **Greedily hoard** wealth by avoiding taxes, accumulating property, and opposing social safety nets.

These values might not show up so explicitly, but they undergird all of the ways we think, teach, and talk about money in our culture.

Budget culture is much more than just making a budget. You don't have to engage in budgeting to be engulfed in the beliefs around it.

These beliefs pervade most of our conversations about money. The custodians of budget culture—many a personal finance guru, investment advisor, money coach, debt counselor, accountant, and wealth manager—have us convinced we can find the right, most perfect way to manage money if we work hard enough. If your finances don't look like you want them to, budget culture convinces you it's because you're not doing it right.

Budget culture rewards restriction and deprivation; ignores the real-life dynamics of income and lifestyle; demonizes spending; and categorically labels certain money moves as "good" or "bad." It promotes hypervigilance around money, and values efficiency and economy above human health, happiness, and well-being. It equates *financial wellness* with making the most money, and *financial literacy* with knowing how to hold on to it. It does all of this because the budget culture standard rests on the premise that money is the goal in and of itself.

The personal finance industry has contrived a fantasy world where it's possible for regular people to overcome tremendous financial obstacles with just a few simple steps and make real progress toward being rich. Budget culture upholds that fantasy as an achievable ideal and the basis for understanding money. Even as individuals continue to fail to realize the fantasy, our approach to money feeds off the never-ending pursuit of this promise it can't fulfill.

This pursuit is how we all get caught up in budget culture, even if we're not actively making a budget (even if, *ahem*, we've never cared about being Good with Money . . .). Budget culture shows up in the ways we all think and talk about money, in the choices we make, and in the goals we aim for.

You might express budget culture characteristics through personal actions like:

- Categorizing your spending (e.g., "eating out," "bills," and "entertainment").
- Labeling expenses as "wants" or "needs."
- Tracking your spending, whether manually or automatically.
- Limiting how much you can spend in a category or within a period.
- Accounting for every dollar in and out of your pocket.
- Seeking financial advice by asking what you "should" do next, like how much you should invest or what size mortgage you should take out.
- Bending your lifestyle to your money, rather than the other way around.
- Following a prescribed budgeting, debt payoff, or other money management method (like Ramsey's debt snowball method or the popular "50/30/20 budget").

The insidiousness of budget culture—the fact that we're all participating without even knowing or trying—is its greatest strength and worst danger. It encompasses our lives and society just like a much more familiar phenomenon: diet culture.

Budget Culture Is Diet Culture for Your Money

The similarities between budget culture and diet culture—both of which encourage deprivation and promote an unhealthy and fantastical idea of success—are striking.

Just as I, like many others who are marginalized in our culture and ignored by popular advice, felt suddenly seen and sane when I first heard the term *diet culture*, so do many people's eyes light up with recognition and relief when they can name the financial pressures they feel under *budget culture* and take the first steps toward healing the tortured relationships with money this culture has imposed on them.

In the same way diet culture sees weight as a signifier of physical health and prescribes food restriction as the path toward its goal of being thin, budget culture sees credit scores and debt balances as signifiers of financial health and prescribes spending restrictions as the first step toward financial wellness—defined, at its core, as being rich.

Budget culture might be a difficult concept to embrace at first, but it's not much more than a new lens to help you see a reality that's been around for ages. Budget culture is the way capitalism shows up in financial education and advice. Just as diet culture is the way an individualistic, competitive capitalist system teaches you to relate to your body, budget culture is how a capitalist economic system teaches you to think about money. By design, capitalism creates an idealized, dominant class—like *thin* or *rich*—and keeps you in pursuit of it while always keeping it out of reach.

Capitalism shows up in personal finance as budget culture just as it shows up in every area of our lives under different names: not just in food and bodies as diet culture, but also in work as hustle culture, in environmentalism as greenwashing, in relationships as patriarchy, and in race relations as white supremacy.

It shows up through a few common characteristics every time. Educator and activist Tema Okun describes these characteristics in her article defining white supremacy culture, among them: perfectionism, individualism, either/or thinking, quantity over quality, only one right way, and more.[5] In budget culture, I recognize these characteristics as restriction, shame, and greed.

How Budget Culture Encourages Restriction

Budget culture wants to convince you that overindulgence is the culprit for your financial woes. Budgeting advice begins with the assumption that spending decisions keep you from paying off debt, buying a home, raising a family, and enjoying basically anything without a well of financial anxiety. Budgets explicitly restrict how much you can spend overall as well as within spending categories; methods like the popular 50/30/20 budget even prioritize types of spending for you (50 percent of your income toward "needs," 30 percent toward "wants," and 20 percent toward savings). Even without those explicit limits on spending, the mindset around budgeting limits choice and moralizes by labeling "wants" versus "needs," and "good" versus "bad" debt or money moves to set you up to constantly question your inner wisdom and feel guilty for your choices—even when circumstances are clearly out of your control.

Case in point: As our country faced record-high price inflation and threats of a recession following the peak of the COVID-19 pandemic, the advice touted in most media centered on tightening your belt. Just like diet culture puts the onus on the individual to lose weight by cutting calories, eliminating demonized foods, and "finding time" to cook at home and work out, personal finance media in 2020 ramped up its advice for the individual to "find money" in their budget by getting rid of debt, building savings, negotiating loan rates, carpooling, canceling subscriptions, and buying generic items at the grocery store. Under both diet culture and budget culture, the struggles people experience—whether they have a low net worth or a high body weight—aren't because of their individual choices but because of the way the culture treats people like them. Prescribing restriction is a way of avoiding collective responsibility and change by telling people to be less of who they are and more of who we expect them to be.

Contrary to the promises of one-size-fits-all budgets, though, financial insecurity isn't about what you spend on Netflix and avocados. It can't be abated by clipping coupons, using a grocery rebate app, or comparing prices before committing to a brand. Financial insecurity is baked into capitalism; a few thrive by extracting productivity from the rest at the lowest possible cost. The personal finance industry thrives on our cultural ignorance of this systemic force. It sells restrictive coping strategies to return customers who, inevitably and by design, are held down by the inequality and instability of our economy despite repeated efforts to change their financial strategies.

How Budget Culture Foments Shame

Just as the diet industry ignores systemic issues like food insecurity and gender discrimination, personal finance education and media ignore the structure of capitalism and focus disingenuously on individual choices and behaviors. Instead of helping us recognize and change oppressive systems, the industry reinforces our individual responsibility for our financial circumstances and incites shame for our imperfections.

These characteristics are part of a much larger trend Yale political science professor Jacob S. Hacker, in his book *The Great Risk Shift*, calls "the Personal Responsibility Crusade," defined as "a political drive to shift a growing amount of economic risk from government and the corporate sector onto ordinary Americans in the name of enhanced individual responsibility and control."

"No longer do political and corporate leaders generally embrace the notion that catastrophic risks represent misfortunes largely beyond individual control," Hacker writes. "Instead of pooling risks through social insurance, those with the power to make policy have been offloading them . . . onto the fragile balance sheets of American families."[6]

The way we talk about money trains us to accept this responsibility without question and feel shame every time we fail to protect ourselves against these risks. But we can't decouple the individual from the social the way some policymakers wish they could. You make choices based on the options available to you, and the system dictates those options. Naming budget culture is a way to highlight that reality. It gives us a language to talk about capitalism as a personal issue, not only a sociological one. Giving budget culture a name is part of recognizing capitalism as an imposed system, not a natural order.

Budget culture makes money all about you: your actions, responsibilities, and mindset. But individual actions can't overcome the shift away from the social insurance Hacker describes. You can't individually eradicate persistent pay gaps, generational trauma, systemic oppression, algorithmic biases, and other forces that keep capitalism working for a select few at the expense of the rest of us. No money management method can square rising housing costs with stagnant wages. No amount of self-control can make up for the costs of so-called professionalism borne by everyone who has to fit their hair, dress, gender presentation, or family responsibilities into a box to keep their job.

Capitalism is a system that classifies us and disadvantages the many for the exclusive benefit of a few. It's a system that requires haves and have-nots, so have-nots had to be created for it to function. Your class and the privilege or lack of privilege associated with it are a direct result of the economic system we live in. The choices you have to make about money exist because of that system. The restriction and discipline of budget culture are a response to the limited choices the system offers, and budget culture's shaming keeps us focused on those individual stopgaps instead of on changing the system.

What Hacker calls the Great Risk Shift, he writes, "isn't a natural occurrence—a financial hurricane beyond human control. Sweeping changes in the global and domestic economy have helped propel it, but America's corporate and political leaders could have responded to these powerful forces by reinforcing the floodwalls that protect families from economic risk. Instead, in the name of personal responsibility, many of these leaders have been tearing the floodwalls down."[7]

As Hacker makes clear: inequalities and unfair challenges have been consistently built into the system to maintain power for those who already hold it. Yet budget culture trains us to feel ashamed of our financial struggles and to blame others for theirs. A budget-free approach recognizes that capitalism works against our needs for connection, security, and autonomy. It means deconstructing the dominance of budget culture ideas, understanding typical financial advice as a tool to prop up capitalism itself rather than help anyone thrive under the regime.

Budget culture idealizes and advises for a definition of richness designed by capitalists to keep capital flowing their way. It encourages resource accumulation and hoarding that rely on things like power at work, freedom from domestic labor, well-rounded education, debt elimination, homeownership, credit, and other things the moneyed, straight white men the system is built by and for tend to have access to more readily than anyone else. We equate these things with being Good with Money because we exist in a system designed to favor them—not because they're inherent signs of responsible stewardship of resources. Traditional and contemporary financial educators, advisors, and content creators have leaned on the mantra of discipline and restriction because it's often worked for them. They dole out generalized advice based on their experience without pausing to realize the system is designed to work for them and against people who aren't like them. Their claims encourage—or at least allow—people to feel ashamed when they don't achieve the results that came so easily to them.

How Budget Culture Normalizes Greed

Where dieting is a response to what writer Kate Harding calls "the fantasy of being thin,"[8] budgeting is a response to what I call the fantasy of being rich. The cultural attitudes that stem from these behaviors—diet culture and budget culture—develop from our constantly seeking a path toward those elusive promises. By upholding the never-ending pursuit of being rich as "financial responsibility," budget culture builds a necessary greed into our relationship with money.

It's not that being rich isn't possible, exactly. The reason this is a "fantasy" that encourages perpetual greed is because "rich" is a moving target. Whatever you think of as being rich probably involves a little more income and a bit more comfort than you have now. Yet when you reach it, you'll probably still feel as if you have a little less than you could (or should). Some experts call this "lifestyle inflation"—the tendency to spend or need more as you earn or have more—but it's more than that. It's not just about how much money you have or spend; it's about the way money drives every decision in your life because of the greed budget culture builds into your relationship with money.

In a 2020 survey by financial advisory firm Willis Towers Watson, 38 percent of employees were living paycheck to paycheck—including 18 percent of employees who earned more than $100,000 a year, well above what many of us would consider a comfortable income.[9] When budget culture convinces you that money is the end goal, that you could always have more, and that there's a right way to get there that you just don't know yet, you get into a nonstop loop of aiming for the fantasy of being rich: a standard that'll always move to be just a little better off than you are now.

Budget Culture Is in the Air We Breathe

Most people never opt into budget culture, whether through active budgeting or a conscious mindset shift. But we're all living it.

Like diet culture, budget culture is a paradigm that captures people regardless of their other political or social views. Like many of my personal finance colleagues, you might be committed to collectivism, social justice, and equality in theory—even in how you vote and the beliefs you state—but you could still be investing in budget culture simply because it's *the way things are* around you. And budget culture's approach to money doesn't seem at odds with your values, because the way you learned about money (if you learned about it at all) didn't connect the dots between the systemic and the personal. That's not likely by accident.

"From the crafty redefinition of existing words (and the invention of new ones) to powerful euphemisms, secret codes, renamings, buzzwords, chants and mantras, 'speaking in tongues,' forced silence, even hashtags, language is the key means by which all degrees of cultlike influence occur," writes Amanda Montell.[10]

The language of macroeconomics and the language of personal finance silo those fields. This disconnect leaves you free to jump on the "social justice" bandwagon behind ideas that align with your values—Black Lives Matter, Love Is Love, Women's Rights Are Human Rights—while fighting those same ideals through capitalist personal financial moves couched in language that equally appeals to your values, like "financial freedom" and "self-determination." The "cult" of budget culture uses the language of empowerment to edge its way into movements for wellness, equity, and social justice, but it doesn't ever address the way its advice works against those causes. Still, its language can make the concepts hard to argue with.

That, in part, is why throughout this book I'll offer alternatives to some common language we use to talk about money. Changing the labels and language you use can be an important step to shifting out of the mindset of budget culture. Of course, adopting language offered by someone else can be quite cultish itself, so read these as suggestions, not imperatives; take what works for you and leave what doesn't.

This culty language, combined with a need for belonging and the constant self-surveillance of our society of control, is how a paradigm like budget culture takes hold. There might be individual cultish gurus we can follow if we're consciously opting into the paradigm. But we don't need a particular institution to set and enforce standards; we internalize them from the culture at large without even trying or realizing it. We hear our parents' opinions about money. We experience challenges or biases because of our financial circumstances. We see friends on social media and characters in shows and movies modeling the same relationship with money over and over until it becomes the norm. We police ourselves and each other through self-judgment and comparison, subtle shame or praise.

Everyone is faced with the anxiety of living a life that costs money, whether that anxiety is a quiet hum or a thunderous roar in your mind. Everyone feels the need to belong and feel like they're doing the "right" things in our society, especially around something so burdened with expectations and mystery as money. Attaching to budget culture beliefs and adopting its behaviors are understandable ways to cope with the anxiety of being human in a capitalist society. But these beliefs and behaviors mask the real problems (and solutions).

Becoming lowercase-r rich can improve life for a lot of people, so that's the goal we've been selling in personal finance for decades. But we're missing the point. No one's basic well-being should rely on their ability to count pennies. Yes, these gurus and their popular methods—including those I touted for years in personal finance media—can help you stretch a dollar to avoid eviction or choose a savings plan to stave off poverty in retirement. But our society needs more than a new brand of budget. We need more than another bandage for individual financial wounds. We need a radical reimagining of what money means in our lives and culture, how we obtain it, how we use it, and how we allocate it.

Budget culture keeps you striving to improve your own finances so you can improve everything money pays for in your life—you have to become rich to thrive in a world made for people who are rich. Dismantling budget culture means remaking the world in a way that lets everyone experience the ease of being "rich," regardless of the numbers in their bank account.

CHAPTER 2

Budgeting Doesn't Work

Veronica Duke found herself a single mom the summer after gradu-
ating high school in 1983. She'd planned to marry her baby's father,
but he'd suffered traumatic brain injury from a motorcycle accident
during her third month of pregnancy and had no memory of her,
their relationship, or the child they were about to have. Veronica was
left to raise the child alone, but she didn't let that deter her from
going to college.

"Between the time [my daughter] was one and about six, I was
in school," she says. "I decided that would be the best way to try to
make things better for both of us and get out of poverty."

Veronica worked part-time while going to school, and she relied
on Pell Grants, student loans, Medicaid, food stamps, a cash assistance program called Aid for Families with Dependent Children,
Social Security benefits from her child's father, a childcare stipend
from her school, and HUD housing vouchers. The assistance was
vital, but the way it was administered meant she and her daughter
lived in constant uncertainty.

A week or two of earning just over the limit in her part-time jobs would make her ineligible for food stamps. The people assigned to help her through those bumps in the road made her feel like she was never doing enough to pull herself out of her circumstances.

Social workers "would give me a pamphlet and tell me how to grow a garden, how to budget my money better," she says. "Not very practical. . . . And then when I went to the food pantry . . . again, I would have to go through that shame and being lectured about not budgeting my money."

Veronica says she did, in fact, "budget" her money, cutting costs any way she could imagine. "I did everything I could to save. I breast-fed and used cloth diapers and made her baby clothes. . . . I remember taking a calculator with me to the store because every penny counted. You could never buy anything that wasn't a necessity."

Still, she fell victim to a system that would use any excuse to withhold support. Veronica for years was shamed and encouraged to restrict her spending, as a single mom working toward a better life for herself and her daughter. When she put those Social Security benefits into a savings account for her daughter, she was penalized with reduced food stamps. When her out-of-state landlord failed to make repairs in time for a HUD inspection, she lost rent assistance. As a student, she wanted to take summer classes so she could graduate faster, move into full-time work, and stop relying on government assistance. But for all the rhetoric around them, the programs weren't designed to help her do that; they were largely designed to shame her for needing assistance in the first place. When she asked her social worker for the help she'd need to attend summer classes, she was denied.

She faced that shame everywhere she went in her small town. "There was just that shame of having a baby and not being married and being at the big cash register and people looking over your shoulder [and seeing] you're paying with food stamps."

Veronica knew what it was like to grow up in poverty, and she didn't want that to be her daughter's story. Her mother had divorced her father, who was an alcoholic, and raised three kids on her own, working multiple jobs and relying on public assistance. Veronica had been working and managing her own money since she was fourteen years old.

"I remember when I did get married [when my daughter was six years old], we moved and we bought a new refrigerator," she says. "We went to the grocery store and we filled it up, and I just was amazed. I hadn't seen a full refrigerator in years and years."

The social workers assigned to Veronica were doing the best they could with the information and resources they had. They were certainly constrained by the conflicts in our welfare programs, but they were also constrained by our cultural approach to money. Budget culture seeped into the way they guided clients, and they did more harm than good by responding to Veronica's food insecurity with recommendations for further restriction.

The trauma of that approach to money has stuck with Veronica even as her financial circumstances have stabilized over the years. "You have that poverty mindset," she says. "I think I still have it sometimes."

Budgeting, Then and Now

The concept of budgeting didn't start with Dave Ramsey, but it's not that far off historically to call him one of the pioneers of the practice. Budgeting as we know it was born not long before Ramsey himself. The need to manage personal expenses is a relatively recent development in human society, and the history of the word *budget* demonstrates just how new it is. Individuals and households have always had some need to manage resources, allocating food and supplies and planning harvests, for example, to sustain their families and communities across changing seasons. But this behavior is not like the budgeting strategies we discuss today, which are explicitly attached to spending earned wages and implicitly rely on individual behavior and sacrifice.

For centuries, the modern English word *budget* and its predecessors in Old and Middle English, Middle French, Middle Irish, and Latin basically described a purse. The word originally meant "a usually leather pouch, wallet, or pack," long before travelers typically carried money in such pouches.[1] This was the word's chief meaning until it shifted to refer specifically to a bag carrying a collection of papers, then to the papers themselves, and then found its way into the names of many daily newspapers in the late eighteenth century.[2] Because of this association with "news," *budget* also came to mean "gossip," and an act of satire in 1733 used that meaning to first connect the word to money.

In the pamphlet *The Budget Opened*, British prime minister Robert Walpole and member of Parliament William Pulteney revealed British government spending and taxes to the public.[3] As this meaning caught on, *budget* referred primarily to government financial affairs throughout the 1800s. For the first time the word referred primarily to a spending plan, but formalizing this type of money management at the household level still remained rare. That's because for most of human history, financial budgeting had been unnecessary and irrelevant. Before the Industrial Revolution at the turn of the nineteenth century, individuals were less likely to work for wages and require money to obtain life's necessities. If you're generally laboring in direct exchange for food and shelter, or growing and producing your own household provisions, money in and out doesn't matter much.

With the rise of wage labor and the growth of cities around industrialized manufacturing through the 1700s and 1800s, people began to earn regular incomes. They also needed to purchase more of the property, food, and clothing that kept their families alive. With a rising awareness of household wages and needs, in the late 1800s people began to use the term *household budget*, referring to the resources available to a family (and, as always, accompanied by complaints about the rising cost of living). The *New York Daily Herald* of January 15, 1874, for example, griped that "it is probable that New Year's gifts will continue to become more and more oppressive as time rolls on instead of growing less so. As it is, they form an item in the household budget which ranks next in importance to the rates and taxes assessed by government."[4]

Amusingly, almost as soon as the concept of a household budget caught on, it was met with the same critique it faces today: that it individualizes systemic problems. From the jump, budgeting advice was a way to shift responsibility for societal concerns onto the individual. The Industrial Revolution ushered in a modern form of inequality and imbalance of power between owners and laborers, creating conditions that sparked labor movements and an interest in socialism and communism. But long before our country was willing to officially recognize and protect laborers through legislation, Western culture was preoccupied with directing working families on how to manage their meager earnings.

With the rise of wage labor also came a new set of gender roles within the household. In middle-class marriages between men and women, husbands were expected to hold employment outside of the home for pay, and wives were expected to bear and raise children and tend to their homes and communities. As we've done time and again throughout history, society recognized the increasing ease in women's lives—their ability to buy premade clothing and factory-milled flour, for example—and created a new bar for them to clear. Women were charged with purchasing food and clothing to meet the household's day-to-day needs, so we quickly developed standards for the right way to shop.

Mary Beaumont Welch, the turn-of-the-century educator and suffragist credited with developing the first college home economics classes, published the first home economics textbook, *Mrs. Welch's Cook Book*, in 1884. Contrary to how we use the term today, the "cookbook" contains few recipes. Instead, it's more of an instruction manual for keeping a house, with descriptions of cuts of meats and types of pastries a home cook should know, utensils in a proper kitchen, and standards for setting a table and serving a meal. Unlike home economics today, which lives up to the name with extensive focus on money, Welch makes just one brief mention of the housekeeper's responsibility for the household budget, opening a chapter called "Marketing" (which refers to shopping at the market): "Every sensible housekeeper should know enough about marketing to select her supplies wisely and intelligently. Economy begins here."[5]

As the field grew, managing the household budget became a normal part of home economics courses and culture at large. By around 1915, the word *budgeting* was most commonly used to refer to the act we think of today: managing a household's expenses. Like other household labor, this was blatantly considered women's work. In a 1915 recap of a home economics course by the traveling lecturer Kate B. Vaughn, the *Oakland Tribune* reports, "The thought Mrs. Vaughn emphasized more than any other, perhaps, was that it requires just as much brains to spend money as to earn it, and that the woman's share of running a household economically and well is just as great as the man's share of providing the home."[6]

The personal finance industry as we know it today emerged after the Great Depression and is credited to the columnist Sylvia Porter, a woman who published anonymously as S. F. Porter, letting readers presume they were learning from a man. Porter started writing in 1934, at age twenty-one, with a newsletter dedicated to explaining US government bonds in plain language and went on to write a column for the *New York Post*, the first of its kind to talk about finance for common people. In her book *Pound Foolish*, journalist Helaine Olen calls Porter "the mother of the personal finance industrial complex"[7] that took off sixty years later. Porter's popularity—and the popularity of household budgeting advice—was fueled at that time by the thriving (white) postwar middle class, who were increasingly regarded as consumers above anything else.

By the 1950s Porter had shifted her persona from savvy investor to conservative housewife, as household budgeting advice for women proliferated. Half a century before we started blaming millennials' financial struggles on female-coded purchases like avocado toast, lattes, and designer shoes, the media was happy to tell women to mind their money by restricting their spending on fashion. In 1950 the *Boston Globe* ran two hundred words teaching the frugal "career girl" how to "budget her bonnets," detailing precisely the amount to spend: $15 per year.[8]

Published talk of budgeting rose slowly throughout the affluent 1950s and 1960s with a focus on the wife's duty to the household. Interest jumped during the 1973–75 recession,[9] when modern middle-class households facing stagflation (simultaneous unemployment and inflation) were suddenly concerned with how to stretch wages that were losing value against rising standards of living. With that frightening economic period always looming in the rearview mirror, Americans' interest in budgeting and personal finance advice has held strong ever since.

Increasing economic insecurity spawned and has continued to feed the personal finance industry. As financial products became more complex in the late 1970s and early 1980s, the industry shifted toward a more blatant focus on wealth accumulation. Alongside stock picks, it began to surface the idea that anyone could become rich if they were clever enough with tools like money market funds, individual retirement accounts (IRAs), and day trading. The exploding stock market of the 1990s perpetuated this claim. "A gain of more than 1,500 percent [in the Dow Jones Industrial Average] in a little more than a generation," Olen writes, "led many Americans and their personal finance and investment gurus—who seemed to multiply by the day—to believe a contradiction: that stock market gains were inevitable, and that their own personal investing prowess was responsible for their stock market success."[10]

A volatile market has shaken that confidence many times since the start of this century: when the dot-com bubble burst in 2000, when the housing market crashed in 2008, when COVID-19 rocked the global economy in 2020. Millennials came of age with a personal finance industry that took a more pragmatic tack than did the investment gurus of the 1990s. My generation followed Ramsey's Baby Steps, did David Bach's Latte Factor Challenge, and downloaded YNAB. All herald the fantasy of being rich, but not with the entitlement and ease of our parents' generation. In this generation of financial advice, prosperity comes from discipline, and discipline starts with budgeting.

Our Disordered Relationship with Money

Despite a growing focus on personal money management in recent decades, Americans' personal financial circumstances are only getting worse.

Only half of Americans are comfortable with their ability to cover unexpected costs.[11] Nearly 60 percent of workers expect to work in retirement, most for financial reasons.[12] Basically no one has saved what experts recommend for retirement. In 2022, $110 billion in federal student loans was in default, affecting 24.8 million borrowers.[13] Money is perennially a major source of stress in the lives and relationships of Americans.[14] Financial stress is associated with increased psychological distress, insomnia, and even coronary heart disease.[15] And that burden falls heaviest on the poorest Americans.[16]

Despite widespread financial stress and signs that point to systemic rather than individual causes, the personal finance industry continues to peddle the promise that individual financial prowess can solve all your problems. It has carried on Dave Ramsey's back-to-basics approach and taken to instructing us to dig ourselves out of these deep debt holes by tightening our belts. Budgeting is no longer reserved for the clever housewife of the 1950s; it's lauded as an inevitable step toward becoming rich.

After nearly a decade of writing about personal finance, where the personal budget is the backbone of every piece of advice, I was surprised to learn that not only is budgeting as advice cruel, as Veronica Duke taught me; budgeting as a practice doesn't even work. As the authors of a 2018 study at the University of Minnesota conclude, "Although budgeting is commonly recommended and many people do keep a budget, little systematic evidence exists on whether budgeting actually helps people achieve their financial goals over the long term."[17]

It's notable that, despite a universal reliance on budgeting as good money management, research into its effectiveness is sparse. The University of Minnesota researchers noticed this, and aimed to fill the gap with studies that looked into whether budgeting actually helps people achieve financial goals in the long term. The researchers led three field experiments (a type of research that takes place in a natural environment, rather than a lab) and one longitudinal study (where scientists collect data from the same people over a long period) to learn how budgeting in various forms impacts spending decisions, spending enjoyment, and goal achievement.

The truth about budgeting contradicts everything the personal finance industry has been teaching.

Budgets Are Unsustainable

Despite the pressure from the personal finance industry, research shows that less than one-third of Americans keep a detailed household budget.[18] Budget culture holds budgeting as the obvious answer to our financial woes and shames us if we don't comply. But no one is complying.

Just like dieting as a method of weight loss, the utility of budgeting for financial security comes down to that persistent truth: we don't do it. And that's not for a lack of trying. Google searches for "how to budget" have risen about 60 percent in the past decade,[19] and searches for the "best budgeting app" are six times what they were ten years ago.[20] But the level of restriction and deprivation and the lack of nuance in budgets—as in diets—makes them unsustainable.

In the first University of Minnesota experiment, participants were randomly assigned a budget for their Black Friday shopping. They got either a budget that explicitly listed a total spending limit or one that only listed limits per person they were shopping for. After Black Friday weekend, they reported their total spending. Those with the clearer total spending limit spent less, but—notably—all participants overspent their designated budgets. "In the short run, setting a budget can help to translate abstract goals into clear standards," the authors note.

But, their second experiment shows, budgeting can also be "unpleasant," which discourages people from sticking to it. "Tracking a budget may reduce the enjoyment associated with spending by increasing pain of paying through a tightened link between costs and benefits," they write. This effect is stronger the less money you have, because spending is more painful when the money comes from a more limited pool.

In this experiment, a different group of people were randomly assigned to track either their Black Friday shopping or their regular shopping. After the holiday weekend, participants rated how much they enjoyed spending on each category. In addition to learning that budgeting reduced enjoyment, they found the lower enjoyment also meant lower intentions to continue tracking budgets in the future.

Through their first two experiments, researchers established that, yes, a restrictive budget can constrict spending in the short term—but it doesn't prevent overspending at all. And the practice of keeping a budget is so unpleasant that it reduces the enjoyment you derive from spending (i.e., living your life), and that lack of enjoyment makes it unlikely you'll want to keep budgeting in the long run.

Budgets Don't Reduce Spending

Still . . . if you *could* stick to a budget—if you happen to have the fortitude so many people lack—surely that would improve your financial situation, right? Probably not, according to these researchers. Budgeting instead encourages a splurge-and-restrict cycle exactly like the binge-and-restrict cycles we see with diets. "People may use perceived progress as an excuse to take a break and may splurge a little," the authors note, giving budgeters "little net benefit."

In their third experiment, researchers followed budgeters and nonbudgeters over a ten-week period. They found that budgeting worked both positively and negatively: when people spent more than they budgeted in one week, they "corrected" by spending less the following week. But the same was true for underspending: When people spent less than they budgeted in one week, they reacted by spending more the following week. In both cases, the reaction was stronger for participants who tracked their budgets closely.

"The net effect," the authors conclude, "was that budget trackers were no more likely to attain their financial goals than those who did not track their budgets."

The researchers' fourth experiment, a longitudinal study that looked at spending adjustments over a longer period using data from a budgeting app, found that active budgeting causes a similar pattern of restrict-and-splurge swings over the long run.

The authors point out that these patterns mirror what we've seen for decades in diet and weight-loss research. Many people see early weight loss from dieting, but a restrictive diet takes all the pleasure out of eating and becomes difficult to maintain, and dieters look for permission to "cheat" or drop the diet altogether, negating the earlier effects.

Budgets Don't Improve Your Well-Being

Studies into budgeting behavior tend to make headlines out of whether participants budget, without noticing or sometimes even investigating a budget's effect on participants' financial or overall well-being. The Financial Consumer Agency of Canada (FCAC) declared a 2019 budgeting pilot "successful" solely for increasing budgeting behaviors among participants who weren't previously budgeting.[21] But a close look at the results shows just one-third of those who left the program with an intention to start a budget actually did so, and just 8 percent of them said the habit helped reduce their financial stress. What, then, is the purpose of keeping a budget? Without seriously considering the behavior's usefulness to our broader enjoyment of life, these studies are about as meaningful as reporting on how many people drive a red car or a white one—it's just details.

Because of the dearth of meaningful research into budgeting, I often consider the similarities between budgeting and dieting in questioning whether budgeting is a useful money management method. We can extrapolate from a much wider body of psychological research on dieting, and see methods relying on restriction and discipline don't work in any meaningful or healthy way—and in fact are often harmful.

A 2020 study published in the medical journal *The BMJ* is just one of the most recent to document that popular diets like Atkins, WW (formerly Weight Watchers), and the Mediterranean diet have minimal impact in the short term, and their benefits disappear after a study ends, when participants are no longer being fed controlled diets. The study, which reviewed 121 dieting trials, found that people are unable to maintain dietary restrictions.[22] As registered dietitian Christy Harrison details in her book *Anti-Diet*, study after study for decades has found the failure rate of intentional weight-loss efforts to be over 95 percent, repeatedly confirming the findings of a groundbreaking 1959 study from Dr. Albert Stunkard. Those who do maintain dietary restrictions and weight loss long-term do so through hypervigilance around diet and exercise, including "weighing themselves compulsively, weighing and measuring food, not taking any breaks from their exercise routine, adhering to strict diets even on holidays and vacations, and basically having all of their time monopolized by their efforts at weight control," Stunkard found.[23]

"In eating-disorder treatment circles," Harrison adds, "we have a word for these behaviors: *disordered*."[24]

Consider another parallel with dieting: researchers in San Antonio in 2017 found an association between food insecurity and rebound eating, weight stigma, and compensatory behaviors like bulimia and over-exercising.[25] Participants with the highest levels of food insecurity were most likely to restrict as well as compensate for eating. People experiencing the most severe food insecurity met clinical criteria for an eating disorder at a higher rate than the general population. That means people who were often hungry because of a lack of access to food still felt so much guilt when they ate what they considered too much that they responded with behaviors that further starved their bodies. That's the power of our culture's reliance on restriction and shame.

This level of scrutiny doesn't yet exist in budgeting research, but Veronica Duke's frugal mindset following her years living in poverty shows how the same thing can happen in budget culture. The restrict-and-splurge spending cycle is already apparent among budgeters in the general population. Add financial insecurity to the mix, and it's not hard to see how the swings of restriction, splurging, and shame would be even more severe when we inhumanely impose budgeting on people who are struggling with money.

Budgets Make Money Management More Stressful

"It just felt too complicated, so I stopped."

Marian Schembari was a twenty-eight-year-old American

freelance writer living in Germany and traveling around Europe when she became frustrated with managing her variable income and downloaded the then-new YNAB software. She appreciated some of the habits she formed while using the app, but she stopped using it after about two months because keeping a budget in the app felt too cumbersome.

"I was constantly having to do math, and it hurt my brain. Even though they're technically doing it for you, they're not really," she explains, because budgeting software is so bad at accounting for variable spending and basic hitches, like spending in cash.

Marian is autistic and has trouble doing simple math in her head, a common challenge for people who experience difficulty with executive functioning, like those with ADHD or autism.[26] That could make money management challenging under any circumstances, but she found herself particularly vexed by the "mental gymnastics" of trying to force money management into even a simple budget.

Even remembering the experience a decade later is upsetting for Marian. "I'm having a weird body response to this," she says, and pauses as she reflects on her experience with the budgeting software. "I'm actually shaking right now. I think because it really made me feel like a failure. I couldn't keep it up, and I felt like I was doing it wrong."

If you've ever tried to keep a budget—or, similarly, to follow a diet—you know exactly the feeling Marian is having.

Many people claim budgeting helps them feel in control and, therefore, reduces financial stress. What's the harm in using a budget if it feels like it's keeping your finances in order?

The harm is what the University of Minnesota researchers found: budgeting actually increases your stress. The harm is the anxiety that comes with maintaining an approach to life that doesn't support your needs and best interests. The harm is the time you spend tracking and planning your spending that is unlikely to yield the results you're after. The harm is the stigma and biases budget culture creates by letting us devalue people—including ourselves—based on financial choices. The harm is learning to ignore ourselves when we want something, deferring to an external set of guidelines to make our decisions for us.

Harrison's description of this impact from diet culture rings true in Marian's experience with budgeting: "Diet culture systematically negates our need for self-care and replaces it with self-control. Diet culture teaches us we don't deserve to care for ourselves or have our needs met. It tells us that the food our bodies need and want is 'too much,' 'unhealthy,' or just plain 'bad.' . . . Diet culture disconnects us from our own needs and shames us for having them."[27]

That doesn't mean budgeting never feels beneficial. Marian downloaded YNAB because she felt like her finances were completely out of her control. She was earning enough to keep up with financial commitments, indulge in plenty of doner kebab, and travel around the continent. But she never knew how much was in her bank account, and she was fed up after her account overdrafted two or three times.

"I felt like a huge failure going into overdraft at twenty-eight. I felt way too old to be making those types of 'stupid' mistakes."

Using YNAB—manually inputting every expense—gave her visibility into her money that changed her habits and made money feel less haphazard. It also showed her where she could make changes to free up money for saving, and she built a "buffer" of a couple thousand dollars in her account for the first time. It felt empowering for a period, but that didn't last.

If you've used a budget, you might have experienced that part, too: the shift toward feeling in charge of your finances instead of the other way around. That's the feeling that keeps people evangelizing for budgeting, especially whatever specific budgeting method or app they use. But, as the statistics show, most people stop following the budget, just as Marian did, because it's nearly impossible to sustain. Unlike Marian, many people also simply don't have access to enough resources to make ends meet, and no way of organizing your money with a budget is going to turn too little into enough. It'll only pile the stress of keeping a budget on top of the stress of not having enough money.

That benefit that Marian experienced from using YNAB, the way Harrison describes restriction as "self-control" that masks as self-care, is a result of feeling as if a budget can quiet the money stress in your brain. It temporarily replaces your constant worry about which decisions to make with a set of strict rules about how to use money. But in the long run, it's more likely that budgeting will cause you to fixate more on money management than make you worry less about it.

Budgets Aren't Designed for Real Life

A lot of budgets are designed with the assumption of predictable income, expenses, and spending, circumstances that aren't the case for a lot of people, especially the people budgets claim to help most, like Veronica as a single mother or Marian as a scrappy freelancer.

"We have this idea that every month you have the same set of expenses," Marian says. "That's just not true. . . . It's not like every month I spend $400 at the grocery store. Sometimes I spend $400 at the grocery store, but sometimes I host people for dinner, and then it's $600. Or sometimes I'm traveling, and I don't spend any money at the grocery store, but my dining-out budget is really high. Or sometimes we eat a lot of meat, and sometimes I don't want meat at all. In the summer, I garden, so my grocery budget goes way down, because I'm eating all the veggies from my garden."

Marian doesn't blame herself or her disability for her struggles with money management the way she used to, but the noise of budget culture keeps her from ever feeling one hundred percent confident in herself around money.

"I still sometimes feel like a failure," she says. "I make mistakes or I don't think through purchases. I still don't think there's a better solution for managing money that doesn't involve all this work and mental gymnastics and math and assigning categories and analyzing every penny."

Budget culture convinces you those financial "mistakes" are your fault. They're your fault because you won't commit to the regimen. They're your fault because you can't comprehend the math. They're your fault because you don't put in the time or effort. Popular budgeting advice assumes anyone can make perfectly economical decisions in a vacuum, untouched by the nuances of life. But as the research shows, budgets fail—just as we acknowledge diets do—as soon as they face the constraints, pressures, influences, and decisions involved in everyday life. You're not a robot, and you don't make financial decisions in a vacuum. How you use money influences and is influenced by every other aspect of your being and your experience in life.

You don't have to engage in the act of budgeting to participate in budget culture. But accepting the premise of budgeting as good money management keeps you tethered to budget culture beliefs. You might avoid budgeting because it's too hard or ignore it because you can get by without accounting for your spending, but you can still hold on to the shame and judgment inherent in the belief that perfect money management should include restriction and control. You can still act on the premise that each individual is responsible for their financial circumstances. You can still strive for perfection and feel guilty for (inevitably) falling short.

When you question the premise of budgeting as good money management, you take the first vital step toward releasing the hold budget culture has on your relationship with money—and on your life at large.

Nine New Ways to Think about Money

In the following chapters, we'll construct a counternarrative to the accepted rules of budget culture by exploring these new ideas that challenge common budget culture tenets.

1. YOU DON'T NEED A BUDGET.

Money should be easy. Budgets offer an illusion of control within the chaos of our systems, but you have to work hard to maintain the illusion. Avoid money management methods, tips, or tools that set spending limits, categorize spending, name priorities for you, label any kind of spending as "good" or "bad" (or "wants" versus "needs"), or in any way make you feel like you're not good with money. Instead of adopting money management methods that ask for more time and diligence, find ways to get money off your mind.

2. YOU DON'T HAVE TO EARN YOUR LIVING.

Reject the capitalist premise that paying for basic human needs makes sense. Income from work isn't superior to any other resource that lets you access necessities. Meet your needs not only through earned income but also by taking advantage of the ways our government intervenes against the forces of capitalism: claim tax credits, utilize public benefits, and be served by tax-advantaged nonprofit organizations. Take advantage of capitalists themselves by leveraging debt to tap into the capital they hoard. Recognize these resources as valid and morally neutral alongside earned income.

3. YOU DON'T HAVE TO WORK SO HARD.

A person's value to society isn't attached to how they work, their ability to do certain jobs, what kind of work they choose, or how much money they're paid for working. Tap into your intuition to choose good work that's in line with what matters to you, and detach your self-worth from external measures like job title and pay.

4. YOU DON'T HAVE TO PAY ALL OF YOUR BILLS.

There's no such thing as a "fixed expense." Bills aren't immutable obligations; they're commitments you make to pay. When those commitments no longer serve you, you can cut them to make the changes you want in your life. When commitments are out of balance with your resources, deprioritizing payments is a valid way to achieve financial wellness.

5. YOU DON'T HAVE TO PAY OFF DEBT.

Choosing how to use debt and how to deal with it are financial decisions, not moral or ethical ones, and carrying debt won't destroy your life the way budget culture makes you believe. Understand the consequences tied to any debt you use, and you can decide how to deal with it in a way that supports your life and goals.

6. YOU DON'T NEED AN EMERGENCY FUND.

Money is just one of the realities of your life; it's not the defining force. Financial fluctuations alone don't constitute an emergency; the most they can do is make you uncomfortable—they cannot break you. A store of money can ease financial stress and let you live life without money weighing in, but you can set your comfort level wherever it makes sense for you.

7. YOU DON'T NEED AN INVESTMENT ACCOUNT.

Our systems of work and government have designed investing to be the most viable path to lifelong security and independence, but investing in a capitalist economy is an ethical minefield that takes advantage of workers, pollutes the environment, and harms society. You're not a bad person if you take this route, but it's worth considering alternatives for long-term financial security.

8. YOU CAN SPEND MONEY.

Restriction isn't an effective money management method. Money is meant to be spent, and you can use money however you want. Yield to your inner voice, and let it guide your money moves, instead of looking to an outside set of rules for what you "should" do. Trust your ability to steward the money in your care in a way that's right for you and the people in your life.

9. YOU CAN GIVE MONEY AWAY.

Whatever you own isn't yours; it's just in your care for now. Money is a tool to shape the life and world around you. When you hold it in your hands, you hold the responsibility to contribute to that world in a life-giving way. Don't fear scarcity when you give money away or use it to benefit someone else. Their gain isn't your loss, because there was never a difference between "your" money and "their" money in the first place.

Three Dimensions of Financial Wellness

I know, most financial educators know, and you probably know by now that—despite what budget culture would have you believe—no number, like your net worth or bank account balance, is a useful measure of your financial health or wellness. Lots of experts have devised new methods and formulas for this measurement, but—as you might imagine—I don't ascribe to any of them. I encourage you to explore various definitions of *financial wellness* on your own, because they can give you more information that could be useful to understand your financial situation. But scales of financial wellness defined by budget culture inevitably measure your proximity to the fantasy of being rich. As we reject that as the goal, we need a new way to measure success and progress.

You have to recognize money as a fluid, interconnected element of your life, and therefore not something that can be attached to a static goalpost. You can't make decisions based on whether they'll move you closer to a defined end goal, because there is no end, and goals will constantly change. Instead, we look at decisions based on how, in the moment or season when you make them, they serve three dimensions of wellness: head, heart, and health.

HEAD

Your head is the part of you concerned with goals and achievements. Decisions that serve the head help you grow and develop. They recognize and utilize your strengths and help you achieve personal, professional, and financial milestones.

HEART

Your heart is the part of you that defines your values, drives your passion, and inspires your care. It sees the world you want to create and the people you want to serve. Decisions that serve the heart help you make the positive impact you want to make and avoid any negative impact you want to prevent. They let you be and honor your whole self and live in line with what matters to you.

HEALTH

Your health is the part of you that admits your humanness. It encompasses your physical and psychological needs, strengths, and limitations. Decisions that serve health provide for your care and safety, and honor your whole personhood.

Most long-standing financial advice starts and stops with the head. More modern advice—especially that coming from millennial and Gen Z personal finance influencers—shows concern for the heart, but tends to stop short wherever it conflicts with budget culture values. Financial advice at large almost entirely ignores health.

As you reflect on your financial situation throughout this book and make financial decisions throughout your life, consider how they serve all three dimensions of your financial wellness. None is more or less important than the others, and none is more or less relevant to money. Your money moves constantly impact every dimension of wellness, so consider them all when you make financial decisions.

Reflection: Your Relationship with Money

Before you dive into the budget-free approach, consider the following questions to explore your existing relationship with money. Look for common threads in your answers to develop a picture of how you've internalized messages about money, how past experiences influence present decisions, and what kinds of emotions about money you've been carrying without noticing.

Messages you've gotten about money

- How did adults around you talk about money when you were growing up?
- What kinds of lessons about money did your parents or other adults teach you?
- What do your family, friends, and colleagues think and say about their financial situation?
- What do your family, friends, and colleagues think about folks with lots of money?
- What do your family, friends, and colleagues think about people who use debt or government resources?

Your experiences with money

- How do your identities (gender, race, age, generation, sexuality, ability, nationality, affiliations, and so on) affect your career, jobs, and relationship with money?
- Have you experienced or witnessed financial trauma or injustice?
- Which financial decisions have you made in the past month? The past year? The past five years? (No need to judge them as positive or negative; just name them.)
- How have your financial decisions served you so far? Are they still serving you?
- Have you set and achieved any financial goals for yourself? What are they?

Your relationship with money

- How do you feel when you talk about money?
- How does thinking about money affect your mood?
- How do you feel when others talk about money around or to you?
- What comes to mind when someone brings up money?
- What kinds of financial habits do you have that you're aware of?
- Where do you sense resistance when you interact with or think about money?

CHAPTER 3

You Don't Need a Budget

The writer Marian Schembari might still feel the tug of budget culture in her self-judgment of her ability to manage money. But she knows she's making better decisions for her money now that she's moved on from stressful budgeting.

"The things that make me 'wealthy' . . . are exactly what I'm doing [now]," Marian says. "Quitting my job. Focusing on a career that I control and that I really love, that allows me to pick up my kid from school and not have to pay for aftercare. It's deciding to have one child instead of multiple children. . . . There are other things that have nothing to do with budgeting that make me feel like I'm doing good things for my money."

Some of the best things you can do for your money have nothing to do with budgeting; in fact, they have nothing to do with money, period. These steps focus on taking care of what author Stephen Covey calls "big rocks."

Covey, the popular businessman and author of *The 7 Habits of Highly Effective People*, popularized the "big rocks" metaphor in the

1994 self-help book *First Things First*, coauthored alongside A. Roger Merrill and Rebecca R. Merrill.

The fable goes like this: A lecturer places a large jar on a table. They first place as many fist-sized rocks in the jar as possible and ask the students if the jar is full. They all agree it's full. Then the lecturer pulls out a bucket of pebbles and pours as many of those into the jar as possible and again asks the students if it's full. They again agree it's full (though, probably more skeptically at this point). Then the lecturer pulls out a bucket of sand and pours in as much sand as possible. After the students are hoodwinked yet again into believing the jar is full, the lecturer pulls out a bucket of water and pours in as much water as possible into the jar.

The lecturer points out that if they'd started with the water, nothing else would have fit into the jar without making it spill over. The point Covey makes in the book is that you have to make room for the important things—the "big rocks"—first, and let the rest fit around them. If you fill your time or energy with the small things—water, sand, or pebbles—your jar is full, and there's no room for the big rocks.[1]

Consider Marian's experience, and see how she's prioritizing her "big rocks" in her relationship with money. She first places her big rocks: family and satisfying work. She lets the water, sand, and pebbles—spending, commitments, and financial goals—fall in place around them.

Advice about managing money often involves an inordinate amount of time spent thinking and worrying about money—the small stuff. That's how budget culture sucks the fun out of money and makes it way harder than it needs to be. Money in and out is a given part of our everyday lives; it shouldn't be such a source of stress. Managing money should feel simple, fun, and freeing, regardless of your circumstances, so you can use it to support the life that really matters to you—your big rocks.

That starts with how you organize and use money day-to-day. This is where budget culture shows up in its most obvious form: the household budget. Most financial advice and plans start with making a budget, claiming it's vital to knowing where your money is at all times and making the "right" decisions about how to use it. A wellness-focused financial planner or coach might guide you in creating a budget, not with the stated goal of restriction but with the intention of giving you visibility and control over your money. That sounds innocuous, but building a budget inevitably builds restriction and shame into how you use money—whether through explicit spending categories, limited allowances, labeling spending as "wants" or "needs," or turning your spend history into graphs that encourage self-judgment, perfectionism, and self-optimization.

I don't endorse money management methods, tips, or tools that set spending limits, attempt to categorize spending, name your priorities for you, label any kind of spending as "good" or "bad," or in any way make you feel like you're not good with money. Instead, I encourage you to experiment with tools, techniques, and strategies that let you manage money with ease and joy. That should be the main goal of any money management method, yet so many start with restrictive behaviors that immediately make you work harder and suck the joy out of your life.

Take budgeting out of the equation. Real ease in money management comes not from having unflinching control over every dollar but from not having to think about money. That's not a luxury reserved for the ultra-rich. In this chapter, we'll look at how to use tools and techniques to set your money on autopilot, from autopay for bills to automatic savings contributions to reminders for upcoming purchases to appointments that create space to hold your financial concerns and goals. Instead of promoting money management methods that ask for more time and discipline, we'll get money off your mind. Money should be easy; don't let budget culture convince you that you have to work hard to do it right.

The Never-Ending Ticker of To-Dos

Let's start by understanding why managing money feels so stressful, regardless of resources or circumstances. It's easy to guess that money is a major stressor for people who don't have enough of it.[2] Not knowing how you'll pay for housing or food, or whether you can provide for the future you want for yourself or your children, is bound to keep you up at night. Even if you can pay the bills easily, living on just the necessities and never caring for yourself with comforting and life-giving indulgences—or, as the teacher Veronica Duke showed us, even a full refrigerator—leaves you never able to take a deep breath. But financial stress doesn't disappear when you have enough to cover everything, because budget culture just raises the bar.

One financial planner who works with high-earning folks told me their clients worry about money just like the rest of us, except their concerns revolve around things like the pressures of the stock market, maintaining their status (which might be vital to maintaining their relationships), and paying for pricey private schools.

And, they say, "For those who have built financial wealth through prudent spending and disciplined saving and investing (rather than due to inheritance or other windfall) . . . the underlying emotion is sort of a generalized anxiety around running out of money."

Even those who ostensibly benefit the most from capitalist wealth hoarding experience immense financial stress because the fantasy of being rich has no endgame.

"In my experience, the wealthier the family, the less transparent families are about talking about money," says financial planner Lisa Hodges, who works with high-wealth clients actively concerned about economic inequality. "They often hide how much money is in the family altogether, how much the child (my client) can expect to inherit. There are often lots of unspoken assumptions about how the younger generation is going to 'squander' the inheritance. The general approach is one of distrust and closely held information. As a result, young inheritors (or future inheritors) are often very ill-prepared for money. They don't really know how much life costs and have no way to emotionally process what effect such a large sum of money can have."

Everything you do involves money—whether that's keeping a roof over your head, seeking a life partner, coparenting with an ex, or coping with a loss in the family—so life's stressors overlap with financial stress at every turn. You can hardly make a decision in your day without consciously or subconsciously considering the financial consequences. That makes money management not only its own dimension of mental work but also a layer that's hitched to every other dimension of the mental load—what's often referred to as emotional labor.

The sociologist Arlie Hochschild first coined the term *emotional labor* in 1983 to describe displaying certain emotions to meet the expectations of a job outside of the home—like a customer service agent maintaining a happy tone to keep a customer calm or a server gleefully singing "Happy Birthday" at a restaurant. It's evolved in popular culture since to acknowledge the same phenomenon playing out in the unpaid labor (mostly) women perform in families and communities without complaint. Emotional labor is the toll of the behind-the-scenes work caretakers do to keep a household running, as writer Gemma Hartley describes in her 2017 article that brought the concept into the mainstream: "reminding [my husband] of his family's birthdays, carrying in my head the entire school handbook and dietary guidelines for lunches, updating the calendar to include everyone's schedules, asking his mother to babysit the kids when we go out, keeping track of what food and household items we are running low on, tidying everyone's strewn about belongings, the unending hell that is laundry. . . ."[3]

This labor is almost uniquely shouldered by women. A 2023 Pew Research Center study found that wives married to men spend significantly more time on housework than their husbands, even when the wife is the primary breadwinner. Even when the wife is the sole earner—the only scenario in which the husband spends more time on housework—he spends about half the time that she does when he's the sole earner.[4] Other research has shown that same-sex couples divide chores more equally, but that split trends more along heteronormative lines once they have children: one partner earns more money, while the other does more house and care work.[5]

My favorite name for this invisible labor comes from Amanda Doyle, cohost of the podcast *We Can Do Hard Things*, who simply calls it "the ticker."

"There is no breathing room in my mental space," Doyle explained about her experience as a mother and wife in one episode. "And it's like a CNN ticker that's like *tick, tick, tick, tick, tick*. Here's all the things you should be doing right now. And while you're doing those, please do all these other things . . . it's like all of the things that come together to architect a life, it feels like those are happening through my head all day long. And god forbid the inevitable happens, where one thing takes twenty seconds longer than it should. And then it throws me off completely, because the ticker keeps running. I'm always and never not behind."[6]

Money management is the ticker capitalism foists on all of us. It's the ticker that runs over the top of the ticker of everything it takes to construct a life. That ticker exists whether you have millions in assets under management or don't know where your next paycheck will come from; money is woven into every decision we make. Budget-centric money management makes this ticker louder, more prevalent, and, as we learned from the University of Minnesota researchers in chapter 2, more painful. You track and categorize purchases, weigh them against allowances, mentally account for changing priorities, move money from one category to another, judge yourself for decisions, seek justifications, note upcoming bills, count the days until your next income, split the check at a restaurant, choose the optimal credit card to use for each purchase. Budgeting ensures the ticker stays turned on, lights flashing, speed dialed up to high, so you, like Doyle, will never not feel behind.

Budget-free money management, in contrast, is about getting you to stop thinking about money. You automate your commitments and goals as much as possible, so you can quiet the noise, listen to your intuition, and spend consciously without ever worrying whether you're using money the "right" way.

Seek Ease, Not Control

That constant ticker that's behind money stress is the reason so many people want to learn a magic-bullet method for money management. Budget culture tells you that if you just get your money under control, that feeling will go away.

But it's not true. You can't get money "under control." The fantasy of being rich nags you to wonder what else you're missing, no matter how much you've already done to bend yourself to the rules of budget culture. Capitalism will always disrupt your peace in the tug-of-war where it plays both sides: keeping you striving for prosperity while depending on your inability to achieve it. Budgets promise to help you feel in control of money, but in reality they control you through restriction, shame, and greed. They give you an out-of-the-box ticker of tasks to master and—failing that—worry about. They suck the joy out of the moment by slotting it into a category and slapping a price tag on it. They dominate your plans and goals, and manipulate your decisions. They give you an illusion of control while causing you to shut out your inner voice and question your every move.

This isn't a healthy relationship with money. If you were treated this way in any other relationship, you'd call it toxic, maybe even abusive. You'd be looking for the door—if you could recognize the abuse. Having been in this kind of relationship with a human man, I know firsthand you don't always recognize what's happening as it's happening. You're told what's "right," and you go along because the alternative seems scary and destructive. You experience moments of control that convince you everything is fine. The noise of expectations and shame deliberately drowns out the voice inside you that knows this isn't where you should be.

Until it doesn't. Until that voice slowly gets louder and you can't ignore its message. You begin to ask questions that cause the whole thing to crumble. That's incredible. And it's terrifying.

Recognizing and divesting from budget culture can be just as slow, complex, and incremental as recognizing and leaving any toxic relationship. As you make space to reflect on your experience and listen to your inner voice, you'll begin to recognize trauma in the same way, too. Pulling the curtain back on a paradigm that's dominated your entire life is in no small way traumatic. As you put distance between yourself and budget culture, starting with nixing the budget, you'll see the ongoing trauma of its restriction and manipulation. Much like a body in recovery from months or years or decades of shame and disordered behavior driven by diet culture, your head, heart, and health will need time to recognize and heal from the damage of budget culture.

The first step on this journey is to recognize that control over your money is an illusion and slowly loosen your grip, letting go of your need to feel in control. A budget-free approach to money doesn't offer a false sense of control; rather, it offers a real experience of ease. When you stop trying to do what someone else says is right with your money, you can start listening to what you already know is right for you.

Budget culture makes you believe you're doing something wrong if you're not working hard to earn, manage, save, and grow your money. But nothing ever has to be hard. If it comes easy, let that be a sign you're doing it right. Ease is just another way of saying you're walking a path free from friction—because it's the one that's made for you to be on.

If you feel friction when you deal with or think about money management, it's probably because you're butting up against some budget culture expectation. Maybe your access to paid work keeps you from earning enough to contribute to goals, while budget culture tells you that you should have a $1,000 emergency fund and shunt 10 percent of each check into a retirement account. Maybe you find immense joy in buying elaborate dinners for your friends, but budget culture says you should be using that money for saving or paying down debt faster. If a money management method doesn't let you experience ease and joy from money on your own terms, it's not the right method for you.

Saying Yes to You

As we've seen in budgeting studies, the restrict-and-splurge cycle of budgeting gets you nowhere. Budget-free money management leaves restriction and discipline out of the plan. Instead, you can let go of the never-ending ticker and use a simple reframe to get money off your mind.

I started to devise my own budget-free approach—long before I gave it a name—shortly after I left my full-time job at the personal finance start-up. Through that work, I'd discovered hundreds of money management apps that were all pretty much the same: all encouraging restriction toward an assumed goal of hoarding money. Just before I left, though, I'd learned about a banking app that made it easy to manage money through an anti-budgeting method and what it called a "safe-to-spend" account. Instead of a total account balance, the app displayed only what was left to spend in your checking account after financial commitments and big spending goals you created were automatically funded. None of the restrictive budgeting methods that are common in most financial apps.

That company no longer exists; it was bought by a big bank that absorbed its customers and discontinued the product like the capitalist giant it is. (I moved to a nonprofit credit union when I found out about the acquisition.) I was devastated to lose that intuitive approach to money management, and it sparked a minor obsession with fixing what was wrong with the personal finance industry.

I couldn't find another app or method like that safe-to-spend account, so I developed a tool I now call a Yes Fund to continue the ease of the safe-to-spend method without using that app. The Yes Fund is a simple container that helps you focus on easeful spending rather than restriction.

A Yes Fund is a metaphorical bucket for spending money—and it has no limit. Just like my original safe-to-spend account, using it is simple:

- **Automate a process for funding your goals and commitments** at levels that make sense for you. That could be through a money management app, your bank account, digital or paper envelopes, or reminders to move money manually, as we'll discuss later in this chapter.

- **The money left in your spending account is your Yes Fund.** That's money you can use freely without restriction or tracking (i.e., it's "safe to spend").

Your Yes Fund is money you can spend or give away without worry, because you know your goals and commitments are covered, and your financial situation will remain where you want it to be. It also quickly gives you information about the consequences of any way you choose to use money: if you spend more than what's in your Yes Fund, it'll impact the money designated for goals and commitments or it'll increase your debt. That's a simple way to get the data you need to make decisions.

A Yes Fund is not another way to restrict how you use money—that's why I put "Yes" in the name (however cheesy it sounds). You don't have to restrict your spending if it exceeds your Yes Fund balance. Adjusting how you use Yes Fund money is always one option. But you could also maintain your spending and make adjustments in other areas—like the income you earn, the alternative resources you use, your financial commitments, or your financial goals. As you'll see in the coming chapters, all these elements of your financial situation are pliable. Instead of turning to restriction, you can tweak in other ways to have a Yes Fund that lets you experience a life in line with your head, heart, and health.

While a typical budget categorizes, tracks, and caps everyday spending, a budget-free approach with a Yes Fund is a way to experience ease in money management without letting it take over your every thought. Instead of predetermining a purpose for every dollar (and inevitably straying from the plan), you'll be able to spend from your Yes Fund without shame or restriction.

Many budgeting methods claim to let you spend without prescribing restrictions. But they tend to do so by encouraging you to self-impose restriction: creating an allowance for each spending category (as YNAB does) or "giving every dollar a job" (as Ramsey encourages). The Yes Fund flips that approach on its head and answers the one question you're truly trying to answer in any given moment: "Can I buy this?" The goal isn't to turn down your desire, but as often as possible to get to a resounding YES.

Budget culture treats restriction as an obvious sign of fiscal responsibility. But *not* spending money has significant consequences you need to consider alongside the consequences of *spending* it. Not spending money could mean restricting your access to community and fellowship. It could mean going hungry. It could mean holding money that could have saved another person's life. It could mean missing enriching and educational experiences.

The Yes Fund is a tool to help you see those consequences more clearly and make financial decisions with them fairly weighed in. Budget culture restricts spending as a way to put the full blame for your financial circumstances on you. But we know it's much more nuanced than that. Abstaining from a generous or indulgent purchase today—or every day—won't determine your financial future. There are much broader forces at play that shape your financial circumstances and are more complex to address.

We have to address those issues (keep reading!), but in the meantime, it's also important to know that your financial problems won't be solved if you buy cheaper shoes and fewer lattes. It's important that you let go of the shame and blame a budget imposes, so you can use money to say yes more often, experience the full life you deserve, and make the impact only you can make.

Get Money off Your Mind

A Yes Fund can replace a typical budget in your approach to money management, but it won't quiet the ticker if you keep up the budget culture habit of constantly tracking your money. To truly reduce your financial stress, get money off your mind through automation.

Automated money management is any strategy that takes decision-making out of the equation. Automation lets you let go of the emotional labor of tracking and remembering to complete tasks, and in many cases takes care of the work for you altogether. You can automate almost everything about your money. Autopay for bills is one obvious example, but that's only a part of it. We're going to talk about ways to get creative with tools, routines, and automation, so you can get your finances off your mind and manage money without thinking about it all the time.

Note that many automation methods are most useful when you have enough income coming in that you can cover commitments, contribute to goals, and still have money left over. Automation is a way to get money management off your mind, but these methods won't increase your resources or lower your bills. If your finances feel severely out of balance, focus first on adjusting your finances to find the balance you want, and you'll find it easier to fit automation into your life. We'll also talk in chapter 12 about how to create a feeling of "enough" when you can't make things balance out, so if these strategies don't feel accessible to you right now, don't worry; there are other steps you can take to find ease.

To get you thinking about how to offload decision-making, here are a few ways to automate money in your life.

Reverse Your Budget

The most straightforward way to automate your money management is to feed your Yes Fund through a method sometimes called reverse budgeting. I've also heard it called an anti-budget, or "paying yourself first." Regardless of the name, this method isn't a type of budgeting at all, because it doesn't involve restrictive rules or spend tracking. Instead, it's a simple way to feed your goals and commitments, so you don't have to worry about whether you can spend money.

Reverse budgeting sets your Yes Fund on autopilot. When you automate contributions to the goals and commitments you've named—whether through an app, your bank account, or a new routine—it's easy to spend freely from your Yes Fund without restricting or tracking. You know you won't need the money to cover bills or savings, so you don't have to count pennies.

Bank Settings

Bank settings are probably the first thing most people think of when they think about automating finances. These include accepting direct deposit for a paycheck or other income, setting up auto-pay for any bills that allow it, and using automated rules to transfer money into various accounts. Direct deposit is a common offering for employees and many contractors. A payer can deposit a payment into your bank account if you give them your account and routing numbers. If you get a regular paycheck, you can use direct deposit rules to split it immediately among a spending account and savings accounts for various goals and plans.

You can set up autopay for bills online either through your bank account or through your service provider, depending on what the service provider allows. Usually it means setting up a direct deposit from your bank to pay the bill on a set date each month. But if you can't do that, you might be able to have your bank send a check ahead of the due date instead. For bills that change month to month, like electricity or water, setting up autopay through utility providers is usually easiest, because they can debit the fluctuating amount.

You can set up automatic transfers into your savings account a lot of ways, depending on what your bank offers. You can do it as a percentage of your direct deposit. You can schedule a recurring deposit from your checking into your savings on a set schedule. And some bank accounts and apps let you set more complex rules, like transferring money into savings every time you spend money at a certain merchant.

Money Management Apps

Money management apps offer tons of creative ways to automate your finances, and many of them are free to use.

A word of warning: most of these apps and tools are completely budget-forward and rely heavily on budget culture messaging to convince you that you need them in your life. And yet technology is a magnificent tool for getting money off your mind and experiencing more ease and peace. So can we use these tools without letting them completely suck us into budget culture habits? I fully support anything that automates financial labor, and I don't have the resources or knowledge to create an app myself. So I work with the landscape that's available and recommend the best (or, sometimes, least offensive) apps to address various financial needs. Financial technology (fintech) companies and products change, merge, and disappear quickly, so go to youdontneedabudget.com for specific, up-to-date recommendations. Instead of naming apps here that'll probably go out of style before this book gets into your hands, I'll share some ideas to get you thinking about what to look for.

Here are some ways personal finance apps can help manage your money:

- Connecting to your service providers, so you get notifications before bills are due, and to your bank account, so you can pay bills automatically.
- Managing an online-only bank account that makes it easy to separate your goals, commitments, and spending without opening a bunch of separate accounts.
- Connecting all your financial accounts, including banking, investment, and debts, so you can easily see your financial picture as a whole and automate savings and investment contributions.
- Keeping all of your public benefits account information and balances easily visible in one place.
- Checking your credit report and keeping track of your score for free.

To find tools that get money off your mind without reinforcing restriction or shame, look for apps that prioritize all dimensions of financial wellness over user engagement. For example, apps that send you alerts when you go over a spending limit, present a graph of your net worth on the opening screen, or email you your credit score daily are more focused on getting your attention than on reducing your financial stress. Look for apps and choose settings that let you think *less* about money by automating money management, not those that make you think *more* about money by adding alerts and tasks to your ticker.

Like most technology that's free to use, some financial apps make money by selling your data or using it to serve ads, so make sure you're familiar with the ways an app uses your personal and financial information and how it makes money before you sign up. You can usually find this information in plain language in a company's FAQs or help center, so you don't have to decipher its entire privacy agreement.

Calendar Reminders

If you like to or need to be more hands-on with money and don't want to let the bank or an app make money moves for you, you can reduce emotional labor and incorporate automation in other ways. Setting reminders in a reminders or calendar app is an easy way to release the emotional labor of constantly thinking about money without giving up all your control cold turkey. Make a note whenever you notice the financial ticker running through your head, and set a reminder to deal with the tasks it presents so you can get them off your mind.

For example:

- Set a recurring reminder on the days you're paid, so you can manually pay bills, make charitable contributions, and move money into savings.
- Set a recurring reminder a few days before each bill is due, so you can manually schedule a payment. To simplify even more, contact your service providers and creditors to move due dates, so you can take care of multiple bills at once and stagger them with your paydays.
- Set reminders a few weeks or months ahead of important birthdays and holidays, so you can plan ahead for any spending and spread the shopping out.

Process Documentation

One thing that makes money management a bigger burden than it needs to be is navigating processes every time you have to make a change to your bank account or pay a bill. Give your future self a gift by documenting processes so you don't have to retrieve the information from your brain or relearn processes every time.

Use an electronic document you can share with others in your household, like a notes app, Google Docs, Notion, or Evernote (apps, too, that might change or disappear in the future—but have so far had greater staying power than most fintech). Document processes and information including:

- Account passwords. For the best security, don't keep these in a basic document; use a secure password manager, like 1Password or LastPass. Or you could include hints in a document.
- In a document, include links to all of your bank and service provider accounts and payment pages, as well as to your employer's payroll provider. That'll make it easy to jump straight to the right place when you need to make a change.
- Document the steps required to complete a task the first time you do it, so it's easy for you and anyone in your household to do it next time. Common tasks you could document include paying a bill online, setting up a bank automation, finding information about financial accounts, managing your paycheck direct deposit through your employer, checking your credit report, or creating a calendar reminder.
- In the shared process document, encourage everyone in your household to make notes when they make changes, like setting up automatic bill pay, so everyone stays in the loop regardless of who's handling tasks.

Here's *my* gift to your future self: Go to youdontneedabudget .com to grab a template to keep track of all your money management processes!

Set a Money Date
Writer Laura Leavitt shares in her essay for my newsletter *Healthy Rich* how she and her husband formed a habit that helps them stay

on top of their commitments and work toward financial goals: they review their finances in a weekly family meeting to keep their major life goals top of mind and make financial progress toward them. The weekly review has helped them prepare to have a child, build a nest egg to move to their dream home, and dedicate a high percentage of income to causes they care about.

"What I've loved about family meetings is that the big things we've accomplished have all crept up on me because they happened in smaller moments throughout our lives together," Laura writes.[7]

Whether you're managing money only for yourself or with your partner(s), family, roommates, or community, regular meetings to check in can reduce your financial stress. Scheduling a regular meeting creates space dedicated to money management, so you can avoid thinking about or discussing money issues outside of that space.

A lot of people like to set a weekly or monthly money date with themselves or their family, like Laura and her husband do. This lets you check in so everyone is aware of your financial circumstances and goals.

As Laura points out, "There are always discussion points that seem just out of relevance, since there's also dinner to eat right this minute or a call to take for work in half an hour. . . . [Our weekly meeting] felt quite silly at first, because we talk all the time. But then we realized the very valuable way a weekly meeting structured our conversations."

A money date gives you time to process and talk about big or small changes you want to make, so you can focus on creating a plan to achieve them. Use a money map so you have a consistent checklist to guide your review.

If you receive a regular paycheck, a periodic paycheck check-in with an HR rep or just a look at your payroll account online is another kind of money date to consider. It can remind you where your paycheck is being deposited and give you visibility into your access to various benefits and retirement planning. Spending a few minutes to do this once every few months can keep you aware of the resources at your disposal and quiet the ticker about meeting your short- and long-term financial goals.

For longer-term planning, you could meet periodically with a financial planner, coach, or therapist. A coach or therapist can be helpful if you want to work through issues in your relationship with money, and a financial planner can help with specific advice for investing and long-term savings.

Money Should Be Easy

As you work out the money management strategies and habits that feel right for you, I can't stress this enough: the goal isn't to optimize yourself or keep up with the latest tools. It's to get money off your mind—pull finances off the ticker and let that burden rest somewhere else (your calendar or apps, for example). If a tool or method adds items to your ticker, it's not useful.

As experiences like Laura's show, "automation" can be as simple as developing the routine of talking about your financial goals. It's less about specific tools or methods and more about adjusting your relationship with money to seek freedom from the burden of financial shoulds, coulds, and to-dos—and expecting money to be easy.

Reflection: Financial Friction

Name places where you sense friction in making financial decisions. Brainstorm automations that would reduce friction or take that decision off your plate. Answer these questions:

- What's a financial decision that frequently causes you stress?
- What makes it hard?
- How could you automate it to remove the need to decide?

CHAPTER 4

You Don't Have
to Earn Your Living

Capitalism is an economic system based on private ownership and profit. We let a minority of people own the resources we all need to survive, and those owners use that power to produce profit and accumulate capital. Under this system, we treat it as normal to exchange labor for access to necessities like food, property, financial products, education, and health care. We unironically call this "earning a living."

Pause to consider the absurdity of that everyday phrase. When we talk about *earning a living*, we are, literally, talking about getting money to pay for the things that keep us alive, like food, shelter, clothing, health care, community, dignity, and safety. When we attach those to the word *earn*, we suggest a person is only entitled to these life-giving amenities if they have the means to pay for them, and, for the majority of people, if they can work for the means to pay for them.

Budget culture fights hard against our innate human understanding that we're all one hundred percent worthy of a life of comfort and dignity simply because we're here. This is how capitalism shows up in what we believe about work. Its focus on profit and capital accumulation is antithetical to a humane system of equitable giving and receiving, so capitalism's survival relies on us to generally believe productivity is a fair trade for a life.

The way this plays out in our lives is utterly inhumane. As the teacher and single mom Veronica Duke showed us, even the "free" resources available to our most vulnerable citizens are severely restricted, and easy to lose if they reach for a whisper of independence. Those resources are almost nonexistent for anyone we deem capable of production, even if the system in which they're expected to produce fails to accommodate their type of humanness. From mothers with caretaking duties to neurodiverse workers masking their true selves to Black Americans battling generational trauma to trans folks enduring daily attacks, our system of work is discriminatory and traumatizing for wide swaths of our workforce. Yet we take at face value that we should strive for capitalism's standard for productivity, and that those who don't meet this standard deserve less than those who meet or exceed it.

Even for those who exceed—and, inevitably, raise—the standard, the expectation to trade productivity for life is absurd. Those of us who do or can earn a living are nonetheless oppressed by a system that expects that of us. While it's not realistic in this system to altogether ignore the need to exchange money for life, we can recognize the many ways to have our needs met without exchanging labor to capitalists.

Recognize Your Resources

Your financial circumstances are based on the resources available to you—ease comes from having enough, whatever that means to you. Suffering comes from not having enough and not having access to any remedy for that.

Conventional budgeting advice looks at your income and asks you to cut spending when it doesn't add up—or work harder to find more income. Budget culture adherents love to tout the so-called simplicity of personal finance: spend less than you earn. That implies an inexhaustible ability to earn enough at all times, which many people don't have. And it treats the constructed mechanism of capitalism like natural law—a phenomenon philosopher Mark Fisher calls "capitalist realism."

Fisher describes capitalist realism as "the widespread sense that not only is capitalism the only viable political and economic system, but also that it is now impossible even to imagine a coherent alternative to it."[1]

That widespread sense is what we have to question.

A typical budget relies entirely on earned income and prescribes restriction when that income doesn't buy everything you need. A budget-free approach suggests it's okay to consume beyond what you earn through work. Income isn't your only resource. If getting groceries from a food bank, for example, frees $100 of cash for you this week, you have more room to care for your needs and work toward your goals. Your existing assets, community and government assistance, and debt are all resources at your disposal to get what you need, and using them is just as valid as using income from work.

Accepting the premise that we need to work to earn everything gives us an excuse to jump to judgment of any spending that doesn't align with our expectations. Ever judged a stranger with a smartphone who's struggling to pay for other necessities like housing or food? Questioned a family's right to be in the restaurant when you know their kids receive reduced-cost lunches at school? Looked sideways at a woman's freshly manicured nails after you've learned she receives government assistance? These are all real criticisms I've heard throughout my life, and I don't believe the people passing these judgments are inherently inconsiderate. They're mired in a culture that's convinced them they have to earn what they have, and it's confusing and frustrating when someone challenges that belief by asserting their inherent right to a living.

It's not a natural law that you must work for money to access necessities; it's just the way our economic system is organized. This system disadvantages large swaths of the population by design and sets all of us up to prioritize work over the life we value. You can break free from that paradigm and make big or small progress for yourself without waiting for change in the system as a whole: take advantage of alternative resources that have nothing to do with earning money.

Veronica wasn't the only woman in her group of friends to become pregnant right after high school in 1983. Another friend came from a wealthy family who'd set up a trust for her. She married the child's father and went on to graduate from college.

"When you have money and your family has resources and if you own property or you own a home or you just have a safety net of wealth, that's very different," Veronica says. "She just was treated much differently than I was."

A third friend became a single mom without any support or cooperation from the child's father. That woman worked as a server in a restaurant and took a job at a factory soon after her daughter was born. She worked full-time and didn't go to college. She worked at that factory until she was old enough to retire.

Veronica was determined to go to college as planned.

"I think I had enough forethought to say that I didn't want to work in a factory like she did," she says. "I felt like that was going to have an endpoint that wouldn't be helpful in the long run."

She enrolled in a community college and was eligible for Pell Grants. She planned to go for two years to earn an associate degree, like her mother had, and become a medical assistant.

"I didn't think I was smart," she says. "I was apathetic about school."

But in her first semester at that community college, Veronica earned grades high enough to get on the dean's list. "I thought: I can do this. It's not bad."

After community college, she transferred to earn a bachelor's degree in biology. In addition to working part-time as a server and a lab assistant, Veronica paid for school and supported herself and her daughter with government grants and loans and public assistance programs. With the difficulties of navigating public benefits, she got by however she could.

"There were times when I started cleaning houses for professors and people I knew to make a little extra money that I didn't report [for food stamp eligibility] just so I could have gas money."

After six years, degree in hand, Veronica became a teacher. She taught first at a community college in North Carolina, where her new husband was stationed with the military. When they moved to Ohio, she got an Ohio teaching certificate and earned her master's degree and began teaching high school so she could be on the same daily schedule as her children.

Though she struggled with financial challenges and the stigma of poverty and single motherhood in the early years of her daughter's life, Veronica was able to care for her daughter and become the first in her family to earn a bachelor's degree because she tapped into several types of resources that are available to all of us: income, assets, community resources, and debt. Without recognizing these resources, she might have never gotten out of the cycle of poverty she'd grown up with.

"You can get in that cycle of thinking that you're never going to get out, and then you have a mindset where it doesn't [seem to] matter," she says. "And then that affects your choices."

Joyful money management has to start with recognizing the resources around you. That includes income, but it's much more than the money you earn from working. Income alone doesn't always cover all your needs or interests. Maybe, like Veronica, you're a student or a parent, or you're living with a disability or chronic illness, or you're already expending all your energy on a job or multiple jobs. Maybe paid work is not the best way for you to contribute to the world or your community. That's why we consider all types of resources, not just income, to make financial decisions.

INCOME

Income is that money you bring in, usually from working, like Veronica's income from part-time jobs. It might also be payments from investment accounts, a trust, or spousal or child support. It's most often money you have to work in some way to earn.

Income is usually the first thing you think of when you think about the resources available to live your life, and this is typically where most budgets and money management plans stop. Before picking up this book, you might have been pulling out your hair trying to find balance between your spending and your income. That comes from the budget culture belief that you have to earn a living. Rethinking your resources doesn't mean discarding the prospect of earned income altogether; you can work and earn as much or as little as you want. But a budget-free approach lets you see the full value of all the resources available to you, so you don't unnecessarily restrict yourself to the money you can earn from working.

ASSETS

Assets are things you own or skills you have that have some kind of potential to expand your resources as needed. They could technically be anything, like items of clothing you can sell on consignment or a guitar you can pawn, but I recommend focusing on the high-ticket items, like property, vehicles, jewelry, electronics, and investment accounts. Those smaller items might come in handy in moments of need, but for the purpose of getting an overall picture of your financial situation, it's easier not to have to inventory everything you own.

Assets can represent enormous value you're sitting on, and you might not even realize it. You could feel constantly strapped for cash day to day, but live in a house you could sell, have a skill you can trade for services, or hold an investment account you could tap.

I withdrew $26,000 from my retirement account when I was thirty-six years old to fund the down payment and upkeep costs for my first house. I knew I could only take up to $10,000 without a tax penalty, but I took more and planned for the tax bill (as debt), because it gave me a path to buying a house that didn't otherwise exist. My new house is just a bike ride away from my sister and her kids, and the yard is big enough to plant a vegetable garden, start a compost pile, plant a wildflower field, and maybe even raise chickens someday. Even as a renter, I was being priced out of the city life I'd enjoyed throughout my twenties. Buying this house in a small town cut my monthly housing cost in half and gave me a stable landing place for the rest of my life (if I want it). The move wouldn't have been possible without tapping into my biggest asset.

Selling your home or withdrawing investments, if you've got them, might not be right for you; maybe your family is living in just the right community and is squeezing every drop of use value out of your home, and maybe you've got a clear life plan that relies on income from your retirement account in the future. But at least noting the value in your major assets lets you make financial decisions with a more complete picture of your options.

You don't necessarily have to liquidate an asset to benefit from it, though. Peer-to-peer platforms offer creative ways to turn your assets into income without giving them up entirely. You could use a room in your house for short-term rentals; use your car for rideshare; or rent out items you own, like tools, baby supplies, or formal clothing. Or you could leverage assets in exchange for community support: be the person in your community with a truck anyone can borrow or the handy skills everyone needs, and trade the goodwill for free childcare when you need a night off, for example. (No need to keep a ledger of these trades; just be a human within your community!)

COMMUNITY RESOURCES

Community resources include things like childcare from friends or family, as mentioned above; or other help from friends, like the help Veronica's friend relied on as a single mother. There are also government resources, like grants, reduced-cost school lunch programs, or unemployment benefits; nonprofit services like food banks, rental assistance, and shelters; and other help from your community, like lawn care while you travel or meal prep after you bring in a foster child. Community resources are any benefits or services you can access that you don't have to pay for out of pocket. They free up your other resources, whether by directly freeing money or giving you free time you don't have to spend working. Budget culture attaches all kinds of shame to community resources as "charity," but this is just a way of redistributing resources so you can get the support you deserve and avoid unnecessary restriction.

Community and government resources exist all around you, and you might be surprised to learn how much you can access and qualify for. Participation in the USDA's Supplemental Nutrition Assistance Program (SNAP), for example, is just 82 percent of eligible people in the country.[2] That's in part due to requirements that are hard to prove and processes that are difficult to navigate—and those are changes we need to make at a policy level. But lack of enrollment can also be attributed to biases and lack of knowledge about the program. One study found that just sending eligible Americans a letter informing them of their SNAP eligibility doubled the percentage of people who enrolled.[3] Sending the letter along with offering enrollment assistance tripled enrollment. This lack of information about eligibility and how to enroll is especially detrimental to the working poor and older Americans, who are even less likely than the population overall to enroll in SNAP benefits they qualify for.

If you're struggling to pay your bills, buy food, afford housing, heat your home, clothe your family, or anything else you need to thrive—or you're sacrificing other types of spending to do it—there's probably a community or government resource that can add ease to your financial situation. You don't have to get through life on grit alone. Yes, you are strong and resilient—and you deserve every boost and helping hand we have to offer.

The communities we build and the governments we elect aren't separate entities we should feel ashamed to need. Budget culture supports capitalism by perpetuating the belief that they are. In truth, communities and governments are ecosystems we exist in. In the same way flora and fauna coexist in every ecosystem around us, our communities and governments support us as we need it, and we contribute to them as we're fit to do. Community support and government resources are particularly important for anyone who faces an obvious barrier to working for income, but don't judge yourself undeserving or above them because you don't think you fit the model of someone who needs community and government to survive. We all need them in our own ways. Take advantage of what's available to you to create the ease and joy you deserve to experience.

I used a food bank for the first time in my life when I was in my "sort of a freelance writer" phase, living in Berkeley, California, and struggling to earn money. My disciplined upbringing connected social services with a lot of shame, but shedding that shame became vital when I only had enough cash on hand to pay for rent or buy groceries, but not both. Picking up a bag of groceries from a nonprofit in the city was a surprisingly delightful experience in this community that prioritized socialized care: my partner and I faced little scrutiny and a short line, we were treated with kindness and humanity, and we left with a bag that included fresh California produce that was a welcome balance to the rice, beans, and pasta we'd been subsisting on with our own dollar. Taking advantage of that resource whenever money was tight let me continue to focus on nurturing my nascent writing career and do work that was right for me, a winding journey that's led to the opportunities I have to do the work I do now.

None of this is to say our social safety nets in the United States are good enough—they're absolutely not, and they're far worse in some regions than in others. We have so much work to do, and we'll talk more about that in chapter 13. But services do exist, and you can take advantage of whatever's right for you.

DEBT RESOURCES

Debt resources are ways you can borrow money to extend your resources, like Veronica's student loans, or my delayed tax payments. In the long run, debt is a liability, not an asset, and you have to understand and consider the consequences of that liability alongside the benefits of using debt as a resource. But understanding and planning around those consequences doesn't mean avoiding debt at all (or any) costs. Debt can be an important way to expand your resources when you need it and help you avoid unnecessary restriction when you don't want to or can't increase your resources in other ways.

Before you pass judgment or give in to shame around using debt, know that it doesn't reflect your level of responsibility or value as a person. Budget culture connects shame to debt when poor people use it, but not when rich people or businesses use it, which creates further inequality in our access to resources. We'll talk about this more in chapter 7, but for now: recognize debt as an available resource, not a moral failing, and remove the shame and blame budget culture connects to it.

Rethink "Earning," and Prioritize "Living"

Your resources build the foundation your relationship with money will rest on and, therefore, the foundation you can build a life on. Recognizing the diversity of resources and support available to you can add a significant amount of ease to how you manage money. Ignoring resources beyond your income can push you into unreasonable sacrifices and shame.

Conventional budgeting methods tend to look only at your earned income and restrict your spending accordingly. They fail to explore the creative ways you can use assets; and they attach shame to community and debt resources instead of recognizing their very real value. By understanding these resources as neutral and listing them alongside your income, you can begin to recognize ways to leverage them to experience the ease and joy you deserve.

Reflection: Rethinking Your Resources

Think about all the resources you've used throughout your life.

- Did the people in your life know you were using each kind of resource? Why or why not?
- What would have been different in your life if you hadn't had access to one type of resource?
- How does your experience color how you see others' use of debt or community resources?

CHAPTER 5

You Don't Have
to Work So Hard

When I was around eight or nine, my parents offered my younger sister and me our first allowance. We were each responsible for a rotating set of weekly chores, and we each got $3 per week for completing them.

I didn't like to do the chores. I remember being asked to wash dishes (from meals I didn't choose), do laundry (full of clothes that weren't mine), and dust (furniture I didn't buy). This labor seemed ridiculous to my childhood brain, which had no reason to care about the appearance of our house and would have gladly chosen boxed macaroni and cheese on paper plates for every meal. I'd forfeit a week's pay anytime I skipped my assigned chores—but that was hardly a sacrifice. I was an elementary schooler with parents to provide food, clothing, and shelter for me, so I had little need for money. The novelty of cap erasers and Airheads from the school store wears off fast, and money loses its luster, especially when you have to trade labor for it.

By the time I was ten or eleven, my parents discontinued the allowance system. The housework wasn't getting done, and money wasn't the right incentive. So they pulled the allowance and instituted a "You do the chores because we told you to do the chores" policy in its place. The lesson? You do work because work needs to be done.

My parents never taught me about our country's economic system or discussed the details of various financial products or money management methods. I assume that's because they were as in the dark about them as many Americans are: just 57 percent of US adults can correctly answer the majority of extremely basic personal finance questions in a survey by Standard & Poor's rating services.[1]

But there's another reason we didn't talk about things like investment accounts and compound interest: financial products and services weren't built for people like us—people who "weren't born rich." Our culture positions financial services as tools for the rich to get richer. We see them as much too complex for the proletariat to understand and inaccessible with our limited resources. The bourgeoisie can enjoy rest and let their vast wealth grow into more wealth; we'll accept our lot and work for our money, thank you very much.

Everything we—me, my family, and my community, but also most Americans—know about money is really about work. We know we need money to survive in the world, and we see work as the only respectable way to get it. We expect we'll never have enough but that we'll be able to get by as long as we keep working. My parents taught my sisters and me how to work hard, and that shaped everything I believed about money.

I've since learned the name for this moral code: "the Protestant work ethic." The concept is rooted in a Protestant Christian belief that hard work and frugality are ways to steward earthly gifts, which the faith interprets as bestowed by God. My family were, indeed, Protestants—Lutherans—so I'm not surprised these beliefs undergirded our way of life. But we never discussed them explicitly and weren't, to my knowledge, even aware of them (given that the term *Protestant work ethic* is primarily used by academics and not the working-class Protestant folks it describes). This belief in the innateness of productivity has become ostensibly untethered from religion and is now simply the American way. Some scholars even credit it with the spread of Western capitalism and the dominance of American productivity.[2]

"[Nineteenth-century German sociologist] Max Weber's revolutionary thesis about the relationship between religion and economic progress has so permeated our society that we're not conscious of the roots of our industriousness," wrote arts and culture critic Charles Ward for the *Houston Chronicle*.[3] "Sure, university professors teach the idea in detail, and some Christians encounter a simplified version in the 'prosperity gospel,' but we're just too busy to contemplate what makes us so productive."

Budget culture rests on the capitalist belief that inevitably morphs from the Protestant work ethic: your value as a member of our society is tied to your ability to produce for profit. The way we think about money in our culture stems from this core belief we dub "work ethic," because without it, capitalism wouldn't survive. This economic system requires masses of people able and willing—or forced—to contribute labor to produce wealth, so the beliefs we've developed to survive measure us based on our ability and willingness to work hard.

Work ethic is so ingrained as normal that we don't usually notice it in ourselves or the people around us. But pay attention. It might not happen explicitly, but we often pass judgment on a person based on our perceptions of their levels of so-called productivity or laziness. And we measure those only on their visible performance of work we deem eligible—which generally means work outside of the home, for pay, and excludes the vast array of unpaid domestic and care work people do within families and communities.

Expand Your Imagination of Work

Imagine this isn't normal. Imagine a world where your worth isn't measured by how hard you work. Imagine that each person begins with the same value because they're human and because they're a member of our society—not only in theory, but in practice. Imagine we're allowed to pass our time in ways that bring us ease and joy. Imagine it's not our collective job to produce wealth and our ongoing responsibility to fight to hold on to it.

Everyone has value in our ecosystem. As Tara McMullin writes in an essay for her newsletter *What Works*,[4] "Our inability to accept that is one of the reasons we have such a hard time inventing a better system to meet our needs than getting as many people as possible into jobs. It's why, even as individuals, we have a hard time going slower, taking a rest, or asking for what we need at work. . . . We can't recover from our broken employment systems and unsustainable working conditions until we accept that all members of our community have value. We need a new cultural and personal narrative about the 'non-industrious poor,' the 'leeches,' and anyone who doesn't work, whether work is available to them or not."

All members of our community have value. This might be easy to accept in theory and about other people. You might think it's ridiculous to suggest you would judge someone's worth as a person solely on their paid labor. But how do you feel about *your* value? Do you accept others' innate value while measuring yourself against an impossible expectation of ever-growing productivity? Do you continue to strive for higher pay and more valued positions? Do you continue to prioritize a company's needs over your own in pursuit of recognition and advancement? That harms others as much as it does you.

"I am on that ladder, too, because we're all on that ladder," said author Sonya Renee Taylor as a guest on the podcast *We Can Do Hard Things*. "No matter where you are on the ladder, someone is below you. There is someone in this world that has a body that is deemed less valuable than yours. And every time you are like, 'I'm going to take another step,' you are ensuring that they stay lower than you. . . . Until you get off that ladder, we will continue to have a world of inequity."[5]

To truly accept that all members of our community have value, you must accept the value you add to your community simply by being. You can't hold yourself to a higher standard of work than anyone else, because that'll always mean giving yourself more credit and value than someone else. You can't hold on to the value we've placed on work ethic, because that'll always mean placing some people above others who don't live up to the expectation of hard work.

Accept that endless, ever-expanding labor isn't the natural order of things. Accept that our economic system has been intentionally designed around extracting labor and hoarding profit. Accept that work as we know it isn't inevitable; it only exists within the system we currently uphold. You can occupy your time in any way that serves your head, heart, and health, and however that looks isn't a reflection of your innate goodness or badness as a person. Other people can do the same, and we have no right to judge their goodness or badness because of it, and we have no right to give or withhold life to them because of it.

I swim in the same waters as everyone else in this culture, and the Protestant work ethic is as much imprinted on my DNA as anyone's. Combined with privilege and chance, my efficiency, stoicism, and persistence according to the standards of capitalism have brought me the life my parents hoped for me—one where I earn double what they did at my age and have the adventures they delayed to raise children. I believed in my right to my relative comfort for years because of the work I exchanged for the money to buy it. For some years, I even believed those who were less willing to put in the same work were less deserving of the same comfort. I grew out of the latter belief pretty early. But the former stuck with me for longer than I like to admit. The glorification of work ethic is insidious. It was apparent in the second-wave feminism of the 1960s, 1970s, and 1980s, which focused on gaining equal rights for women in paid labor rather than fighting for fair recognition and compensation of work performed (by people of any gender) in caring for homes, families, and communities.[6] Today, it underpins millennial hustle culture, my generation's attempt to use the tools of capitalism to dig ourselves out of the recession-sized hole that capitalists' recklessness dug for us as we entered the workforce.

"You do work because work needs to be done" is the attitude behind the ridiculous politics that have stuck us with a federal minimum wage that hasn't budged in a decade and a half. Operating on work ethic means you make do with what you get and don't ask for more or better. It means work is your duty, not labor you can choose and deserve compensation for. That makes earning and managing money a matter of discipline. You don't expect more, you don't spend more than you make, and you never ask for help.

Expanding your imagination of work and money starts with disconnecting how you value yourself from the kind of work you do and the money you earn. Connecting your innate worth to how you work can make you feel like there are right and wrong choices for how you earn money—and that, in turn, can make you feel like there are right and wrong ways to use money. This belief supports the budget culture narrative that you have to earn certain kinds of spending. That sets you up for a spiral of shame about how you earn and use money, and none of it is fair.

Your worth has nothing to do with your job title, your pay, your ability, or how you choose to occupy your time. Tap into your intuition to choose work that's right for you and the purpose you want to serve, and detach your self-worth from external measures.

When you downgrade work from a measure of morality to its proper place as a way to occupy your time, you can seek what I call good work. Good work is any way of occupying your time that serves your head, heart, and health. It might be a job for pay, community service, family care, or anything that lets you be just who you're meant to be in each moment. Good work supports the kind of businesses you want to see in the world, serves people you care about, makes the positive impact you want to make, and avoids any negative impact you want to help prevent. It lets you bring your whole self to your work, because the work you do is in line with the kind of person you are and want to be. It utilizes your strengths, supports your learning and development, and makes room for things you want to achieve in your personal life. When you work for someone else, good work pays fairly, provides for your health and safety, and respects and honors you as a human being—beyond your ability to produce.

Good work is what author and podcaster Jenny Blake describes in her book *Free Time: Lose the Busywork, Love Your Business* as "easeful work," explaining that it's work that aligns with your natural talents (not that "the work itself is easy or without challenge").[7]

Blake describes two ways to think about challenging work, one that's fulfilling and one that simply fulfills the expectations of the Protestant work ethic: lowercase hard work and uppercase Hard Work. "Lowercase hard work is rewarding. It's challenging, and it pushes us to the edge of our stretch zone, where we discover flow. Uppercase Hard Work is worn as a badge of suffering, one that mostly leads to burnout."[8]

Reject Productivity Culture

Many money management methods assume the main goal of work is to make as much money as possible, which can conflict with your ability to gain joy and fulfillment from what you do. "Earning more money" is the cultural prescription when we look at our finances and find further restriction is not feasible. Expanding your resources through work can come in handy, but it isn't always the right goal for everyone, and it's downright inaccessible to some.

When you accept that work doesn't define your value, you can approach work not as a duty to "God" or community but as one way of occupying your time. Our economic system makes paid work unavoidable for most people if you want to access basic needs like food, shelter, and security, but it's equally vital that you address other dimensions of wellness as well. An activity that occupies as much time as work does—half of our waking days[9]—ought to support not only your need to access resources but other important needs, too: a need for belonging, purpose, respect, and self-actualization. I invite you to expand your imagination of work beyond simply productivity and occupy your time in a way that lets you be who you are and make the contribution you want to make to your community and the world.

This means shedding the assumption that your time is meant to be productive. Possibly the hardest part of rethinking your relationship with money is the inevitable step of rethinking your relationship with productivity and reimagining a world where your body isn't a tool of capitalist production.

In *Rest Is Resistance*, a manifesto against capitalism and "grind culture," author Tricia Hersey writes, "Rest saved my life."[10] Hersey's encouragement to rest, daydream, resist grind culture, and imagine the world you want to see is uncomfortable to take in. The thought of stopping, of not working, is so counter to what we're trained to view as inevitable that it befuddles your mind.

The premise feels right when you first hear it: "Grind culture thrives on us remaining in our heads, unable to allow the technology of our divine bodies to soar and develop," Hersey writes. "There is massive knowledge and wisdom lying dormant in our exhausted and weary bodies and hearts."[11]

But when you try to imagine actually claiming the rest you have a right to, you can turn your brain into a pretzel. It's not easy to square the liberation Hersey writes about with the work ethic that feels like our prime directive as Americans.

"Everything we know about rest has been tainted by the brainwashing from a white supremacist, capitalist system," Hersey writes. "As a culture, we don't know how to rest, and our understanding of rest has been influenced by the toxicity of grind culture. We believe rest is a luxury, privilege, and an extra treat we can give to ourselves after suffering from exhaustion and sleep deprivation. Rest isn't a luxury, but an absolute necessity if we're going to survive and thrive. Rest isn't an afterthought, but a basic part of being human. . . . We must reimagine rest within a capitalist system."[12]

Hersey goes on to explain that rest is hard to square in our minds—and, in particular, in the minds of Black women and others from whom rest has been stolen for generations—because our minds have been traumatized by capitalism. We're inclined to ask, "How do you make money if you're resting?," imagining rest in the way capitalism defines it: a break from work. What Hersey describes isn't a break from work, or a onetime detox to recharge for future productivity. It's an "unraveling that will require our participation for our entire lives." It's a daily practice in which you embody rest as resistance against the programming capitalism has instilled in you and your culture.

That programming Hersey calls grind culture is what I see as the productivity component of budget culture. In the same way budget culture embodies the fantasy of being rich, Hersey describes how the fantasy of success undergirds grind culture's lie: "I clearly remember the moment it clicked for me how a capitalist, patriarchal, ableist, anti-Black system could never make space for the success I wanted for myself. The 'success' grind culture props up centers constant labor, material wealth, and overworking as a badge of honor."

The Trap of Passion Work

Choosing good work isn't the same as chasing what's known among nonprofit workers and academics as "passion work." It's easy in service-oriented or advocacy work in particular to focus only on values alignment when you're looking for a job or starting at an organization. Many well-intentioned workers take on a role of service regardless of their position, always making others' needs a priority over their own. They're willing to accept low pay, untenable hours, or poor working conditions if they work for an organization supporting a cause they care about. Passion work is often disguised as work that cares for your whole personhood but is actually just hustle culture within an organization whose mission you support.

Skepticism about capitalism and profit causes some folks—more and more with each new generation—to ignore the finances of work altogether and focus narrowly on values alignment or passion in their work. But the three dimensions of financial wellness are inseparable. Work that ignores your head or health doesn't truly serve your heart.

"The rhetoric that a job is a passion or a 'labor of love' obfuscates the reality that a job is an economic contract," writes Simone Stolzoff for the *New York Times*. "The assumption that it isn't sets up the conditions for exploitation."[13]

This stance isn't fair to anyone—not to the people who work in the organization and not to the communities you serve. Whether you're looking for your first job, leading an organization, or building a company yourself, consider all dimensions of financial wellness to ensure you and the workers around you are able to do good work within the organization. In this way, good work can feed the person performing it as much as the people served by it and contribute to the highest good for everyone.

Ownership over Your Occupation

The most unfortunate truth about capitalism is just how hard it fights your efforts to take on good work. The system doesn't exist without exploitation, so it relies on the lies of hustle culture and budget culture to keep us working hard.

In chapter 13, we'll explore some collective action we can take to encourage broad change and fight worker exploitation on a societal level. But for now, let's acknowledge the reality that you quite likely work for pay or expect to for a major part of your life. Within this system, you can resist exploitation on an individual level and choose or make work that serves every dimension of financial wellness by claiming ownership over how you work. Ownership puts you at the helm, so work can be a fulfilling pastime and not a precarious commodity that forces you into constant compromises.

Ownership, in this sense, isn't about hoarding resources or power. Owning your work doesn't mean becoming the oppressor you're protecting yourself from. It's not necessarily about legally owning a business or being a boss. It's about a set of beliefs that lets you eschew the premise of the Protestant work ethic and reclaim autonomy in work that serves you. It lets you break free from the belief that your well-being depends on an employer and reminds you of the immense value your labor contributes to an organization, regardless of your title or seniority.

You can take ownership in any position by reorienting how you approach work. Instead of accepting the submissive position of employee to any employer, look for opportunities to join or create a working environment that honors your strengths and needs, supports workers' rights, and flattens the hierarchy among bosses and workers.

ENTREPRENEURSHIP

The author Jenny Blake is dedicated to designing a life optimized not for profit but for head/heart/health alignment. She wrote the book *Free Time* and has built an online community of what she calls "heart-based business owners," entrepreneurs who run businesses for more than just money.

"Free time and heart-based business is about integrity, working in alignment with our values, and setting our time free through smarter systems," Blake explains. "Sometimes even freeing our time before the money shows up, before we match it precisely to how to earn more abundantly, with joy and ease. We are taking some risks here. We are making a point to say that free time is the way, not something that only follows far in the future, after we've worked ourselves into the ground."

Entrepreneurship at its base lets you take full ownership of a business and benefit financially from the work you do, and that's what attracts a lot of people to this way of working. But Blake's Free Time Framework is an example of how this approach to work can also give you ownership of your time—and, therefore, your life—in a way many employees don't have access to. The ownership you gain as an entrepreneur means the freedom to choose work and working conditions that support your financial and overall wellness.

FREELANCING

Freelancing is similar to entrepreneurship, but people tend to use the label "freelancer" when they work in a position of service to another business, rather than their own. It can be a way to gain the autonomy of entrepreneurship while maintaining some of the support and companionship you might enjoy as an employee.

Both Daniella Flores and Sarah Prager have written for *Healthy Rich* about seeking freedom in freelancing as queer people. After enduring layoffs, toxic bosses, and the biases against women and LGBTQ+ folks in the workplace, Sarah found immense freedom in freelance writing work.

"I pitch articles I want to write about LGBTQ issues I want to cover," she writes. "I only pitch them to LGBTQ-friendly editors at LGBTQ-friendly publications. If I have a negative experience, I don't write for them again. I'm never tied down with a long full-time contract, and every time I work with a new client, I have a chance to negotiate my pay and choose not to accept it if it isn't enough."[14]

As Sarah illustrates, freelancing offers a different way to approach work that gives you autonomy, flexibility, and access to opportunities traditional jobs don't offer. It's easy to get stuck in a job or life you hate because you feel like you don't have other options; freelancing is a way to expand your options. Freelancing can help you explore a new craft you haven't studied formally, leave a job that makes you unhappy, work on your own terms, add variety to your workload, make extra money or learn a new skill in retirement, work around caretaking responsibilities, or make a career transition.

Daniella used freelancing and remote work to support a cross-country move for them and their wife. Daniella is nonbinary, and their wife is a trans woman; a move from Missouri to Washington State let them live in a place where their identities are affirmed and protected. Their cost of living doubled, but they decided the change was worth the better quality of life they could have on the West Coast—even after the couple were down to one income following Daniella's wife's 2020 layoff.

"I had multiple side hustles and passive income streams to fall back on for extra financial security," Daniella writes. "Those multiple income streams, along with $30,000 in savings, gave us enough financial backing to get [to Washington State]."[15]

Despite several freelance jobs, sometimes combined with full-time work, Daniella doesn't submit to hustle culture. "[My wife and I] don't hustle, we dabble," they write on their blog, appropriately titled *I Like to Dabble*.[16] "Dabbling brings excitement in experimentation and gives your energy the freedom to create amazing things. More money is not the ULTIMATE goal here; time and freedom are."

WORKER COOPERATIVES

A cooperative is a business owned and governed by a collective of member-owners who are stakeholders in some way—usually as workers, customers, or community members. A worker cooperative is a business owned and democratically operated by its workers, while a member (or consumer) cooperative is owned by customers and community members. The model gives each member an equal voice and distributes profits among members according to their contributions to the business, rather than to an elite group of owners based on their ability to purchase ownership.

In a worker-cooperative model, workers own a number of shares of the business, often determined based on hours worked to directly reflect their contribution to the business. Each member gets one vote, and decisions tend to be made by democratic vote, rather than by hierarchy. Depending on the size of the company, you might vote for a board of directors, which includes representation from not only executives but also workers and managers; or you might vote directly on business decisions and working conditions. Members decide how to use or distribute profits; you might reinvest a surplus by adding an employee benefit, or distribute it to member-owners.

A worker cooperative lets workers gain literal ownership in a business, so they can fairly benefit from the wealth their labor creates and participate in decisions about working conditions in the business. Because worker-driven governance comes from the collective, it can be concerned with outcomes beyond profit. This kind of organization tends to be beneficial not only for workers but also for customers and the surrounding community, economy, and environment, because worker-owners are stakeholders in all of these.

The international translation agency Guerrilla Media Collective, founded in Spain, showcases how a co-op model lets a business contribute more holistically to the lives of workers and the community they serve. Its governance model explicitly recognizes three types of work as vital to its success: livelihood work that's paid for by clients, pro bono work that contributes to its free "plurilingual knowledge commons," and so-called reproductive or care work that happens behind the scenes and keeps the business thriving. In a traditional corporate business, "productive work," like sales and client work, would likely be held in higher esteem and rewarded with higher pay and better benefits. Care work—what the organization calls "reproductive work," like project management, employee success, and quality control—would be relegated to low-paying positions, and pro bono work might not be done at all. By creating a model that recognizes the value of all three types of work, Guerrilla Media Collective makes space for each, and ensures workers are compensated for all of it.[17]

It's possible to convert your current workplace into a worker cooperative, but that usually involves employees buying the business from current owners. If you don't want to do that, look instead for an existing worker or member co-op when you're searching for a job, or consider this model if you're a small business owner ready to expand and hire employees.

UNION MEMBERSHIP

A labor union is an instrument to strengthen workers in the fight against capitalist exploitation. It lets you band together with other workers at your company or in your industry to set standards for pay, benefits, working conditions, complaint procedures, and processes for hiring and termination; and unions have an ability to collectively bargain with employers on behalf of employees.

Union membership doesn't give a worker literal ownership in a business the way a cooperative does. In that way, unions are still basically a tool of capitalism: they maintain the division between workers and capitalists, rather than abolish it. But they're a pragmatic response to the existing imbalance of power between workers and employers; not everyone has the ability to start their own business or transform the structure of the company they work for, but every American worker has the right to organize or join a union.[18] Through an organized labor union, you can gain power to demand that your work support your needs and best interests (and those of your fellow union members).

Union density—the percentage of workers who are part of a labor union—dropped dramatically in the latter half of the twentieth century after gaining steam in the first half. In 1983, union members made up 20 percent of the US labor force; by 2022 membership was down to just 10 percent. The bulk of modern union members work in the public sector, where union density is 33 percent. Just 6 percent of private sector workers—the vast majority of US workers—are union members.[19] As I write this book, public support for unions is rising, but this new labor movement faces an uphill battle against capitalist interests.

"If you are in a union, look around—there is the labor movement. It's you and me," writes labor reporter and Writers Guild of America member Hamilton Nolan. "We do not deserve this wonderful and powerful tool any more than the 90 percent of workers who do not have it. It is our moral responsibility to pass this tool on to them, so that they can join the same fight that we are all in."[20]

If you're not in a union and would like to unionize your workplace, visit youdontneedabudget.com to find resources to guide you through that process.

INFORMAL ORGANIZING

Regardless of the structure of your work, you can seek solidarity with coworkers to ensure a safe and fair workplace for everyone. In our current work culture, informal solidarity might be the best tool at your disposal.

I managed a team of five direct reports when I was a lead editor at a nonunion digital media start-up. I'd started early with the rapidly growing company as a staff writer and was quickly promoted through a few positions to become a manager of a team of two, then three, then four, then five people—many of whom had been my peers months before. I don't know if I ever became a good manager, but I know I was well-liked among my peers, I was close with many of the people on my team, and I got along well with everyone.

I was away from the office for three days for an event when the company dropped a surprise on our team that I had to scurry to handle. I checked my text messages at lunchtime to see a worried text from one writer asking, "Did you know about the noncompete contract?"

I hadn't even had a chance to check my own email to find the formal, detached request from our HR department. After we'd been employed for years with the company, executives had retooled our job descriptions to require a noncompete clause in our contracts. The clause they were asking us to sign was standard noncompete language, and it was restrictive. As noncompetes are designed to do, it would restrict our future job prospects and make it very hard to leave the company if we hoped to maintain an income.

At the time, I wasn't quite the anticapitalist I've become since. I felt quite loyal to the company and rooted for its success. But my coworkers saw the noncompete through skeptical eyes and immediately questioned it. Because I was the person who'd been placed between them and upper management, they came to me to figure out if they could possibly keep their jobs without allowing the company to hamstring their careers with this greedy, paranoid move. Their fear moved me, and it never occurred to me to be the middle manager I was probably expected to be: just quiet their concerns and tell them to sign the thing. Instead I set up a meeting with our CEO (with whom I worked closely) for the next day to find out on behalf of my team what this was, and why we were being asked to sign it.

The CEO soothed my immediate anxiety, but that didn't change the impact signing this agreement would have on our career prospects. Three of us on my team met to discuss what was wrong with the agreement, what we'd be willing to sign, and which details were nonstarters. Then we asked for a meeting with HR to negotiate.

I didn't realize what I was doing at the time, but this was collective bargaining. This was employee organizing, even though we'd never even entertained the idea of forming a union at our nascent, tight-knit company. With our combined strength as three valuable employees on a revenue-generating team, we negotiated changes to the language in the default contract. Our final contract updates were rewritten to loosen restrictions and leave us room to take our talents to competitors if we wanted to. That was an incredible win for employee rights—but none of us had approached it as activists. We were just anxious workers giving support and space to each other's concerns.

If I knew and felt what I know and feel about work today, I'd have fought much harder to abolish the noncompete agreement from our company altogether. I could have spoken up in defense of employees who didn't have my clout because of biases and circumstances that impacted how they showed up at work. But it's not always necessary to take on the burden of activism. Simple conversations with and care among coworkers can chip away at worker exploitation and contribute to better working conditions for everyone. Stay in touch with coworkers you trust, and don't be afraid to have conversations that question anything a company asks of you. You're probably not the only one experiencing concern, but it's in the company's best interest to make you feel like you are. (That's why, for example, a company might send individual emails about a new policy instead of holding a meeting, or why some company policies won't allow employees to discuss salaries.) Get your concerns out in the open in any way that feels safe for you, and use the combined power of workers to force your employer to concede a tiny bit of ownership over the labor you provide.

Don't Work Hard; Do Good Work

Budget culture gives you two options to pursue the fantasy of being rich: restrict more or earn more. It teaches you to measure your value based on your net worth and productivity, but what if, instead of productivity, you measured the success of a day based on the joy you experienced, the strengths you honed, the values you honored, and the lives you impacted? Letting go of budget culture's binary lets you resist uppercase Hard Work and acquiesce to the ease, peace, and joy of good work.

Reflection: Finding Good Work

What work do you currently do (paid or unpaid)? How does it support your financial wellness? Answer these questions about the work you do:

Does your work:

- Respect and utilize your strengths?
- Offer opportunities for learning and career development?
- Make room for personal goals and interests?
- Support the kind of business you want in the world?
- Serve people you care about?
- Make the positive impact you want to make?
- Avoid or prevent outcomes you'd consider bad?
- Pay fairly?
- Provide benefits like health insurance, paid leave, and retirement contributions?

- Enforce health and safety measures?
- Offer flexible and remote work, so you can determine how to make your best contribution?

If you answered no to any of these questions, imagine work that would check all of these boxes. What would have to change at your current workplace? Where might you look for work elsewhere to meet your needs?

CHAPTER 6

You Don't Have to
Pay All of Your Bills

"The 'great pause' [in 2020] made us all kind of question and just ask, 'Is this as good as it gets?' " Jennie Mustafa-Julock says of experiencing the social and economic shifts spurred by lockdowns and social distancing in the early part of the COVID-19 pandemic.

Jennie and her wife Meredyth, who work as life and business coaches in their eponymous business, Jennie + Meredyth, were living in an apartment in Chinatown, just north of downtown Los Angeles. Before they became business partners, Jennie worked full-time in the six-figure business as "Coach Jennie," and Meredyth was a special education teacher and then a school administrator for seventeen years, three years with KIPP SoCal Public Schools in LA.

"We had upgraded to the point of, like, we can barely afford this," Jennie says of their LA cost of living.

Through an event the two cohosted for Coach Jennie clients in January 2020, designed to help clients name and commit to their next big goals, Meredyth revealed to the group and simultaneously to herself that she was ready to leave her career in education.

Working in public schools, and particularly in special ed, is demanding work, but Meredyth wasn't fleeing a grueling job. She loved KIPP more than any job she'd ever had.

"I had been searching my whole career for a school that was *home*," Meredyth says. Of KIPP, she says, "I adore them. I think it's one of the best schools ever. They do everything right. And I left it. . . . Part of me had to feel like, okay, I can rest easy; I know it's out there. I know there's a school that is doing right by kids, doing right by teachers, by families, [and] that's when I left."

When Meredyth had become the school's assistant school leader (the charter school version of an assistant principal) in June 2018, the school had been "in the red on all data points" measuring student culture and academics. By early 2020 she'd turned it around through better professional support for staff and teachers, and responsive support for students with different needs; the school was in the green on all data points and outperforming all other public and private schools in the neighborhood. She'd done her job and was ready to move on.

"We weren't prepared for that," Jennie points out. "It's not like we had six months of savings and all of that kind of stuff ready to go. And we use the word 'retired' all the time [to describe Meredyth leaving her previous career], but we weren't drawing from some retirement fund."

Once Meredyth had named her goal out loud, though, it became urgent. This isn't a pair who are willing to wait around for the right time to make their dreams come true. They had to figure out how to move this goal forward, as they encouraged clients to do, "no matter what." They agreed Meredyth would leave her job after the 2019–20 school year. Within just over five months, their household income would drop significantly.

"We knew that we had to do something dramatic in order to afford that," Jennie says.

The couple couldn't make this change and continue to pay the rent and bills on their LA apartment. They needed a way out of their restrictive financial commitments.

In the early days of California's COVID-19 lockdown, Jennie had picked up the habit of watching YouTube videos about school bus to RV conversions, affectionately known as "skoolies." It began as entertainment, but the couple eventually started talking about picking up an RV for real—for occasional weekend trips, because they love to be on the move. But with Meredyth's impending "retirement" and their need for a dramatic financial solution, they connected the dots.

That spring, they financed a 112-square-foot Airstream Nest—"the bougiest, cheapest option," Jennie calls it—and an SUV to haul it, broke their LA lease for a fee, and hit the road, headed east for the first few months. Meredyth joined the coaching business full-time as CEO and equal partner, and the couple embarked on the next phase of their personal and professional lives.

Taking another school year or two to save up money so they could make the transition and keep paying rent was never a serious option, however "responsible" that route might seem. Jennie had been building her business for fifteen years by that point, and it hadn't been profitable for many of the early years. She'd worked on the side for some income, but, she says, "I wasn't really financially contributing to our family. So in my mind it was fifteen years of her going to work . . . to fund my ability to chase this dream."

Now it was Meredyth's turn. "When she had a new dream," Jennie says, "there was no postponing that because of money."

There's No Such Thing as a Fixed Expense

A lot of the ways you hear about life and household expenses makes them sound like obligations you can't get out of. Getting this message about the cost of living can make you feel trapped by your finances. We even often use the term *fixed expense* in personal finance to describe the cost of housing and bills. But, as Jennie and Meredyth discovered, those costs don't have to stay "fixed." If they'd viewed their living expenses as unchangeable obligations, Meredyth might not have ever gotten the chance to go after her new dream. Because they saw the flexibility of these costs, they were able to make the changes they needed to create the experience they were after.

Seeing bills and living expenses as obligations can make you feel like you need to stay wherever you are: a relationship, location, job, or other situation that's not right for you. You might take work that doesn't serve you in order to pay the bills. To stop money from dictating your life, stop thinking of expenses as obligations, and think of them instead as commitments. Those are agreements you can control.

Commitments are a choice you make, so they're a choice you can change anytime. When you make commitments, you're in charge of your financial circumstances, instead of in reaction to them. That means, when your financial situation doesn't feel right, you can make all the big or small changes you want.

Your bills, housing costs, and other living expenses are commitments you had to make at one point, so they're commitments you can drop at any point, too. You could uncommit to a cable subscription by switching to a streaming service, for example. You could uncommit to your auto loan payment by selling your car. You could uncommit to your big student loan payment by setting up income-driven repayment. You could uncommit to your rent payment by moving into an RV.

As you make choices throughout your life, you make big and small financial commitments along the way. In exactly the same way, you can cut those commitments to make the next change you need to make. No one chooses your commitments for you, and bills aren't inevitable once you sign up. You can make a change anytime you want to adjust your experience.

What If You Don't Meet Your Commitments?

To make an informed decision and make sure your family or household is prepared for any changes to your commitments, you have to understand the *consequences* tied to each of your commitments. If you were to stop paying on any one of your commitments, what would happen? For example . . .

- What are the consequences of paying rent late, or not at all? Check your lease for a grace period and late fee, and check with your local renters' rights or tenant resource centers to understand the eviction laws, protections, and processes in your area.

- What happens if you don't pay a utility bill? Late payment fees might be listed right on your bill, or you could learn the information in your account with the servicer online. How long can you go without paying before the services are cut off? What does the servicer allow for payment plans? Does your city or state have protections against cutting off certain utilities for nonpayment?
- If you cut your commitment to a regular therapy appointment, how might that impact your well-being?
- If you don't pay a debt, or you pay late, what'll it cost you? Know the interest and fees connected to your debts. Also be crystal clear on the lender's right to take any collateral you put up, like your car or home. And don't forget about the nuisance of debt collectors if your debt goes into default.
- If you want to get rid of your mortgage payment, how would selling your house impact your life, your family, and your work? Where could you live instead?
- If you want to get rid of your car loan or lease payment, how would selling your car impact your life, family, and work? What are your options for walking, biking, and public transportation in your area?

Understanding these consequences helps you prioritize your commitments and make life decisions with a broader view of your options. It can help you see which commitments aren't serving you and find a path to cut them from your life, and it can help you prioritize which commitments to cover and which to let slide for those times when you don't have the resources to cover them all. Getting this full view of your commitments can also help you seek the best alternative resources for your circumstances. If you have access to assistance with utility bills, for example, you could use that to reduce the burden of that commitment for a while, so you can prioritize others.

Review your commitments periodically as part of your regular money management practice, rather than waiting until you're struggling to make a payment. That can help you spot opportunities for community or debt resources early, help you balance out the burden of your commitments, and give you ample opportunity to ponder big questions about what you want to do with your life and your resources.

Choosing, Prioritizing, and Cutting Commitments

Choosing commitments based on what you can cover with your resources is the simplest way to make sure you can cover them. But, of course, circumstances change. A change to your job or salary could reduce or increase your available resources; or you might start working toward a new goal that changes how much you want to allocate to commitments; or you might have to accommodate an unexpected expense, like a major car repair. As those changes happen, you'll prioritize and cut commitments to get them in balance with your resources and make sure you can still work toward your financial goals.

"In balance" means being able to cover your commitments, work toward your goals, and have a satisfying Yes Fund within your available resources. Remember: that doesn't mean simply "spending less than you earn," like most budgeting methods. It means taking full advantage of your assets, community resources, and access to debt to pay for the experience you want (and deserve). It also means treating the purchase of a new couch or sending a kid to camp with as much respect as paying a credit card bill, or more. Managing money requires tradeoffs. Budget culture expects you to always trade away pleasure and comfort; a budget-free approach acknowledges those as necessities. We'll talk much more in chapter 12 about adjusting the parts of your money map to find the balance that's right for you.

A lot of circumstances make it challenging to choose commitments that fit within your resources. A high-cost-of-living area can mean you'll have to devote a large amount of monthly resources toward housing. If you're just getting started in your career, your income might not cover all the commitments it takes to live comfortably or care for a family. You might be receiving disability income and are restricted from earning more or accessing additional resources. These kinds of circumstances can lead to an imbalance in your finances and make it difficult to find a satisfying amount to spend or to work toward financial goals.

If you're in a situation where you can't get your commitments in balance and you can't cut any more, you might have to prioritize which payments to make and which to ignore or leave for later. This kind of financial triage can dredge up a lot of budget culture baggage. Budget culture attaches shame to not being able to pay bills, because it supports the narrative that we're supposed to earn a living. The shame you feel about getting behind on bills is the voice of budget culture telling you that you don't deserve comfort and security because you can't earn the money it takes to buy them. That's absurd. Letting go of that culturally embedded shame isn't easy, but start with that: it's absurd. Whatever reason you have for not allocating resources to a particular commitment is legitimate; a bill from a service provider, debt collector, or landowner doesn't make their desire to be paid any more legitimate than your inability to pay.

Even once you shed the shame, though, there's the practical matter of all those companies expecting payments from you. That's where understanding the consequences tied to your commitments comes in. Understanding those consequences can take some of the stress and risk out of triaging your bills, because you can choose, cut, and prioritize payments based on their consequences. If paying rent means keeping a roof over your head, for example, you'll likely prioritize that bill over paying off credit card debt, where a missed or late payment just means more debt and a lower credit score. If filing bankruptcy can remove thousands of dollars in commitments each month, it could be worth it to increase your spending to buy food or clothing to suit your family.

You don't have a moral obligation to pay a bill once you've made a commitment to it. A commitment might come with certain legal responsibilities you have to navigate—but that's all it is: something you have to navigate. Jennie and Meredyth signed a lease for their apartment in LA, and they broke it early to move into their Airstream and save thousands of dollars on housing. The lease came with a clause that let them end it early if they paid a fee, so that's what they did. Credit card bills come with interest and fees as consequences for not paying by a stated due date. Utility companies cut off access to utilities if you've got old enough unpaid bills. Despite the baggage budget culture attaches to those events, they aren't the universe handing down punishment because of your moral failing; they're just consequences you have to navigate because of a financial commitment. Some of those consequences significantly upend your life, some are pretty inconvenient, and some are just minor annoyances. When you look at your bills as potential tradeoffs—rather than compulsory amounts with due dates—you can largely set the money part aside and make choices based on how their associated consequences will impact your life.

Having commitments consistently out of balance with your resources could mean watching those consequences snowball. It's not convenient or comfortable to ignore a lot of your financial commitments for a long time. If you're regularly finding yourself in financial triage mode, take a look at your money map to see where you have control and influence to make changes. (We'll talk about that in more detail in chapter 12.) Commitments tend to make up the bulk of a household's monthly expenses and financial challenges, so they're a good place to start. Look at your commitments to see where you can make changes. Dramatic changes, like finding a different place to live, could make a dramatic impact on your finances and comfort level. But smaller changes can have an impact, too. So don't ignore opportunities like negotiating debt payments or cutting cable.

You might notice I haven't asked you to track your everyday spending or find ways to save money on groceries or eating out or to cut back on shopping for clothes. Budgeting methods like to home in on this kind of spending (which they call "discretionary"), where it's easy to add restriction. They'll have you track your everyday spending, then encourage you to cut those categories as much as possible to address any financial issues. But that kind of spending barely scratches the surface of financial challenges in our culture. Contrary to what financial gurus might have you believe, no one goes broke buying avocado toast. I focus on commitments, not spending, on purpose. This lets you look at the places that take up the majority of your resources and focus any changes where they can have the most impact. (Do you know you'd have to buy about sixteen lattes a day to equal the median cost of rent in the United States?[1] Makes sense to tackle that housing cost and leave your Starbucks habit alone.)

Listing commitments isn't about giving your money a job or telling it where to go or whatever budget cliché. It's about wrapping your head around the commitments you've made so you can recognize the influence and control you have to make the life you want.

There are a lot of nonfinancial factors to consider when choosing commitments, as well, and it's important to account for all dimensions of your financial wellness. Only you and others in your household can say what makes the most sense for you, but naming your commitments and understanding their consequences can help give you a clear picture to work with when making decisions.

Reflection: Controlling Your Commitments

How does reimagining your expenses as *commitments* change how you relate to them? Can you name opportunities for changes you hadn't considered before? Where in your life do you feel the most and least control over your commitments?

CHAPTER 7

You Don't Have to Pay Off Debt

I'm often stunned by what people actually believe about debt. Many of us have so internalized budget culture that it feels like a fact of nature that debt is bad and people with debt are bad.

In mid-2023, I shared my student loan balance in a story for *Business Insider*[1] and explained why I'm in no hurry to repay my federal student loans, decrying the way our culture treats debt as a shameful moral failing. Someone responded to the story online, "Debt is not a shameful moral failing, but not fulfilling the obligation made when signing is."[2]

My loans weren't in default. I was current on my payments. I'd been using the options the guarantor—the federal government—had made available to repay the loan, including deferment, a pandemic-related pause, and income-driven repayment plans that sometimes made my monthly payment commitment $0. I was 100 percent fulfilling the "obligation" I signed on to fulfill, but this reader seemed to believe it was a moral failing simply not to prioritize fast and efficient debt repayment.

This was the attitude that permeated the debate around President Joe Biden's quest to cancel a portion of student loan debt for millions of federal borrowers beginning in 2022. If debt were canceled, critics could no longer shame balance holders for nonpayment. They turned to the narrative that you're simply a bad person if you borrow money and don't repay it, *even if the lender says you no longer have to repay.* They constructed a narrative that borrowers have a *moral* obligation to repay debt.

The obligation to pay off debt is a dangerous message that's foundational to budget culture, much like the obligation to lose weight undergirds diet culture. It causes so many of us to feel shame about using debt resources, exacerbating our already unequal access to those and other resources. As long as we carry debt, budget culture shames us for any spending decision because we don't use every available resource to eliminate debt as quickly as possible.

As my friend Jen Smith learned, though, debt payoff isn't necessarily a path to financial freedom or better enjoyment of life. For many who focus on this goal, it's just another form of budget culture's impossible quest toward financial perfectionism.

After spending two years following Dave Ramsey's Baby Steps to aggressively pay off student loan and consumer debt balances, Jen and her husband experienced what she calls a "debt-payoff hangover." When that debt was gone, she craved another financial goal.

"I had created this idol in my life of the debt," Jen says. "It was a negative idol, but I had still been kind of worshipping this idol for two years, and then it was gone and I had nothing left to worship."[3]

Her next financial obsession? Like many in the personal finance space looking for the next thing to do, Jen turned her sights on the quest to subsist off investment income: financial independence/retiring early (FIRE). She contributed so much to her workplace 401(k) that an HR rep checked in to make sure it wasn't a mistake. When she was laid off a year later, eight weeks before giving birth to her first child, she and her husband finally paused to ask whether this was a goal they actually wanted to pursue. They realized they'd been inflicting so much restriction on their life for a goal someone else had defined.

"That was very much the catalyst for me, reexamining the FIRE movement and looking at it with renewed eyes," Jen says. "And I see a lot of people [saving for FIRE] just to have another idol to worship."

Jen and many others get caught up in debt elimination because they've absorbed the budget culture message that it's the right thing to do. Does it feel "right" because of an inherent concern for making right with credit card companies? Not likely. It's because budget culture emphasizes debt elimination and shames debt resources as another way to keep us striving to be perfect individuals within a system riddled with imperfections.

Debt Isn't a Moral Failing

A 2015 study from Pew Trusts found that eight in ten Americans hold some kind of debt, with 39 percent holding unpaid credit card balances.[4] Sixty-nine percent say nonmortgage debt (like credit cards or personal loans) is a necessity for them, but they still would prefer not to have it, reflecting the shame our culture attaches to debt. Sixty-eight percent of people also say debt has afforded them opportunities they otherwise wouldn't have access to, like investments or purchases.

"These findings suggest an uneasy comfort with debt—a sense that it is needed and possibly even advantageous—but is still not desired," the Pew Trusts report says. "Furthermore, although most Americans consider debt a necessity in their own lives, they view it as a negative force in the lives of others."

Seventy-nine percent of people in the study said other people usually use debt irresponsibly, and 85 percent believe other people use debt to live beyond their means. When other people carry debt, we imagine it's the result of frivolous overspending—and we know that's how others view our use of debt. Because of that culture of shame and blame, it's hard to use debt as a resource without feeling bad about it.

You might believe we only shame the kinds of debt financial gurus like to categorize as "bad"—consumer debt, like credit cards and personal loans. You might feel justified judging people who use this kind of debt or consider yourself irresponsible if you use it. Many financial experts theoretically support taking on "good debt" that could support wealth building, like mortgages and student loans. But our culture has shame reserved for those when it comes down to it, too. Remember how no one bailed out the homeowners facing foreclosure during the 2008 financial crisis? Remember how President Biden's student loan cancellation was stopped by multiple lawsuits in 2023? Assistance for homeowners in 2008 might have kept nearly four million families in their homes[5], and student loan cancellation could have provided relief for forty-three million borrowers[6]—both with enormous benefits for our economy at large. But our antidebt bias is so strong that millions of Americans got behind decisions that left borrowers in the dust.[7]

We somehow imagine using debt as a way of what some call "living beyond our means," and we blame irresponsibility and indulgence. You should have known better than to accept the mortgage with an ever-increasing interest rate. You should have chosen a lower-cost school closer to home if you were going to major in the humanities. You should have gone without that dress, that night out, that present for your kids, if you weren't going to be able to pay off the credit card before the end of the month.

That stance falls apart, though, when you realize debt is, in fact, one of the "means" available to you. It's one of many types of resources available to support your life under capitalism, as we discussed in chapter 4. With that understanding, using debt can't cause you to live beyond your means any more than using your paycheck can. Framing debt as a result of living beyond your means is one way budget culture reinforces a cycle of shame and restriction.

Even if you can't shake the belief that debt is bad when it's used for so-called frivolous purchases, you should know most people don't use debt that way. The most common type of debt Americans hold is a mortgage, and nearly as many have an auto loan as have credit card debt, according to Pew Trusts. Even most credit card debt isn't the result of overconsumption. Nearly three-quarters of people who hold credit card debt accumulated it because of day-to-day-expenses, medical emergencies, or unexpected expenses like home or car repair.[8] A minority of people use credit card debt for anything budget culture would label "discretionary." Eleven percent have debt from retail purchases like clothing or electronics, which are both necessities if you want to live and work among humans. Another 11 percent have debt from vacation or entertainment—also not frivolous, though budget culture uses the wants-versus-needs framework to label them as such. Nearly 10 percent of American adults have some medical debt, with the greatest burden on disabled and Black Americans.[9] Debt isn't, in fact, a vehicle for overconsumption in our culture; it's a means of capturing resources in a culture that expects way too much of everyone and pays way too little to most.

Just as with everything else in budget culture, proponents of debt payoff cite basic individual responsibility: you signed an agreement and borrowed the money; you must pay it back. The concept that a responsible person ought to repay any money they borrow sounds straightforward—until you layer in the realities of our society:

- **Wealth and income gaps** increase some people's need for credit to meet everyday commitments and participate equitably in job and social markets.
- **Legal discrimination** in credit scoring taxes marginalized people with higher interest rates that increase how quickly debt balances grow.
- **Predatory marketing and promotions** distract borrowers from the risks of the complex agreements they sign.
- **An insufficiently regulated business model** incentivizes lenders and credit card companies to encourage you to carry a balance that costs you money.
- **Intentionally complex debt products** operate on systems of scoring, interest, fees, billing dates, minimum payments, and compounding that most people don't have the capacity to unravel during a financial decision.

The notion of individual responsibility assumes you're entering a credit card or loan agreement in good faith, and it's easy to argue that any decent person should do that. But the lenders and credit card companies are not entering these agreements in good faith. They're designing products—right up to the line regulations allow them to—that depend on you being what financial experts label as "irresponsible" and ensure they get exponentially more than they give. The hypocrisy in budget culture's moral compass is that we allow financial companies to collect on debts in ways that ruin individual lives but don't allow individuals to ignore debts to the minor inconvenience of financial companies.

Debt payoff doesn't have to be your highest priority by default. Once you strip debt of the shame and blame our culture piles on it, deciding how to deal with debt is just a matter of weighing costs, benefits, and priorities.

Understand How Your Debt Works

Just as with commitments, the key to making choices about how to use debt and how to deal with it is understanding the consequences of any kind of debt you take on. When you understand how your financial products work and how they can impact your life, you can make decisions about how to handle them that are based on a simple cost-benefit analysis, rather than on shame and expectations from budget culture.

To decide how to deal with any debt you carry (and what kind of debt you want to use as a resource in the future):

1. Know the characteristics of each debt product.
2. Know the consequences of each type of debt.

3. Consider how those consequences will impact your life (which you can live with and which you need to avoid).

4. Make a plan to deal with your debt.

We often talk about having debt as one homogenous thing, but it's made up of lots of products that act and impact your life quite differently. Understand how each of these products function, so you can use debt and deal with it in a way that serves your head, heart, and health.

STUDENT LOANS

If you attended college and borrowed to pay for it, student loans might be your biggest debt for several years. That can be stressful, particularly for borrowers who are early in their careers. But it doesn't have to be. The consequences of carrying student loan debt depend a lot on what kind of loans you have.

Most people who take out student loans use federal student loans—those are issued and backed by the US government through the Department of Education and managed by authorized private servicers. A smaller number of people take out private student loans, which are issued by private lenders, banks, and credit unions.

Private and federal student loans have some similarities. They're both designated for paying for college tuition and other education-related expenses. They both usually come with a deferment period, so you're not expected to make any payments while you're in school. But the loans are otherwise pretty different, as are the consequences of carrying each type of debt.

Private loans require a credit check, and you or a cosigner need to qualify to take them out. By contrast, undergraduate federal loans are issued based on need. Federal loans also come with a lot of relief options private loans don't offer. You can apply for income-driven repayment plans that reduce your monthly payment according to your ability to pay, and limit or eliminate the interest you can accumulate. And you can qualify for various debt cancellation options, including the most well known, Public Service Loan Forgiveness (PSLF), for those who work in government or nonprofits. Private loan relief options are very limited. Some lenders let you defer payments for a short period due to financial hardship, and some have options to skip an occasional payment. But they don't offer income-driven plans or cancellation options.

If you have private student loans, you'll probably have a deferment period, so you aren't required to make payments while you're in school and usually up to six months after school. During that period, your debt accrues interest, so the debt balance grows. But you won't default for not making payments. Federal student loans come with that deferment period, too. Unsubsidized direct loans accrue interest during the deferment period, but subsidized direct loans do not. Many borrowers have a mix of unsubsidized and subsidized loans.

Once you're required to make payments on student loans, you'll fall into a payment plan. With private loans, your plan is pretty much locked in when you sign the agreement to borrow: you'll have a repayment period of a set number of years and a minimum monthly payment to make. Look into your lender's deferment options so you know what's available if you ever have trouble making a monthly payment. With federal loans, you have more repayment options. Every borrower is automatically put into a standard repayment plan, which gives you ten years to repay and sets your minimum monthly payment accordingly. But you can apply for income-driven repayment, which caps your monthly payment based on your discretionary income. This can offer a lot of relief for many borrowers, and might even bring your payment as low as $0 per month—so you can avoid default without the burden of a monthly payment—and the remaining balance is canceled after a set repayment period.

If you work in government, education, or nonprofits, you might qualify for PSLF or Teacher Loan Forgiveness for federal loans. The government also offers other loan cancellation programs for graduates who work in certain sectors, like health care and education, and take jobs in underserved areas or serve in the military. If you believe you work in any qualifying field, contact your loan servicer regularly to ensure you take the necessary steps to qualify once you're eligible for cancellation.

If you miss student loan payments for ninety days straight, your loans are in default. With private loans, this could mean your debt could eventually be sold to a collection agency, or you could be sued by the lender and have your wages garnished or turn over assets to cover the debt if you lose. With federal loans, the government could automatically garnish your wages, intercept tax refunds, and levy your bank account to recoup payments, and it doesn't have to take you to court first. You'll be in a much better position if you apply for income-driven repayment when monthly payments are too high, before you find yourself in default.

Defaulting on any debt impacts your credit score negatively, but carrying student loan debt and staying current on minimum payments—even if they're $0—doesn't weigh heavily on your score compared to other types of debt.

Note: Student loans are a hot topic in the federal government as I write this. If all goes well, paying for college and dealing with federal student loan debt will see major changes in the coming years, and this information might be outdated by the time you read this. Here's hoping! Check youdontneedabudget.com for the most up-to-date information on student loans.

CREDIT CARDS

Credit cards are a type of revolving debt, which means you only borrow money as you spend it. Once you repay revolving debt, the amount becomes available to you again within a credit limit.

Credit cards are particularly complex because of their typical repayment structure. When you get a bill, the payment due by the due date isn't the total amount of credit you've used; it's a minimum payment that's usually around 2 to 3 percent of that. So there are two ways people carry credit card debt: you might make your minimum payment with every monthly bill but carry the rest of the balance month to month, or you might not make a payment at all. Either way, as long as you're paying off less than the full amount you spend each month, you're carrying a balance—i.e., holding credit card debt that grows with interest.

Making minimum payments is enough to keep you in good standing with your credit card agreement, but it leaves the rest of your balance to grow and is a slow (nearly impossible) way to elimi-nate credit card debt. If you make just minimum payments:

- **Your balance will grow with interest.** Interest is money added to your balance, and it's tacked on periodically as a percentage of the debt. So the interest you're charged in April will be more than what you were charged in March, for example, even if you don't spend more, because the balance grew in a month just from the interest added in March. Average credit card interest rates fluctuate with the economy; at the end of 2023, the average rate was 21.5 percent.[10] There's no maximum allowed rate, but a typical credit card rate runs between 16 and 35 percent.

- **It'll affect your credit score.** Carrying a balance on your credit card affects your credit score because credit card companies typically report your debt and payment activity to credit bureaus. A balance could indicate that you use a lot of your available credit or that you have high debt overall, both bad for a credit score (more on that later in this chapter).

- **You'll run out of credit.** If you continue to use your credit card and don't repay the balance, you'll hit your credit limit and not be able to spend on the card anymore. You could open additional cards, but eventually that resource might run out, too, as your credit score goes down.

Your other option with credit card debt is to ignore it altogether. If you ignore your credit card bills and make no payments or less than the minimum payment by the due date, you'll be assessed late fees in addition to the accrued interest and effect on your credit report.

Your credit card agreement might also include a penalty interest rate, which is a higher interest rate charged to your balance for around six to twelve months if your payments are late. All of those costs are added to your existing balance, so the gist is: when you don't make credit card payments, the amount of debt you owe increases.

If you ignore your credit card bills long enough that a creditor figures it's not worth dealing with your account anymore—usually around two to three months—it might sell the debt to a debt buyer, a company that's legally authorized to acquire and collect on accounts. A debt buyer pays the credit card company a tiny portion of your balance—around 4 to 6 cents per dollar. Then you owe repayment for the original balance to that company instead of the original creditor. These companies, commonly called "debt collectors," usually report this action to credit bureaus, so going to collections is another hit to your credit score. They'll also use all the tactics legally (and often illegally[11]) available to them to contact you and intimidate you into making payments.

INSTALLMENT LOANS

Installment loans are a catchall for any kind of loan where you borrow a lump sum up front and repay it in installments over time, usually monthly payments. Personal loans are a basic type of installment loan that aren't tied to a specific purpose (like student loans are). You can borrow a lump-sum personal loan to use for any purpose, and you'll agree to repay it with interest for a set monthly payment within a set period.

Installment loans are usually amortized, which means the interest is calculated in advance and spread across your repayment period, so every monthly payment is the same. If you pay extra each month, you can pay the loan off early and pay less interest. Personal loans are often slightly less volatile debt to carry than credit cards because they can be harder to get. Most personal loans require a good or excellent credit score and proof of income. As long as your loans are *unsecured*—don't require you to put up an asset—you don't risk losing any assets if you don't repay. Defaulting on these loans would have similar consequences to defaulting on credit card debt: the debt might be sent to collections, you could be sued for repayment, and you'll take a hit to your credit score.

MORTGAGE AND AUTO LOANS

Mortgages and auto loans are common examples of a kind of installment loan called a *secured loan*. Those are any kind of loan where you have to put an asset, called *collateral*, on the line to qualify for the loan. For a mortgage, your home or property is the collateral. For an auto loan, your vehicle is the collateral. When you borrow money to buy those assets, you agree to turn the asset over to the lender if you don't repay the loan as agreed.

Mortgages, auto loans, and other secured loans can be the riskiest kinds of debt to take on, because you risk losing an important asset if you don't repay. Late payments on these loans can impact your credit score just like other loans, and you'll accrue fees on top of interest. If you don't make payments for ninety days straight—or another period designated in your loan agreement—the lender has a right to seize your asset. For an auto loan, they can repossess your car; for a mortgage, they can foreclose on the home.

In response to the fallout of the housing crisis, mortgages in the United States are highly regulated to make it harder to get a loan if a lender expects you to have trouble repaying. That makes a mortgage a fairly safe kind of debt to take out if you have access to it, but you do have to make decisions based on your financial situation about the size of a monthly payment you're willing to take on for the long term. Auto loans are still less regulated and have been easier to get with a low income and low credit score. That could mean a dealer might steer you toward a car purchase that isn't a good fit for your financial situation. It's always important to understand the monthly payment amount that makes sense for you before you agree to a loan and to know your options for dealing with the consequences tied to the loan in case your financial circumstances change. (Your money map can help with both of those!)

GOVERNMENT DEBTS

Government-backed loans are types of loans you take out through a government agency, like student loans through the Department of Education; or mortgages through the Federal Housing Administration (FHA loans), the Department of Agriculture (USDA loans), or the Veterans Administration (VA loans). You borrow the money and manage the debt through private servicers, but the federal government guarantees the loan repayment. That reduces the lender's risk, so these loans are available to people without excellent credit.

You might also deal with government debt that you owe directly to a government agency. This can happen if you owe taxes you don't pay by tax day or you owe back child support, for example. That kind of debt is usually due immediately, so you're considered delinquent until you repay it or set up a payment plan. Government debt isn't always reported to credit bureaus, and it doesn't usually accrue interest the same way private loans do, but you'll probably be charged a onetime fee to establish a payment plan and a monthly fee until the debt is repaid.

Just like with federal student loans, the state or federal government has pretty broad rights to seize your money or assets if you owe debt to the government. They tend to give you a lot of leeway to set up a payment plan first. But if you don't do that, they can typically order wage garnishment, take money from your bank account, capture tax refunds, and seize valuable assets to pay down the debt. Most states protect your primary home and a necessary vehicle from seizure, but any other valuable things you own could be fair game.

What Do You Give Up When You Pay Off Debt?

Once you understand the consequences of holding different kinds of debts, you can decide which kinds of debts you'll use as a resource and how you'll deal with any debt you already have. That could mean planning for a way to repay it or figuring out how to live with the balance. There are plenty of rational and personal reasons that'll determine how you decide to deal with debt, and they're all valid. The key to dealing with debt in a healthy way is understanding those consequences we talked about and weighing them against the consequences of using your money in another way.

There's an important fact about debt that most payoff-focused strategies ignore. As financial educator K. Kenneth Davis, aka The Trans Capitalist, points out on the *Healthy Rich* podcast, "When you pay off debt, what do you get back? Nothing."[12]

Spending that money or saving it for a future purchase gets you something in return. It can fund the life you want. For the transgender folks Davis works with, that can mean access to an expensive gender-affirming medical transition, which could save lives or increase job prospects. For others, it might mean buying a flight to visit family, enrolling in class at a community college, or paying rent in a neighborhood closer to work.

As you consider whether to pursue debt payoff (and which, if any, payments to prioritize), look at the other areas of your finances. Which goals and experiences do you sacrifice or delay if money goes toward debt? Using money for debt payoff could mean sacrificing:

- **Other financial goals.** Even financial gurus admit fast debt payoff isn't the best fiscal strategy. If you're trying to grow your money through investing or a retirement fund, those typically earn a greater average return than the average interest you'd save paying off installment loans early. Optimization aside, though, you might just prefer to save money toward future purchases or experiences instead of prioritizing debt payoff.

- **Your standard of living.** You'll hear this less from financial gurus: you might enjoy life more if you spend money instead of using it to pay off debt. Not making a big monthly debt payment could mean more money in your pocket now for things like higher rent to live in a safe and identity-affirming community, quality food, a gym membership, therapy, cultural experiences, and nicer stuff that adds to your comfort.

- **Self-actualization.** As Davis teaches, spending or saving money for future spending might give you opportunities to live your most authentic life, and that's a major thing to sacrifice in the name of being debt-free. Spending money now might give you access to a better job or education, better schools for yourself or your kids, food stability for your family, or other things that support your head, heart, and health in ways that debt-payoff plans often ignore.

- **Surviving inequality and discrimination.** No individual actions can eliminate the inequalities built into our culture and systems. But you can make choices that help you survive them, and those choices might involve accumulating debt and spending money. For example, you might have to pay for specialized health care out of pocket if it's not covered by your insurance plan. If you need family planning services like adoption, in vitro fertilization (IVF), or surrogacy, you might face costs our culture doesn't typically account for. You might use money to support your community or family members, especially if you've been afforded upward class mobility they haven't experienced.

Debt Doesn't Have to Be a Pain

Instead of complying with the budget culture obligation to eliminate debt at all costs, look for ways to reduce the burden debt can place on your day-to-day life. Just as with automating money management, find ease by getting debt off your mind.

Here are a few ways to lessen the burden of your debts:

- **Use built-in relief options.** Take advantage of debt-relief options drawn into your borrowing agreement, like deferment, forbearance, consolidation, income-driven repayment, and cancellation for student loans.
- **Make just the minimum payments.** Credit card debt is a much more aggressive kind of debt that doesn't come with many built-in relief options. You can lessen the burden of that debt by making just the minimum payments to avoid penalties without too much of a monthly commitment (but understand the consequences we talked about).
- **Replace credit cards with more favorable debt.** For example, pay off credit card balances with a federal student loan refund, or use a type of personal loan called a *debt refinancing loan* or *debt consolidation*. Those bring your debt under a single payment and (ideally) a lower interest rate.
- **Deprioritize debt payments.** You always have the option to forgo making debt payments altogether. Depending on the kind of debt, that means risking a lower credit score, going to collections, being sued for a payment plan or wage garnishment, or losing a major asset like your home or car. Most of these consequences are probably not in line with your best interests, but there might be circumstances where they make sense for you.

Understanding what happens when you do or don't repay various debt products lets you weigh your options fairly, choose what's right for you, and plan carefully for the impact.

Filing Bankruptcy

One more important way to lessen the burden of debt in the United States is to file bankruptcy. If you can prove that debt from personal loans, credit cards, or—in rare cases—student loans creates an undue hardship on your financial situation, you could use bankruptcy to eliminate or reduce your responsibility. Bankruptcy is wildly misunderstood and highly shamed in budget culture. It's neither the get-out-of-jail-free card many people believe it to be nor the burden on innocent financial companies opponents paint it as.

"The bankrupt are pretty much like other Americans before they file: slightly better educated, more likely to be married and have children, roughly as likely to have had a good job, and modestly less likely to own a home," writes Jacob S. Hacker in *The Great Risk Shift*. "They are not the persistently poor, the downtrodden looking for relief. They are refugees of the middle class, frequently wondering how they fell so far so fast."[13]

Bankruptcy's purpose is to get you out of debt payments that are too burdensome in your life—but it can be a fairly burdensome process itself. It's nearly impossible to file without hiring a lawyer, who might charge hundreds or thousands of dollars, and the process takes about three to six months.[14]

This process is a legal way to discharge debts that cause you "undue hardship," either by paying off all or some of them with assets you own or setting up a payment plan through a government trustee. If you have to sell assets, that'll include anything of value you own that a judge deems not necessary to live and work—like a savings account, ATV, or collectibles. Your home, car, and retirement account are usually safe (but those details vary by state and federal circuit court district).

You're not likely to be able to discharge student loans in bankruptcy, but it happens sometimes. The courts get to interpret the "undue hardship" part of the law, so various regions use different criteria. Most courts around the United States require that your circumstances make it impossible for you to make payments, they aren't changing anytime soon, and you've made good-faith efforts to repay (like asking about payment plans).[15] If you have federal loans, though, any circumstances that would qualify you for bankruptcy would easily qualify you for low or $0 payments and zero interest through income-driven repayment, which is much easier to set up, doesn't involve any court, and won't hurt your credit.

Experts tend to recommend bankruptcy as a last resort, not least because it can severely impact your future finances. Unsurprisingly, lenders and credit card companies don't want to extend debt to someone who's legally declared they're unable to repay other debt. Bankruptcy stays on your credit report for ten years, so it could affect your ability to buy or rent a home or take out loans or credit cards in the meantime. Keep in mind, though, that bankruptcy typically has about the same effect on your credit score as a poor payment history—so if you're going to stop making payments on your debt anyway, bankruptcy might not have such a downside. A bankruptcy lawyer or financial planner can help you figure out the effect a case might have on your particular circumstances.

Understanding Credit Scores

One inescapable reason many people are concerned with how to deal with debt is its impact on your credit score. Worrying about your credit score is a hallmark of budget culture—an obsession with tracking and optimization and subservience to financial institutions. But so many systems rely on this metric to determine your access to resources, and even to jobs and housing. So it's useful to know how your score works, so you can understand its impact on your relationship with money.

Your credit score is a number that ranks your past reported financial behavior based on a formula that hopes to account for your ability to be the kind of consumer a company wants as a customer. Building a positive credit history can make some financial goals, like buying a house or a car, easier, because lenders use your credit history and score to set terms for borrowing.

A credit score isn't a useful measure of how "responsible" you are with money, though it's often described this way. You can work hard and pay bills and do everything budget culture considers being "responsible" with money, and still have a low credit score because you haven't participated in the system in a way that makes you the kind of customer a lender or credit card company wants. In other words, credit scores rate your financial behavior, yes; but they also rate your willingness to use credit—which is key to lenders and credit card companies making money off you as a customer.

We all start out with no credit history and no credit score. You build a credit history (which is country-specific) as soon as you do anything that's reported to credit bureaus. In the United States, building a positive credit history could include things like opening a credit card or borrowing student loans. You might also build a negative credit history by having unpaid rent or bills.

Lenders treat having no credit score just like having a low credit score. You could go through your whole life without participating in credit or lending in our financial systems. If you never borrow money or take out credit cards, and you pay all your bills on time, you might never have a credit history reported to credit bureaus. But your history might be checked even when you're not applying for credit, like if you apply to rent a home, buy car insurance, or get a background check for a job where you'll handle finances.

Building credit doesn't have to mean using credit cards or even taking advantage of a lot of debt. By understanding what makes up a credit score and which activities make it onto your credit report, you can choose credit-building moves that ensure ease in your relationship with money.

CREDIT REPORTS

Credit scores are calculated based on information included in your credit reports. Those are detailed listings of your credit history compiled by credit bureaus. (The major bureaus in the United States are Experian, TransUnion, and Equifax.) You have a legal right to see your credit report from each of those three bureaus once every twelve months. Those reports don't include a credit score, but they let you see what's been reported so you can make sure the information is accurate. Not all financial behavior is reported to credit bureaus, and this sets up many low-income and low-wealth communities for a cycle of reduced access to credit.

What's reported?	What's not reported?
Applying for a credit card	On-time rent payments
Applying for a loan	On-time utility bill payments
Credit card balances	Employment and income
On-time and missed payments on credit cards and loans	Checking your credit score (no matter how often)
Delinquency, default, and collections	
Bankruptcy	
Unpaid utility bills	
Unpaid medical bills over $500 in collections for one year or more	

CREDIT FACTORS

You don't have any single credit score, even though you might hear this metric described as if it's a singular thing. Different companies calculate a credit score for you when they check your credit history for a particular purpose, like applying for a loan or credit card. Most major lenders use a proprietary formula to calculate your score, but they tend to use similar criteria, weighted in a similar way.

The most popular formula for calculating a credit score comes from the Fair Isaac Corporation—also known as FICO. Your FICO score considers (and weights) five elements:[16]

- **Payment history (35 percent):** Whether you've made credit card and loan payments on time, as well as any reported unpaid bills (but not on-time payments). Late payment and nonpayment will significantly bring down your score.

- **Amounts owed (30 percent):** Also called credit utilization, this is your balances compared with your total available credit (like your credit card limit). Creditors want to see that you use cards, but using your full credit limit could indicate a higher risk of not being able to pay it back. Experts recommend keeping utilization between 1 and 30 percent.

- **Length of history (15 percent):** How long you've used debt, based on the age of your oldest active credit or loan product—the longer the better. Loans fall out of your credit history as you pay them off, and credit cards fall off if you close them.

- **Credit mix (10 percent):** Variety of credit products you have, like installment loans versus credit cards. A greater variety is better for your score.

- **New credit (10 percent):** Recent applications for credit cards or loans. Applying for new credit typically brings down your credit score for about thirty to ninety days, and your score can rebound after that. This is most important if you're about to apply for a mortgage.

VantageScore is another popular scoring model that some financial institutions use. Its most recent formulas and scores are similar to FICO scores, but it's frequently updated and has begun to include some alternative data, like reported rent and utility payments. If you look up your free credit score through an app like Credit Karma, you'll see a VantageScore. If you get your credit score through a banking app or your credit card company, that's usually a FICO score. The most-used versions of both VantageScore and FICO scores run from 300 to 850. A score of 800-plus is considered excellent, while anything below 580 is considered poor.

BUILDING A POSITIVE CREDIT HISTORY

Needing credit to build credit is a catch-22, but there are a few strategies you can use. These can help whether you're building credit from scratch or rebuilding credit from a low credit score.

- **Open a credit card.** Credit card use weighs heavily in a credit score, so opening a card is an easy way to build a credit history. (It also comes with the risk of accruing debt that's difficult to repay, which could strap you with a low score.)
- **Open a secured credit card.** Qualifying for a credit card could be difficult if you have no credit or a low score. A secured card, like a secured loan, lets you back up your credit with collateral—in this case, cash. You generally have to pay a deposit of as little as $100 to $200 and start with a limit of that same amount.
- **Become an authorized user on someone else's card.** Yet another way to use credit cards to build a credit history, this is most often recommended for children or teens to build credit early. Any usage on the card, even if it's not yours, will be reported the same on your credit history as that of the original card holder.

- **Use a credit-builder loan or account.** These bank products are designed solely for the purpose of building credit. Loans are for small amounts like $1,000 to $2,000, and you don't get all the money up front. It goes into an account, and you get access to portions of the money as you make monthly payments, which are reported to credit bureaus.

Reflection: Dealing with Debt

Consider the debt you hold and the impact it's had on your life so far.

- What has your debt allowed you to do that you couldn't have done otherwise?
- Have you been prioritizing debt-payoff goals you don't actually care about?
- Have you been neglecting other goals that are more meaningful to you?
- Does your debt feel manageable to you? Why or why not?

CHAPTER 8

You Don't Need
an Emergency Fund

Ramat Oyetunji knew the panic of being laid off. An immigrant to the United States from Nigeria, she earned her bachelor's degree in mechanical engineering from the University of Maine and started her career in the oil and gas industry. Less than a year later, disruption in the industry led to layoffs that left her without a job to protect her from deportation as a foreign national. This became the nudge she needed to work toward a life more aligned with her heart—it hasn't been without challenges, but it's led her to good work she loves to do.

Ramat applied to an MBA program at Maine and got a graduate assistantship that paid her tuition, room, and board, plus a $600 monthly stipend. She graduated in three years and started working as an engineer for Procter & Gamble. Three years later she followed her passion for finance and changed careers to become an investment advisor at Edward Jones in 2008. By September, she was laid off again when the housing crisis plunged us into the Great Recession, and she returned to engineering.

Ramat was never satisfied with her work in engineering, and she quickly started plotting to stop relying on the work for her comfort. She was in her early thirties when she returned to the field, and she hoped to save enough money to be financially independent by age forty-five. The stress of working through the COVID-19 pandemic pushed her to bump her goal up by a year. She watched her family suffer health crises throughout early 2021 and hit a wall when she actually fell asleep in a virtual meeting one morning.

"I was mortified and upset," Ramat writes in her 2022 book *One Year after F.I.R.E.* "My health suffered. My mental, physical, and emotional states were impacted. My outlook on life and what was important changed."[1]

She'd been saving toward financial independence for ten years already and had reached $1 million in investment holdings the year before. "It wasn't my 2011 goal of $100K [per year] in passive income, but it met my definition of financial independence: the ability to generate enough income to cover my expenses without working," she writes.

Even with those massive savings, she hadn't been ready to give up her job and her six-figure salary yet. "But after pulling through the crisis, I realized I was heading for a major breakdown," she writes. She considered a leave of absence but realized it wouldn't provide the rest she needed; it would only have her worrying about the work she wasn't doing. Determined to find peace, she finally decided to leave her job.

Walking away from her career in July 2021 meant Ramat would shift from earning a salary of $155,000 plus bonuses in her engineering job to withdrawing $40,000 per year from her investment accounts. Access to those resources is certainly something to celebrate, but it was a serious leap to make that kind of change to her resources.

"Sometimes you are more ready than you think you are, and with all the planning in the world, it still requires a leap of faith to make a bold move," Ramat writes.

Since leaving that soul-draining work, Ramat turned her focus to her own business, The FI Woman, as a personal finance counselor and purpose-driven investment educator.

Ramat pursued a version of financial independence that's not unlike budget-free living. Although much of the FIRE movement is bogged down with prescriptive budget culture advice, the spirit is exactly the same as we're pursuing here: releasing the hold money has on your life.

Jessica at the *Fioneers* blog defines this sort of pursuit of financial independence, known in the industry as *Slow FI*, as "a philosophy that focuses on using the financial freedom that you gain along the path to FI [financial independence] to design a life you truly love."

"People on Slow FI paths are focused on working less (or doing something they actually enjoy to generate income)," Jessica writes. "They do this so they can invest more time in the things they enjoy and value: health, relationships, hobbies, travel, learning, curiosity, etc."[2]

Despite opposing most forms of wealth accumulation, I'm in favor of building a store of savings you can use to protect the freedoms capitalism would otherwise wrest from your life. For most of us, that store of money might be just a small savings account to help you weather some transitions throughout life; for others, it might be the complete financial freedom Ramat sought through FIRE. (You don't necessarily need to take the step of growing this money through investment like Ramat did; we'll discuss that in the next chapter!)

Drop the Word *Emergency* from Your Financial Plan

Building a store of money is the simplest way to create financial ease for yourself and embrace a belief in abundance and security, regardless of your financial circumstances. Setting aside some money that's not earmarked for anything and is always there when you need it lets you live life without money calling the shots. That's the real freedom financial independence can offer.

I call this store of money a comfort fund. I deliberately use that label instead of the popular term *emergency fund* to help you make an important shift in your relationship with money. Building an emergency fund implies that a change in your financial circumstances constitutes an emergency in your life. A budget-free approach rejects that narrative. The most financial fluctuations can do is make you uncomfortable—they don't control you. Money is one of many realities in your life; it's not the defining force. Calling your store of money a comfort fund is an ongoing reminder of that fact. It's also a small step to quiet one piece of the ticker that can cause daily stress and make money management challenges feel more severe than they are.

Dropping the word *emergency* from your financial plan is a way to remind yourself that an unexpected change to your financial circumstances is not only not an emergency but also not even necessarily a bad thing. Losing or leaving behind what feels like financial security might be a challenge in our culture, but it could also be the first step to a more joyful life, like it was for Ramat. It could even, as another woman discovered, be a step that saves your life.

Lisa Orban was married to an abusive husband for three years. In 1990, at twenty years old, she left after he threatened to kill her and their two young children. Her financial situation in the marriage? "Bad, in a nutshell," she recalls. Her husband was the main breadwinner, and he managed the family's finances.

"Whenever there was a chance that I might make enough money or make more money than him or do anything to upset his financial apple cart, so to speak, he would come in and sabotage it," she says.

She lost multiple opportunities because of his meddling, including the chance to go to college. She had moved with him from her hometown in Illinois to Arizona, where she'd won a four-year scholarship to study psychology. But before she could start, he contacted the university and told them she'd decided to drop out.

"Imagine my surprise when I go to registration day and find out that my scholarship is gone," she says.

He wouldn't let her use the car alone, and at one point even took her mailbox key. And he kept control of the checking account. He knew how much money she earned, and he would accompany her to the bank to deposit her paychecks. He signed up for credit cards in her name. By the time Orban left and filed for divorce, she was $80,000 in debt and didn't even know it.

Money represents freedom in a capitalist system. So it's no surprise that the vast majority of people who experience intimate partner violence also experience financial abuse or control,[3] and often stay in an abusive relationship because they're afraid to lose the perception of financial security the relationship offers.

"More often than not, the abuser has made the victim feel as if they are dependent upon the abuser—that without the help of the abuser, the victim could not survive financially in the world, and it is only by the grace of the abuser that the victim has a roof over their head and food on the table," says Michelle Kuehner, a survivor of domestic violence who is now a financial advisor.

Lisa didn't make a plan to leave her abuser. She did what many survivors do: run blindly for their lives. "[We] look for a moment—a credit card left unattended, a check that unexpectedly arrives that you somehow got access to, a Christmas bonus from your work that your spouse doesn't know about," she says. "These are things you look at, and you go, 'This is it. This is my chance.' "[4]

The lack of a social safety net in our society means those small windfalls Lisa described are often the only way out of an untenable situation. But it's important to understand that while money can help you mitigate an emergency situation in your life—like leaving an unsafe relationship or weathering an unexpected illness—money itself cannot constitute an emergency. You deserve these freedoms, whether they sound to you like basic rights or luxurious comforts, and you can go after them regardless of your financial circumstances or plans. A comfort fund, if you're able to build it, is just a way to help soften your landing when you take that leap.

Money Is Meant to Be Spent

"I like the idea of a comfort fund versus an emergency fund," says Anastasia McRae. "With the use of the word *comfort*, I have more agency. In an emergency, I just need to react to stop the boat from sinking. With comfort, I decide how much pain I want to endure and can prepare for it. So if my comfort fund is not where I'd like it to be, I can navigate with a different mindset than when in an emergency."[5]

That mindset shift is exactly the point of changing this one word. You can use the money in a comfort fund for anything that contributes to your comfort; it's not only reserved for an emergency. You can use comfort fund money to move across the country or buy a new car. You can use it to transition to self-employment or look for a new job. You can use it to file for divorce, weather a layoff, or avoid depriving yourself if your income slows down. A comfort fund ensures that money isn't the deciding factor in your day-to-day or major life decisions, like where you live, where you work, when you have children, or who you're in a relationship with.

To carry on Anastasia's metaphor: a comfort fund can plug a hole in your boat if you're taking on water, yes. But that's not its only purpose. It can also afford you new seat cushions, so you're not chafed and bruised with every ride. It can help you move to a different marina when your neighbors are keeping you up at night. It can replace the motor when it goes out unexpectedly. It can make up the down payment on . . . a tugboat, so you don't have to row so hard anymore? Clearly, we've reached the end of my boat knowledge, but you get the picture: we call this a comfort fund because its purpose is to add comfort—ease, joy, and dignity—to your life.

This language is important because it reminds you to give yourself permission to use the money for anything that contributes to your comfort. The thread of greed that runs through budget culture encourages a habit of hoarding under the guise of good money management, and it threatens you with a fear of scarcity to discourage spending. That fear can keep you always worried about the next thing that'll come along. What if you spend funds on something less severe now, and you don't have them when you really need it?

That fear is what led my friend Erik Noren to accumulate nearly half a million dollars in a savings account and continue to avoid spending on comforts he needed and longed for, like a car to get around his city or furniture to hold him over through the major supply chain disruptions during the pandemic.

"[I just] keep putting the money aside because I don't know when I'm gonna need it," Erik tells me.

Friends and financial experts have urged him to put the money in an investment account for added insurance and potential gains, but that feels too insecure for Erik. "All I'm hearing is: I don't have control of my money, and I don't know whether or not, when I need it, there will be less than what I gave to them because of some market thing."

Erik grew up in a working-class family in a small town in southern Ohio and, like many of his peers, adopted a fear of scarcity. His mom lived paycheck to paycheck and frequently borrowed money from Erik when he was a teenager and young adult. She always repaid, but it bothered him that she didn't meter her spending better.

"Growing up, it just felt like the people around me weren't very responsible," Erik says, "so I think I turned very responsible [as an adult]."

"Responsible," according to Erik's internalized budget culture, meant working hard, spending very little, and holding on to as much money as he could. He earned a bachelor's degree in just three and a half years and earned a master's degree in computer science before moving to Washington, DC, to work for, among others, the

US Secret Service. His dream had always been to live in New York City, and he frequently took the train north to the city to stay in Times Square.

"I remember as a closeted [gay] kid reading stories of people moving to NYC to be in a place where they could live as themselves and have community," he says, "and that planted the seed in my head that I should do that, too." In 2011 Erik took a job in New York and made the move, landing in a Times Square apartment not far from his new office. By 2020 he was earning six figures and had stashed nearly $500,000 in two savings accounts, in addition to a 401(k) he'd been maxing out each year.

When the firm he worked for went remote in 2020 because of the pandemic, Erik left the city that was the epicenter of COVID-19 in the United States and moved west, settling in Tacoma, Washington. For the first time in two decades, he lived in a city that required a car, but prices were skyrocketing under pandemic-era demand, and he couldn't bring himself to spend the money, despite his comfortable nest egg.

Erik had started saving using direct deposit from his paycheck, building an "emergency fund" for himself. He liked that the automatic savings made it easy to know how much money he could spend without worry while still knowing he'd have money "if something bad happens."

"And then I just kept putting a higher percentage into it until, like, three grand a month goes into that account [now]," he says.

Many people start budgeting because they don't trust themselves to spend all the money available to them. Erik doesn't have that worry.

"Every time I would spend money on myself at a large amount," he says, "I would immediately have regret. [I'd wonder] did I spend too much, was this too much? Should I have done something different? And I'm watching the prices for the next couple of months to see if I overpaid, was I taken advantage of. The stress of that feels awful."

Erik is constantly measuring "opportunity cost" like this and talking himself out of spending money on things he needs. With car prices highly inflated by the end of 2020, he worried about overpaying for something that would be cheaper later, so he decided he could go without for a while. Two years later, he still hadn't made the move.

"If I were less self-conscious about spending on myself or . . . if I had a different personality entirely, then I probably would be spending that money much more frequently. At least I would have a car by now."

Too many people like Erik suffer through untenable situations while sitting on a well-endowed "emergency fund" because their needs don't feel like an emergency. Using the term *comfort fund* reminds you you're worthy of the comfort money can buy, no matter your income, how you work, or how you spend. And you get to decide what those comforts are; don't let budget culture set your standards for you.

A comfort fund, like an emergency fund, can protect you from disaster, but, unlike an emergency fund, it can also help you take advantage of opportunities.

By moving out of their LA apartment and into an Airstream, the coaches Jennie and Meredyth Mustafa-Julock turned their modest comfort fund into a new lifestyle that gave Meredyth a new career and supercharged their business. They weren't running from anything in their old life, though; they were running toward new possibility.

"We see so many people wait until they retire at sixty-five to start having a life, and that just never interested us," says Jennie.

"It's not that we were unhappy," says Meredyth. "But all of a sudden, this whole new potential unlocked. . . . A new realm of happiness opened up. And as soon as we realized that, we were like, *Okay, we need that, like, tomorrow. So how do we bring it into action?*"

How Much Money Should Be in Your Comfort Fund?

The amount you need in a comfort fund is completely up to you—choose the number that makes you comfortable right now. The right amount is different for everyone, so I can't offer you a convenient formula. Set a target amount for now that lets you breathe easy and make life decisions without money weighing in. If that's a big, meaty, FIRE amount like Ramat set, then build toward that number. (You can always change your mind, like Jen Smith and her husband did, and you'll still have a fund that adds significant comfort to your life.) And if the number that's comfortable for you now is $0? Let it be $0. Only you can say what's comfortable for you in this moment.

In 2010 I took a leap and left my known life behind with a $0 comfort fund. I left my then husband, and the following year I left my home in Wisconsin to travel and live outside of the state for the first time in my adult life. I was twenty-five years old and fueled by the fearlessness that leaving a stifling relationship instills in many women. My new partner and I moved to California with barely a plan and little more money than it would take to move into an apartment. The prospect of waiting another second to take those leaps while we stashed a prescribed amount of money would have been preposterous at the time. We needed change, and we felt comfortable pursuing it with $0.

Ten years later, we made a similar leap under totally different circumstances. I left the full-time job I'd held for four years and moved from the town it'd taken us to in Florida back to our home in Wisconsin. This time we planned ahead for months and made the move with nearly $15,000 in our comfort fund. I was thirty-five years old and accustomed to a stable income by that time. I was no longer invigorated by the prospect of flinging myself across the country with no job lined up and no financial cushion. The thought exhausted me.

Each of these decisions was right for me when I made them. Listen to your intuition to set a comfort fund amount that feels right in this season of your life, and continue to adjust it as your circumstances change. That includes those moments when you tap into your comfort fund and might need time to replenish it. In 2023, my partner and I bought a house and a business within eight months of each other, and we tapped our comfort fund (along with my IRA) to make it happen. That dropped the fund below our target for a while, so part of deciding to use it was adjusting our barometer for comfort to accommodate the major lifestyle changes we wanted. The fund can afford you comfort in those moments of transition, but only if you allow yourself to use it and trust in your ability to continue to feed it.

Listening to your intuition and being in flux with the seasons of your life might make it seem like you don't have to think about the amount in your comfort fund. The number you set isn't important—but it's important that you set a target amount, so you can avoid the trap Erik fell victim to: oversaving and hoarding money without a purpose. Set a target amount for your comfort fund, and stop feeding it once you hit the target. Redirect your resources to other goals, spending, or giving until you use the funds and need to replenish them.

You could tie your comfort fund target to your income or expenses, as many experts recommend for an emergency fund, but be careful not to get caught up in the idea that you can only touch this fund if you lose your income. You could also tie it to a goal you have that will be easier with a financial cushion, like working for yourself, moving to a new town, or adopting a child. You could base it on past experiences of life changes or major decisions. You can simply commit to contributing an amount that feels feasible for you each month for a set number of months. Or you can set a goal based on what your gut tells you is a comfortable number for where you are in life right now. Your money map can help inform the amount of money you want to store and the most practical way to do it. Continue to listen to your gut and adjust that amount as your circumstances change.

How to Build Your Comfort Fund

When you have resources to direct to savings, building a comfort fund is as simple as setting the money aside in an easy-to-access checking or savings account.

Step 1: Use your money map at the end of this book to set a comfort fund target, achievable contribution plan, and desired timeline. Adjust those as needed.

Step 2: Set aside savings when you're able. You could do that by:

- Automatically directing a portion of your income into a comfort fund savings account.
- Setting aside mini windfalls, like holiday gifts and tax refunds.
- Maintaining your commitments after your next raise and directing the surplus into savings.
- Working a side gig temporarily to bank the target amount faster.
- Deprioritizing commitments or debt-payoff goals to redirect money toward your comfort fund.

Your comfort fund is a living creature. Use the financial cushion when you need it, and continue to contribute to the fund to maintain your target amount as you go. Adjust according to changes in your life; you don't have to contribute the same amount every month, and some months you might not contribute anything at all. Keep your comfort fund goal and progress up to date on your money map so this is always part of your financial plan and you can easily rebuild after dipping into the funds.

Taking Care of Yourself in the Meantime

Chances are you might already experience the kinds of challenges or opportunities comfort funds are meant to address. If you don't already have a comfort fund stashed away, that's a tricky situation to be in (and one that typical financial advice somehow, annoyingly, fails to address). Sure, you might be able to save $1,000 or $10,000 by the end of the year—but what if you need extra funds in the meantime? How are you supposed to build a comfort fund while dealing with financial triage? And how do you deal with financial needs before the comfort fund is there to back you up?

You have a lot of options, but what's best for you depends on your circumstances. Don't let money be the thing that keeps you in a dangerous or intolerable situation. Lean on every community and debt resource you can find to get out, and balance your financial plan later, like Lisa did. Letting your finances fall into chaos in order to remove yourself from an unsafe situation or an uncertain future is not irresponsible by any measure. Take care of yourself first, and worry about the money later. Leaving a financial disaster in your wake as you escape a situation that does direct harm to your head, heart, or health makes sense. If money is the thing holding you back from making that move, that's budget culture overriding your gut instinct. Quiet the noise, and listen to your intuition to find your next move.

If your situation is annoying, vexing, or unsustainable, but not dangerous or urgent, like Ramat's, you have a little more leeway to make adjustments without a financial typhoon you have to address later. Don't let the tolerable nature of a bad situation lull you into doing nothing to change it, but determine what you can handle temporarily while you make strides in other areas. For example, can you handle an unpleasant job in the short term if you pull back and perform at the bare minimum? Could you live with nitpicking parents rent-free if you chip in a few chores you wouldn't otherwise care about? Again, listen to your intuition—you know the difference between an annoying situation and an intolerable one. A job where a boss harasses you on the regular and has faced no consequences is intolerable. Claim unemployment benefits, use debt resources, cut your rent commitment, and move in with a friend, so you can leave the situation immediately. A job where a boss is disorganized and egotistical and won't listen to feedback is unsustainable, but you might live with it in the short term so you can direct money into a comfort fund and search for other options.

Once you set yourself up to weather a bad situation in the short term, you can turn your energy reserves to making a plan to leave it in the longer term. Some steps you might take that could help you move into a better situation faster:

- Research any available community and government resources so you're prepared to use them as soon as you need them.
- Bolster your options for debt resources. For example, you might open a new credit card while you have a stable income and are paying bills on time, in case you don't have access to that additional credit after deprioritizing commitments to transition from one income to another.
- Eliminate or pause commitments to reduce the amount of resources you need to get by month to month.

These are generally short-term fixes and aren't sustainable if you have long-term financial goals, especially any that require a high credit rating. But they are options to remove financial barriers that might be holding you back from making the kinds of changes your life needs. A well-tended comfort fund is the long-term fix that can stop money from dictating your options.

Reflection: Finding Financial Comfort

Think of a time when you've faced what felt like a financial emergency.

- How does the shift in language from "emergency fund" to "comfort fund" affect how you think about your savings?
- Did you pull money from savings? What feelings came up? How did you feel about the way you used the funds?
- How did that event impact your relationship with money afterward?
- If you've never faced a financial emergency, what effect does this language shift have on how you view others' spending or saving behaviors?

CHAPTER 9

You Don't Need an Investment Account

Before the Dave Ramseyfication of personal finance centered financial advice on budgeting, advice in this industry was almost exclusively guidance for investing. Even now, if you're going to pay a professional for financial advice, you're most likely going to hire an advisor to guide your investing decisions. Ask any social media influencer or slightly wealthy neighbor for a money-management tip, and they'll probably tell you to start investing (after admonitions to pay off debt and make a budget). That means conversations about money are often explicitly aimed at the 52 percent of American families who invest in the stock market, who are disproportionately white and high-income earners.[1]

Despite this disparity, budget culture treats investing for long-term wealth building as an inevitability. Conventional financial advice tells you you're foolish if you don't invest, because investment gains are framed as "free money." And why would you let your money sit under a mattress or spend it on something fleeting if you could instead put it somewhere that would, seemingly by magic, turn it into more money?

But of course investing is much more complicated than magical free money. Investing in our economy is a system that rests on the worst characteristics of capitalism and perpetuates wealth inequality: the wealthiest 10 percent of US households own 69 percent of the wealth in our stock market,[2] and the profit motive of publicly traded companies is inevitably antilabor. But plenty of systemic forces make it difficult to opt out of investing altogether. So let's talk about it.

Most people I know are intimidated by the idea of investing. Many of them have money in the stock market through retirement funds and other vehicles, but they don't really know what it's doing, and they don't know how to find out. Many Americans' understanding of the stock market is limited to media coverage that offers dense economic updates with no context or education, leaving us to rely on the interpretation of politicians—also humans who don't understand economics and have lots of incentives to skew the information in one direction or another. This can cause us constant anxiety about markets that aren't even built for us and don't truly affect our everyday lives.

But investment accounts aren't the only way to hold wealth. You can participate in the system in a variety of ways and balance ethical concerns to varying degrees. Throughout this chapter, I'll share some ways to get creative with long-term financial planning, so you can choose what kind of participation makes sense for you.

A Tale of Two Investors

One way to look at investing in our economy is that there are two kinds of investors: let's call them *traders* and *savers*.

There are tons of distinctions between these two types of investors, but the most important is the reason they invest. To a trader, investing is a way to get richer. To a saver, investing is a form of long-term savings. Almost all of us are savers. If we're interested in investing or are already investing, the purpose is long-term financial security. Generally, that means having resources in retirement, so we can stop working for an income at some point and still have money to meet our commitments.

Despite the firehose of information from cable TV, savers don't need to be stock market experts. You typically just need to know a few things about investing to get started and keep your savings humming for the long term. I want you to know just three things about investing:

1. Investing is unethical (but sometimes unavoidable).
2. You don't need the stock market.
3. You're not a trader.

1. Investing Is Unethical (but Sometimes Unavoidable)

Investing is a tricky topic when you're concerned with being a good and ethical steward of money in our society. I'll complicate this advice shortly with some information to help you make sound investment decisions, but my basic stance is: there's no purely ethical way to build wealth. Thankfully, we're not aiming for "purity" here; we won't re-create budget culture's shame by attempting to find a different way to strive for perfection. In this system (and, likely, under any human circumstances), no one can or should strive to live a perfectly ethical life.

Most expert advice will tell you investing is a must for long-term financial stability, and they're not completely wrong. Because of the lack of elder care, disability care, end-of-life care, and basic income in the United States, most people rely on long-term savings to pay for life's essentials after they stop working. And several twentieth-century policies make investment accounts the most fiscally secure and advantageous place to hold those savings. I'll talk about why shortly.

The personal finance industry attempts to wash over ethical concerns about investing and convince us we can achieve long-term financial stability without compromising our values, but it's not true. These ethical problems are baked into the system we rely on to survive, and it's difficult not to participate. You deserve the comfort, safety, and dignity of planning for your future, supporting loved ones in need, and knowing your basic needs will be met when you stop working. So I'll teach you what I know, so you have the information you need to make a decision that balances your needs and values.

INVESTING EXPLOITS WORKERS, CONSUMERS, AND THE ENVIRONMENT

In the simplest terms: investments gain value because the underlying companies make profits by selling goods or services for more than it costs to produce them. Those costs include workers and environmental resources, so a profitable company needs to spend less money extracting resources and paying workers than it earns selling goods and services.

This system makes investing necessarily exploitative. Any profit a company makes means workers produced more value than they were paid for, or resources were extracted for a low cost, or a company sold goods or services for prices that exceeded their value. The mostly unfettered incentive to increase stock value leads to things like unlivable wages, environmental destruction, and high inflation, among other societal harms.

WHAT ABOUT SOCIALLY RESPONSIBLE INVESTING?
Many investors or would-be investors—especially among millennials, as we make our way into income brackets that call for investing—have become aware of this exploitation. Many of my cohorts are worried about investing in funds that put money behind multinational corporations that exploit labor around the world and extract resources from our environment without restraint. We don't want to grow wealth by supporting firearm manufacturers that lobby against commonsense gun control. Many of us want to keep our money out of the coffers of companies that produce, sell, and market alcohol, tobacco, gambling, and other vices that are out of sync with our personal morals. We want to use our dollars to do good in the world . . . and yet we know stock market investing is considered the smartest way to grow wealth, and we want to be smart.

So, as any market does, the market for financial services has responded with options to grow our wealth through public companies while soothing our guilt about supporting a system built on inequality and violence. Three major categories of so-called sustainable or socially responsible investing have emerged to appeal to various priorities, but they don't seriously tackle the fundamental issue of exploitation:

- **Environmental, social, and governance (ESG) investing:** The clunky acronym ESG describes an investment strategy that accounts not only for a company's financial factors but also for the impact of its actions on the environment, the communities it touches, and how it's run internally. ESG funds, like any other, prioritize profits; but they consider how environmental, social, and governance factors will impact profits over time.

- **Socially responsible investing (SRI):** This broad term is sometimes used as an umbrella for sustainable investing, but more often refers to the practice of choosing and restricting investments based on personal values. Advisors can guide clients to use an SRI strategy to build a portfolio according to their personal preferences, and some firms create socially responsible funds with a particular focus, like green energy or gender diversity.

- **Impact investing:** This term is also sometimes applied more broadly, but it specifically refers to investing in companies that are dedicated to making a specific impact on the world, like eliminating poverty or developing sustainable food systems. Advisors can guide clients in using impact investing strategies to build personalized portfolios, or firms might create impact investing funds that curate companies that meet certain criteria, like the United Nations Sustainable Development Goals.

Firms often offer these investment options as "ESG funds," "SRI funds," or "Impact funds." These are mutual funds or exchange-traded funds (ETFs), which means they're baskets of securities from a variety of companies. Investors buy a portion of the fund instead of individual company stocks. Fund managers set the parameters for which securities make it into their funds. The parameters for sustainable investing aren't standardized in the industry or regulated by the government; they're set for individual funds by the private firms that manage them. As long as the ethical guidelines for sustainable investing remain ad hoc and profit remains the priority for both fund managers and investors, labels like ESG and SRI don't carry much weight. We've seen corporations make this move over and over again for decades—pasting Certified Organic labels on factory-farmed food, rainbow-washing their social media accounts every June, and launching underfunded diversity initiatives in the summer of 2020. It's all marketing to changing tastes; it doesn't drive real change.

As an investor, you can look into the criteria for a particular fund or work with an advisor to set your own socially responsible parameters, but there's no government body overseeing what can and can't be included, and it's tough to know the criteria a corporation uses to consider itself socially or environmentally responsible. An investment advisor's only regulated responsibility is as a fiduciary—ensuring it manages your money and advises you in your best financial interest. Translation: their job is to earnestly try to make you money. That means sustainable funds and even personalized portfolios of sustainable investments will likely remain inherently exploitative, regardless of their veneer of social responsibility. Financial advisors and institutions in any capacity are usually set up and trained to focus on growing wealth. In investing, that means picking profitable companies. Producing profit inevitably means extracting value from workers, consumers, and resources without providing equal value in return; that's an inherent problem with the system.

None of this is to say you're a bad person if you contribute to a retirement account. You're challenged with surviving in a system that gives you few other options. But it does make this a tough decision to wrestle with ethically. If you have the fortitude to question our system and look for alternatives, consider what your financial plan could look like without stock market investing.

WHAT CAN WE SAY ABOUT CRYPTOCURRENCY?

After a boom during the COVID-19 pandemic in 2020 and 2021, interest in blockchain, cryptocurrencies, nonfungible tokens (NFTs), and decentralized autonomous organizations (DAOs) grew nearly to a point of being undeniable before values began to wane and media coverage slowed. But these technologies are still developing. The extent of their impact is uncertain as of this writing, but curiosity about the potential of cryptocurrency investing is here to stay.

As a technology, blockchain is fascinating (though an incredible strain on environmental resources). I'll let you explore that on your own; it can easily fill its own book. As an investment, though? Leave it to the traders. Cryptocurrency and other blockchain applications fall into a category called *speculative investment.* Those are assets that have no proven history experts can analyze to forecast how their value might change in the future. Investments in these assets are based on speculation that demand for them will increase—hopefully soon and hopefully by a lot. Think of nineteenth-century land speculators in the western United States, early dot-com investors, and Beanie Baby collectors. For some, it pays off; for most, it doesn't. Speculative investment is a gamble, no matter how much knowledge you bring (or believe you bring) to the game. The people who win in this game do so because they start with a lot of money they can comfortably lose in the majority of their bets.

Cryptocurrency isn't yet widely adopted or regulated, so its value isn't anchored to any predictable economic or social behavior. That unpredictability causes the major swings that make the investment exciting; value can, indeed, skyrocket overnight. But it can just as quickly free-fall with no clear path to recovery. Because of this behavior, cryptocurrency investing in its current state is more akin to playing your state lottery than to a long-term financial strategy.

2. You Don't Need the Stock Market

If it feels right for you, you can opt out of traditional investing. It's not a common move, and you should do it with a clear understanding of its impact on your long-term financial options. But if a profit-driven investment account doesn't feel like the right place for your money, consider some alternatives for long-term savings that could help your money grow without supporting the exploitation inherent in traditional investing.

All these options come with complexities and risks, and they still involve varying levels of structural inequality—that's almost inevitable if your goal is building wealth. But they could simplify a lot of the ethical complexities of investing and help you secure your future while using money more in line with your head, heart, and health.

PEER-TO-PEER LENDING

Peer-to-peer lending has been around for a while, and most platforms act a lot like banks and feel pretty close to any other type of investing. But one platform has broken the mold in recent years, and its model is promising for both borrowers and lenders.

SoLo Funds is a community finance app that lets individuals request micro-loans to cover unexpected expenses, offering a "tip" of any amount in return. Other individuals on the app fund the loans and earn a little bit of a return through tips. Borrowers set the amount of the loan, the repayment period, and the tip amount; they're in complete control of the process. They can include in their request an explanation of how they'll use the money: to pay rent, to take a vacation, or to pay a phone bill, for example. Borrowers are scored on the platform based on their SoLo Funds history (no credit checks or other outside reporting), so you can get a sense of the likelihood your loan will be repaid on schedule.

SoLo Funds cofounder Rodney Williams explains, "We're bringing this human emotional factor into the decision-making, which I think [our society has] lost. But I do think people will make better decisions [about who to lend to] than the institutions."

Williams says the average annual return on SoLo Funds loans is higher than the average return similar investors get through DIY investing on an app like Robinhood because it's less complicated and more connected to human finances than micro-investing apps are. Just like those apps, you can make hands-on decisions about where to direct your money, and you can get started with just a few dollars at a time, so the option is accessible to the majority of those who the stock market isn't built for. But SoLo also lets you use money to directly help someone in need.

"It's like a mixture of GoFundMe [and] an investment product," Williams says.

Peer-to-peer lending through an app like SoLo Funds can be a generous way to use your money while also growing it to secure your future. With plans to add auto lending, larger loans, and a credit card, this type of community finance could quickly become a viable alternative to traditional capitalist financial institutions.

INVEST IN SMALL LOCAL BUSINESSES

Investing in small private businesses could grow your savings while supporting business owners in your community locally or online. If you have a significant chunk of money to contribute, your investment could make the difference in an entrepreneur getting their idea off the ground.

Investing this way still functions much like investing in the stock market, because the growth of your savings relies on profits in the business (or a sale, whose valuation relies on profits). So you still have to wrestle with the downside of labor, resource, and consumer exploitation to some degree—but that exploitation is often much less than with larger, publicly traded corporations, which aren't stakeholders in the communities where they operate.

A bigger difference with investing in a small private business is that it's riskier than investing through funds, because it puts all of your resources in one place. That one business has to succeed, or your money is lost. Investing through the stock market, by contrast, lets you spread your money across several businesses and sectors, so any single failure has a smaller impact. The upside to private investing is that you can have more influence over how the business is run, and thus more agency in how much you earn.

BUILD AND SELL A BUSINESS

Instead of (or in addition to) investing in someone else's business, you can build a business of your own to sell one day. This is a classic way of working to earn income while building an asset you can cash out at the end of your career so you have money to live on after you stop working.

There's a ton of hype around entrepreneurs who start businesses, especially in the tech industry, with the intention of finding private investors, growing fast, and cashing out quickly. That's not the route I'm talking about here. Depending on your access to time and financial resources, you could bootstrap a local or online business and sell it for a modest but significant amount that offers an opportunity to another entrepreneur and lets you move into your next phase comfortably.

Software engineer Anna Maste and her mother, Marianne Edwards, did just that when they built and sold their small business, Boondockers Welcome, for seven figures, enough to fund Marianne's retirement. As Anna tells Alexis Grant for the podcast *They Got Acquired*, the business leaned on both women's expertise—Anna's ability to code and Marianne's enthusiasm for RVing—to develop a community in which RVers could connect with hosts who would let them stay on their property overnight, instead of at camping sites—like couch surfing for RVs.[3]

While Anna was on her year-long (Canadian) maternity leave with a newborn, she followed her curiosity and learned how to build a membership site. The pair launched Boondockers Welcome in 2012 and built an audience for the site using an email list Marianne had developed from her work writing ebooks for RVers and campers. Two years later, Anna quit her day job to focus on the business and spend more time with her kids. She worked a few hours a week on the business while Marianne watched her kids. When the kids were older, working on her own schedule meant Anna could walk them to school and pick them up every day. That labor distribution, along with Marianne's RV expertise and community, earned her 50 percent ownership in the business.

The pandemic brought a surge of interest in RVing and camping, and Boondockers Welcome experienced fast growth in 2020. Several private equity firms and businesses contacted the mother-daughter pair about buying the business, and they eventually sold in 2021 to a similar business looking to expand its base of hosts. They earned mid-seven figures in the sale, and Marianne's share let her enjoy her retirement. To that point, she'd only built a "modest" retirement fund, having waited until her late forties to start saving.

"I always looked at my retirement savings as money to keep invested without touching it unless absolutely necessary," she tells me. "One never knows what the future holds—how long will we live, in what health, how much care will we require, and at what cost?"

The funds from selling the business let her retire comfortably and spend with less trepidation. "Selling the business has allowed me to feel comfortable spending some of those savings on fun things without worrying if there will be enough left for old age," she says. "The biggest change we've made has been to designate a generous annual travel budget and then try our best to spend it."

RENTAL PROPERTIES

Purchasing and managing rental properties can help you earn additional income you can put into savings, build an asset you can sell, or earn income late in life when you're not employed. Like buying any property, this requires access to a massive amount of capital or a loan, so your financial circumstances will dictate whether it's an option for you.

Using housing as an investment gets you out of the stock market, but it comes with its own set of ethical concerns. Housing has become unaffordable in many cities around the country precisely because of real estate investors hoarding stock (and public officials refusing to act on the problem). Putting yourself between families and life-saving shelter in order to make a return on your investment is tough to justify, even if it might be the best way for you to support your family in the long term. That's the environment capitalism thrusts you into. But you can use the opportunity to not only benefit yourself but also provide safe, respectful, affordable housing for tenants in your community.

One of my friends who earns the bulk of his income from rental properties in Madison, Wisconsin, told me he'll keep up with "market rates" for new renters, but he never raises rent on a tenant once they're in, no matter how long they've lived in his building. He has some tenants who've been in one place for fifteen years, so they pay the rents they came into more than a decade ago. This practice doesn't maximize the money he could extract in a city with a high demand for rentals, but it lets him make a comfortable living—enough to cope with the city's rising cost of living. And it lets him do that while honoring his values of fairness and equity the best he can.

3. You're Not a Trader

As promised, this is where I'll complicate my own advice and offer a little bit of guidance for traditional investing. Despite the ethical implications, the lack of a long-term social safety net in our country makes traditional retirement accounts the most viable option for a lot of people, and you're well within your right to decide challenging the system isn't worth a lifelong struggle for you or your family.

I also know participating in the system can be an important part of liberation for many people living in the marginalized identities our economic system has invented, used, abused, and oppressed for centuries. As I learned from The Trans Capitalist, K. Kenneth Davis, one way of beating the system is to not end up in the position it's designed to put you in. "Capitalism is our economic system. It's not going anywhere," Davis says. "It's going to be here for a long time, because too many people benefit from it. But the thing is, since it's such a racist and oppressive institution, there's no way you can survive unless you know the rules of the game."

Challenging the system doesn't have to mean divesting from it entirely. As with all the financial issues in our society, the ethical challenges of investing are much bigger than what any one person does with their money. The challenges are tied up in our financial and social systems that make it impossible for many people to make alternative choices. Being a good steward, in this case, doesn't have to mean taking a chance on your future. You can use the products available within this system to improve your situation and find other ways to challenge or change it for those who come after you.

For example, creating a more robust social safety net would mean workers by and large wouldn't have to rely on savings for financial security. With sufficient Social Security and health care access, for example, many of us wouldn't need to invest at all. And even for those who continue to invest, the exploitative nature of capitalism could be mitigated with heavy regulation that ensures fair wages, environmental protections, and affordable prices. Profits always technically require some amount of exploitation, but regulation can bring the equation into balance to shrink the gap between workers and capitalists. The way you show up in your community as an educator, advocate, voter, and public servant can support this kind of change.

This type of stewardship isn't about how you use money; it's about the impact of the money you use. You can work to create fairer choices for the people who come after you and make long-term financial security more of a certainty and less of an ethical dilemma. We'll talk more about how this can look in chapter 13.

If you're going to invest, learn the basics so you can do it without feeding into budget culture. Don't chase the fantasy of being rich; instead ask how the system works so you can use it in a way that supports your needs *and* your values.

Here are a few key tips to invest like a saver and minimize the harm you participate in:

INVEST THROUGH A RETIREMENT ACCOUNT

A tax-advantaged retirement savings account is the way many Americans are introduced to investing.

If you're employed through the government or a rare private organization, that account might be a pension. A pension is a *defined-benefit plan*, which means you're guaranteed to receive a predetermined fixed income from the account after you retire. Employers usually make the bulk of contributions to pensions throughout your employment.

Most workers since the 1980s, however, save for retirement through a *defined-contribution plan*, which is what most people imagine when they think of a retirement plan now. Instead of a guaranteed payout after retirement, you contribute a set amount of money as a percentage of each paycheck, and your employer often matches your contributions up to a set percentage. Your savings and income at retirement depend on how much has been contributed and how investments perform over time. Defined contribution plans in the United States include the 401(k) for for-profit companies and the 403(b) for public schools, churches, and charitable organizations. Outside of an employer, you can also contribute to an *individual retirement account* (IRA), and you can talk to an accountant about additional retirement plans designed for the self-employed and small businesses.

If you're an employee and you've gotten any financial advice, you've probably been told you'd be a fool not to contribute to your company's retirement account (if one is offered). This advice comes from budget culture, and it ignores not only the ethical implications of investing but also your personal financial circumstances and needs. Only you can know which money moves strike the right balance for you, so consider how saving for retirement fits into your overall relationship with money.

There are several reasons you hear so many people idealize retirement accounts:

- Contributions come out of your paycheck automatically, so you don't have to rely on individual willpower or planning to grow your savings. (Note that many companies have moved to automatic-enrollment retirement plans on the assumption that this is what's best for workers, which means you could be automatically making these contributions without doing anything. Check your pay stubs and talk with your boss or HR rep to make sure you know what's going on with your money.)

- Employers often match your contributions up to a percentage of your paycheck. Financial gurus like to call this "free money" you throw away if you don't contribute, but let's call it what it is: a portion of your compensation held hostage if you don't conform with budget culture expectations.

- Retirement contributions get you a federal tax deduction up to a certain amount each year—and financial experts love tax breaks!

Retirement accounts come with tax advantages other types of investment accounts don't enjoy. Most commonly, you get a tax deduction on contributions you make to a retirement account, and you don't pay tax on the money gained in it through investments over the years. Instead, you withdraw the money as income in retirement and pay income taxes on it then. Most people owe less in lifetime taxes by saving this way. Retirement planning, especially if you work with a financial planner or wealth manager, is largely about finding a balance between the risks and rewards of investing, and manipulating accounts to take advantage of tax breaks. It's absurd to imagine Americans' long-term independence and health depends on this kind of financial maneuvering, but that is the way the system's designed.

DON'T PICK INDIVIDUAL STOCKS

A huge danger with the way we tend to talk about investing in this culture is that most people don't make the distinction between traders and savers. Many savers get sucked into tools and advice designed for traders.

Business news from the likes of CNBC, Fox Business, and Bloomberg broadcasts to consumers, but it's really only intended for professional traders. The rest of us shouldn't be watching financial markets so closely—nor can we usually interpret the news in a useful way if we do. Investing apps like Robinhood and Webull that make it easy to buy individual stocks and crypto are also designed based on the behavior of traders, but they intentionally appeal to a lot of savers. These products claim to "democratize" investing by letting anyone buy pieces of stocks for small dollar amounts. But they encourage savers to act like traders, which puts your money at greater risk.

Savers aren't meant to trade individual stocks and bonds. Those are risky moves, even for professionals, and they tend to only pay off for investors who have a lot of extra money to gamble with.

The safer way to invest is with what are called *mutual funds*—collections of stocks curated to balance risk with returns and maintain relative stability over the long life of an investment portfolio. Studies have shown that the least risky kind of mutual fund is an *index fund*, a mutual fund whose stocks represent the companies included in a particular stock index, like the S&P 500, a list of five hundred leading companies in the stock market that covers about 80 percent of the total US market value. The value of an S&P 500 index fund share reflects the weighted value of all those companies, so it's tough for the performance of one company to make a huge impact on your overall savings. If, instead, you buy a bunch of shares in one company because experts expect it to gain a lot of value soon, you risk losing money if the company doesn't perform as expected.

Several studies have shown that index funds and similar products called *exchange-traded funds* (ETFs) consistently outperform even professionally managed mutual funds, where professional traders choose stocks for you.[4] So know that, unless your goal is to gamble for the sake of entertainment and occasional wins, savings is more stable in the long term in a simple (boring) index fund.

TALK TO (THE RIGHT KIND OF) FINANCIAL ADVISORS

Only about 25 percent of people turn to financial professionals when making financial decisions. People are more likely to turn to family and friends, or even Google, over a professional.[5] That's probably because financial professionals have traditionally worked in an industry gated off for the rich—and because they cost money. Even modern financial planners who set up firms with a mission to serve a more diverse base of clients still rely on fees, which makes their services inaccessible or impractical for many basic financial questions.

But *financial advisor* is technically a catchall term that encompasses anyone who can provide information or guidance around money. If you're employed, two important people can help you make long-term savings decisions without costing you a thing:

- **HR or other company representative:** This person in your organization or company can't offer individual financial advice (i.e., where to invest), but they're an important resource to help you understand any retirement plan benefits you have access to and how to manage them. They should be able to direct you to information that'll explain how to enroll in or opt out of a plan and where your contributions are being invested.
- **Retirement plan custodian:** This is the representative for an employer's retirement plan provider. They also can't provide personalized advice, but they can answer questions your HR rep can't. They'll let you see what types of funds the plan uses, so you can know whether

your savings is in pricey managed funds or low-cost index funds, and how to set up your investments (usually through an online account).

When you speak with these advisors about long-term financial planning, consider these questions:

- **When are you eligible to enroll in a retirement savings plan at work?** Not every job lets you contribute and get the company match as soon as you're hired; you might have to work there for thirty to ninety days first. Find out when your eligibility starts, so you can set a reminder to meet with HR and set up your account (and document how to access it!).
- **Does your employer match your contribution?** If so, up to what percentage of your paycheck?
- **Will you be enrolled automatically?** If so, at what percentage? How can you make changes to your automatic enrollment settings?
- **Do your investments incur any fees?** If your employer's retirement plan is invested in actively managed mutual funds, not only do they risk worse performance, but you'll also pay higher fees that can eat up a significant portion of your savings. Find out what's being charged (usually as a percentage of your savings), and ask how you can make changes.
- **Where can you manage your account?** Most retirement plans come with an online portal, where you can

sign up for an account and make any changes you want. Don't take that as an invitation to become an active trader, but learn how to use the account to understand your fees, move your savings into low-cost index funds, and take the savings with you if you leave the job.

For personalized financial advice—i.e., someone to tell you exactly which funds to put your savings into and maybe even make the moves for you—you'll need a financial planner. If you go this route, look for a fiduciary, fee-only financial planner. They're certified and regulated to provide investment advice in line with your long-term goals. Look specifically for "fiduciary" and "fee-only," because other types of advisors could be incentivized to direct you to riskier investments to earn a commission. If the planner or their firm is a registered investment advisor (RIA), registered with your state or the SEC, they can manage your investments for you.

A financial planner can help with more than just retirement planning, but they're a particularly valuable resource for long-term planning because they're trained to help you sort through the complexities of investment accounts. Some financial planners also help with short-term financial goals, like saving for big spending or dealing with debt. Just go in with an understanding of your relationship with money and the head/heart/health goals you want to achieve. Every financial planner I've met starts with making a budget, so you'll have to assert your budget-free approach up front. Check youdontneedabudget.com to find recommendations for anticapitalist financial planners who'll be more willing to hear your concerns and work with you to make a budget-free plan for your long-term financial wellness.

Reflection: Are You an Investor?

- Does an investment account feel like the best place for your money? Why or why not?
- What effect might *not* investing in the stock market have on your life in the short and long term?
- Have you gotten investment advice from experts or friends in the past? How has that affected your decisions and feelings about money?

CHAPTER 10

You Can Spend Money

"I don't do No Spend Months. In fact, I rarely participate in No Spend Challenges," writes Penny, the anonymous blogger and mother behind the personal finance site She Picks Up Pennies.[1]

And yet in January 2023, Penny was inspired by an Instagram trend and challenged herself to start the new year with a no-spend month, a popular exercise among personal finance enthusiasts in which you commit to not spend any money on so-called nonessentials for thirty days. A no-spend month is like a Whole30 diet or a restrictive cleanse, but for your money.

"I love the feeling that comes with a new year. Or even a new month or a new week," writes Penny. "There's something about Fresh Start Energy that I love."

It's tough to resist the urge to overhaul your relationship with money at the start of a new year. Budget culture presents this annual opportunity to think about where you've been and where you want to go next, and that inevitably includes naming your shortcomings and making a plan to fix them. (If you can't think of any, don't worry! There's an influencer out there who can give you some ideas!) That makes January a popular month for a no-spend challenge, and Penny got swept up in the excitement on social media.

"I am a sucker for a well-crafted list. I also have a soft spot for graphic design. . . . There are so many beautiful, simple, and stream-lined no-spend-month trackers floating around Instagram that I couldn't pull myself away from their siren song."

But, as with any restrictive budget, the challenge didn't last long for Penny—frankly, it barely started. She'd decided to do it, and she'd spent a couple of weeks thinking more about her spend-ing than usual. But when she was faced with opportunities for spending, she took them—because the benefits of spending out-weighed the supposed benefits of succeeding at perfect restriction. For example, a few days into the new year, her husband ordered twenty dollars' worth of screen protectors from Amazon for their kids' electronics. It was "actually a really smart money move," she notes, because of the cost of repairing or replacing the devices if the screens were to break. Penny's second "fail" in the challenge was to spend seven dollars at McDonald's after a trip with her son to the bank, about ten days in. And, finally, she got an email from a longtime friend with an invitation to meet for lunch.

She was about to say no so she could honor her commitment to no spending. "But then I realized the one thing I needed more than to meet some arbitrary measure of financial fitness was to take my $9 and go have a Mediterranean bowl at the local gyro place with my pals," she writes. "My soul sang." Penny calls that lunch with friends "the final nail in my No Spend Month coffin," and she ended the challenge after that.

When you're struggling to use money the way you'd like to in your life, most financial experts tell you to start with some kind of restriction. Some might recommend a full-on no-spend challenge like the one Penny attempted, and some might push you toward a budget that doesn't end your spending but instead attempts to plan and control it. Making a budget might seem like a no-brainer when you want to feel more in control of your money. But conventional budgeting methods rely on restriction, discipline, and perfectionism in a way that doesn't work for most people. They ignore an important truth about money: it's meant to be spent.

Money that isn't spent is just paper (or numbers in a database). It doesn't have any meaning or value by itself.

"The real reason why I don't jump into these challenges like the frugal fanatic I am," Penny notes, "is because I'm not sure I like the ultimate lesson. Money isn't good or bad. Money has no moral value. And yet these challenges certainly assign one."

Capitalism and budget culture would have you live in a mode the nineteenth-century philosopher Karl Marx describes as "the less you are, the more you have,"[2] hoarding capital at the expense of living a life. The message is that the fantasy of being rich is within reach as long as you follow the rules. But those rules are, in fact, designed to keep you small—spending less and therefore doing less, owning less, and *being* less of who you are.

No-spend challenges and ongoing budgets train you to believe spending is bad, and you're a failure for giving in to it. What Penny learned is that spending money is often the right choice—not only when it's a frugal choice, like it was with the screen protectors, but also when it can create connection and foster joy, like it did with her son and her friend. Penny also realized money's status as morally neutral means it shouldn't carry positive moral value, either.

"Let's say that I could participate in the challenge only joyfully," she writes. "Imagine a world where I got to the end of the month and took a high-speed victory lap around my dining room table or around my social media circles. I'm not sure money is supposed to feel triumphant, either. Money is a tool meant to help us add joy to our lives, not become the source of our joy."

Letting go of the satisfaction you feel from restricting is just as important as letting go of the shame you feel from spending. "Succeeding" at restriction might make you feel like budgeting works for you, but it's just the flip side of shaming yourself for spending.

Practice Conscious Spending

Letting go of the perceived control a budget gives you might feel scary, because budget culture has taught you not to trust yourself around money. How can you manage money without imposing restrictions?

Once you've rejected the premise of budgeting, you have to learn to trust yourself to spend money without destroying your life (as budget culture convinces you that you certainly will). Using money in a way that feels satisfying and productive for you involves understanding that money doesn't control you, as we've discussed in previous chapters. And trusting yourself to use money is what I call *conscious spending.*

We know setting restrictive limits on how to use money for things you love and value is impractical. My goal with money management isn't to create new kinds of restrictions or give you another difficult chore to manage. A budget-free approach is about being able to say yes more often when you're wondering whether or not to spend money. But budget culture's lionizing of restriction has probably messed with your ability to know how you truly want to use money. Trying to reject budgeting without a way to trust yourself could throw you right back into a cycle of splurging and restricting.

To avoid that cycle, we'll look at conscious spending practices to help you easily see how a spending decision will impact your overall financial picture, and relearn to trust your gut.

It's possible you've heard language like "conscious spending" before—as "mindful" or "values-based" spending. Budget culture often uses these concepts to encourage restricted spending, and I want to be clear: that's not what I'm encouraging here.

Budget culture frames mindful or values-based spending as a way to control your spending by becoming disciplined against forces that cause you to spend money. Financial gurus use the word *afford* as a get-out-of-jail-free card under these frameworks. They can claim to let you do whatever you want with money as long as they attach this one word. "Buy what makes you happy, as long as you can *afford* it." Tacking on that disclaimer lets advisors peddle restriction and shame without explicitly setting limits or critiquing your choices. They lean on individual responsibility by leaving you to decide what you can afford—while never explaining what it actually means to be able to afford something. The word likely means something different to everyone, which makes it meaningless as financial advice, and useful only as a technicality to place blame. Be careful about framing your spending decisions with this concept; like other budget culture ideas, it crumbles when you put it to the test, and it isn't a useful decision-making tool.

Using money in a satisfying way will, in fact, mean less spending on things that aren't aligned with your head, heart, and health; as you practice conscious spending, you'll probably find lots of ways our culture entices you to act in capitalists' best interests instead of your own. You'll learn how to address forces like anxiety, depression, or fear at their root instead of quieting them with consumption. With conscious spending, you'll discover opportunities to refrain from using money when you don't truly want to—but you'll also start embracing opportunities to spend money when you *do* truly want to. Conscious spending doesn't involve restriction at all; it's about knowing what you want and what you don't want (and, often *but not always*, being able to articulate why).

The Myth of "Wants versus Needs"

Attempts to control spending often start with deciding whether something is a "want" or a "need." The idea is that you can spend on needs without guilt, but you should make sacrifices to afford wants—or forgo them altogether. The problem with these categories is they're pretty much impossible to define. Their real function is to give you a framework for restriction and shame.

You need to eat. Does that mean you *need* the organic, pasture-raised eggs, or is that a *want* that drives you toward irresponsible spending? Do you need to live with integrity, for example, with your values of environmental consciousness and protecting animal welfare, or do you want to? Do you need eggs at all, or do you want to eat a satisfying meal, when your need for calories could be met with cheap porridge? Do you need certain culinary ingredients to spend an afternoon baking with your grandkids, or is that an indulgent want? Is it reasonable for the definition of wants versus needs to change depending on a person's access to income or wealth? (Think of Dave Ramsey telling people with debt they should never eat at a restaurant.)

The wants-versus-needs framework doesn't add clarity to spending decisions; it adds judgment. Just like attempts to label foods "healthy" or "unhealthy," it creates a way to ignore your inner voice and justify restriction. Maybe even more, it gives all of us permission to decide others aren't worthy of respect or support because they could always be more disciplined or restrictive.

Why We Buy Things

Even though it's the antidote to restrictive budgeting, the freedom of conscious spending doesn't mean boundless indulgence. When you tune in to your head, heart, and health, you're unlikely to find that overconsumption is what you're looking for. Binging and splurging are no more in line with your financial well-being than restriction and discipline are. Instead, what you gain when you take this mindful approach to money is freedom from the stress of traditional money management and freedom from second-guessing your own competence.

Conscious spending requires you to develop a solid understanding of yourself and what drives your decision-making. This isn't separate from any other self-exploration you might do; knowing yourself better helps you use money in a more satisfying way. As you go through your day, ask yourself why you make the money moves you make. Investigate how these decisions tie into other parts of your identity, personality, and life experience.

Many factors influence the various facets of your financial well-being, though they're not widely discussed in personal finance education. As you explored at the end of chapter 2, you bring the history of yourself to every financial decision. Your decisions can be swayed by trauma or privilege you've experienced, and lessons you've learned explicitly or implicitly. You also bring present conditions to your decisions. Your mental health, hormonal cycles, mood, hunger, and day-to-day experiences can all impact your next money move.

And, of course, spending decisions are heavily influenced by marketing in our culture. Regardless of how you're feeling or what you're needing, advertising and branding can sway you toward financial decisions that are in the best interest of the seller, whether they're in your best interest or not. These conditions might be within or out of your control, but becoming conscious of them can help you see the forces behind your financial decisions and use money with intention to create the experience you want.

Practicing conscious spending is about yielding to your innate wisdom to guide your money moves, instead of looking to an outside set of rules to determine what you "should" do. You might call this wisdom your inner knowing, your inner voice, your gut, your highest self, God, the Holy Spirit, Self, the universe, Source, intuition, a still small voice, or a gentle whisper. Whatever it feels like to you, your inner voice is the part of you that knew what you wanted and needed before the world drowned it out. It's the part of you that cares for your head, heart, and health, whether you tend to them or not.

Divesting from budget culture is all about learning to listen to that inner voice and trusting that it knows you better than all of the voices shouting at you from the outside. (After all, it *is* you!) From this place, you can use money in the way that's uniquely right for you.

Practices and Experiments

Raising your consciousness to become a conscious spender is a big and endless endeavor. This practice doesn't come with a set of milestones you can hit, and you can't go into it with expectations for yourself. Raising your self-awareness and tuning in to your inner voice requires ongoing practice and experimentation—but it doesn't have to be hard. Just about any mindfulness practice that speaks to you will hone your self-awareness toward conscious spending.

Here are some experiments you can try:

CREATE CHECKPOINTS FOR REFLECTION

Rather than a prescriptive spending plan, set yourself up to learn from your spending as you go. Build automated checkpoints to remind yourself to reflect on your financial decisions. That could be a weekly meeting, like we talked about in chapter 3, or something to make you pause in the moment before or after spending. Consider:

- A note in your wallet that asks, "What does money do for you in this moment?"

- Transaction notifications from your bank or credit card company.
- Dinner conversation prompts that include "What was your favorite way you used money today?"

USE A SPENDING DIARY

A spending diary is a tally of all the ways you use money—but it's not just a list of transactions. It's an exercise to reflect on your use of money and tap into how it aligns with your needs and values. Long-term spend tracking can be cumbersome and encourage perfectionism and restriction, so I recommend you only use a spending diary temporarily, and focus on your experience, rather than the numbers.

Take a week or a month or any number of days to jot down where you spent money, what you got out of it, how it made you feel, and how it impacts your finances and greater experience. The numbers don't matter here as much as the reflection on your relationship with money.

Here's an example of how this might look, using Penny's experience of getting lunch with friends:

- Spent: *$9 at the gyro place.*
- What: *Mediterranean bowl.*
- Why: *Friend invited me to lunch.*
- How I felt: *Guilty at first, then happy to spend time with my pals. My soul sang.*
- Impact: *Reinforcing my friendships and remembering money doesn't have a moral value.*

Use these questions to start your own short-term spending diary:

- How much did I spend and where?
- What did I get?
- Why did I have this opportunity for spending?
- How did I feel during and after the experience?
- What impact did it have on my finances and life?

IMAGINE YOUR IDEAL DAY

Being more conscious about your spending doesn't mean you'll discover some profound purpose for your money that forces you to give up everything about the life you're living now. For most people, these practices will probably help you discover purpose in the ways you already use money and to weed out things that no longer serve (or never served) you.

Dr. Susan Biali Haas writes in her book *The Resilient Life*, "Purpose comes in lots of different shapes and sizes. Our world tends to glamorize things that are big and flashy, without recognizing the immensely important contributions (and purposes) of the people who quietly, faithfully show up for their non-glamorous lives, day after day."[3]

To tap into what feels purposeful and meaningful for you, Haas recommends a reflection in which you imagine a day in your ideal life. Imagine your ideal life five or ten years from now, and answer these questions:

- Where are you living? Who do you live with? In what type of living space?

- Who are your neighbors? Who are your friends? How are you engaged with your community?
- What do you do in a typical day?
- What gives your life meaning and purpose at this time?
- What gives you the greatest joy?
- What is your life about, if you could summarize that in one sentence?

Once you've crafted this ideal future day, Haas asks, "Finally, what will you need to do in your life, from today forward, to increase the probability that this meaningful, purposeful future might come to fruition? Is there one primary thing, or several?"

This exercise is a way to tap into the experience you want and become conscious of whether the ways you use money support or impede it.

NOTICE YOUR HORMONE CYCLES

If you menstruate, cycle tracking is an important way to understand the overall health of your body and mind. Though research has debunked the myth that hormone cycles make you necessarily irrational, it is true that changes throughout the menstrual cycle impact your energy and emotions and, therefore, decision-making. Tuning in to your cycle can help you understand and embrace how it impacts the ways you use money at various points throughout the month. The approximately twenty-eight-day menstrual cycle takes your body through four phases, each of which involves estrogen hormone levels that have a distinct impact on your energy, emotions, and drive.

"For most of our lives, we've been taught that we must feel the same, work the same, be the same person twenty-four hours a day, 365 days a year," says Caitlin Molony, a menstrual cycle educator. "The patriarchal and capitalist systems we live in seep into even places where you'd think the menstrual cycle would be honored and respected."[4]

Molony says you might feel more productive during the *follicular* and *ovulatory phases*, those one to two weeks after your period. You might feel less motivated and more introverted during the *luteal* and *menstrual phases*, the days often referred to as "PMS" and "getting your period," respectively. Energy and mood tends to go up during the follicular and ovulatory phases and wane during the luteal and menstrual phases. Those physical and emotional changes can impact how you work, what you eat, what you do for recreation, and what you need for comfort—all of which impact how you use money. Studies have found menstruators to be less loss-averse during ovulation, when self-confidence is boosted, which can mean making more rational (less fear-based) economic decisions[5]; and more impulsive during the luteal phase[6]—i.e., less likely to restrict and more in tune with how to use money to care for yourself.

If you primarily experience a testosterone cycle, you'll likely have higher levels of testosterone in the morning and increasingly lower levels later in the day. Testosterone levels also tend to go down as you get older, especially after age forty. Those daily fluctuations might not be noticeable, but low testosterone in general could show up as irritability, disengagement, crankiness, and a tendency to be more emotional.[7] Similar to changes during the menstrual cycle, you can learn to notice these emotional changes in your body and understand how various emotions drive your spending decisions.

DO "MONEY MINDSET" WORK

So-called money mindset exercises can be useful to help you recognize the beliefs you might carry from childhood or other experiences. Use questions like those from the reflection in chapter 2 to tap into the ways your experiences have instilled biases toward or against certain ways of using money.

The most common way people describe money mindset—again, another way to refer to your relationship with money—is a belief in either abundance or scarcity. An *abundance mindset* means trusting in having enough, while a *scarcity mindset* means fearing not having enough. Experiencing poverty or years of restriction could foster a scarcity mindset, but so could experiencing wealth with the expectation of growing or holding on to it.

Much of the reflection you've done throughout this book can help you understand your relationship with money and how it impacts the ways you use money. You can find tons of other money mindset exercises online; just be aware as you explore that these are often accompanied by language focused on becoming rich, which doesn't have to be your financial goal. Check youdontneedabudget .com for my recommended money mindset sources.

DO YOGA AND SOMATIC EXERCISES

"[As adults], we begin shutting off the impulses of free movement and the needs and desires of our physical bodies that once were natural responses to our sensations and emotions," says somatic educator Cristy de la Cruz. "We are likely to be reprimanded when we're young for not being compliant. It's almost a survival instinct to turn down the signal of our sensorimotor system to avoid punishment."[8]

Redeveloping that bodily awareness as an adult can help you recognize messages coming from your body—which often holds memories and wisdom you can't access with conscious thought. (This is why many of us call our inner voice "listening to your gut." You might physically feel a response to an idea or event in the pit of your stomach, for example.)

"Somatic awareness is about noticing the places in our bodies where the feelings arise while working with money," says de la Cruz. "While some people believe we should name the feelings, I prefer to describe the sensations instead. One reason is that naming an emotion usually has judgment attached to it. . . . Money can bring up emotions that are difficult. When we realize emotions will not harm us, and we can move through them by watching and breathing, it frees up our energy to make better decisions for the long term. It also brings our frontal cortex back online, so we're less likely to make hasty decisions out of fear."

A movement practice like walking or yoga is a simple place to start feeling into your body. De la Cruz also recommends a simple body check-in practice you can add to your financial check-in or decision-making process:

1. Notice your body and the position you're in. Notice sensations on your skin. Notice scents in the air. Notice comfort or discomfort. Notice where your feet touch the floor. Notice how breath moves in and out of your body.

2. Notice thoughts and emotions that float to the surface. What feelings are you connecting to this financial

situation or decision? Where do those feelings sit in your body (a heavy gut, a tense jaw, a fluttering heart, etc.)?

3. Ask yourself, "What would feel good to my body right now?" Listen for the answer—do you need to adjust your posture, roll out your shoulders, loosen your jaw, blow your nose, blink your eyes?

By taking a couple of minutes to listen to your body before you make a money move, you can care for yourself from the inside out before letting the pressures of the outside world dictate your direction. If financial stress shows up as tense shoulders, for example, take a few minutes to roll out your shoulders and loosen the tension instead of taking it into the grocery store with you. Listen to what your body is asking for, and you can care for it without letting money call the shots.

INCORPORATE REST

Building an intentional practice of rest and true self-care will help you set your mind loose from the hectic expectations and stresses of our culture. Letting your mind wander the way Tricia Hersey recommends in *Rest Is Resistance* can be a simple way to make space for what your inner voice is saying.

"Let the space that dreaming asks for channel you back to your true self," Hersey writes. "The tender human being bound up by a violent duty to overwork to justify your worth. The dreaming is our work. The resting is our goal."[9]

PRACTICE MEDITATION OR PRAYER

Meditation and prayer are explicitly designed to help you connect with the divine, whatever that means to you. A regular practice teaches you how to tune in, so your inner voice is closer to the surface in your day-to-day life.

"Being transparent about everything, prayer helps me gain understanding about my journey," Kiana Blaylock writes in her essay for *Healthy Rich*. She calls prayer a "financial habit" in her life. "Long story short, God is my bestie who always has the best advice. . . . Through prayer, I know I will be connected to abundance and all my needs will be supplied."[10]

A Gift to Your Future Self

Spending outside of your day-to-day costs can feel scary, even if the spending is on something you know you want. If your resources don't leave you a lot of leeway, a big, out-of-the-ordinary expense can throw your finances out of balance for months. But you can ease the burden of big spending by setting aside the money in advance.

A lot of money management plans call this strategy "short-term savings," which doesn't make sense to me. *Saving* evokes and encourages restraint and hoarding, and—most vexing—these plans often force you to name a savings goal and target date even when those don't fit your plans. None of this makes money easy or joyful, and it certainly doesn't support conscious spending. Setting aside money for big spending is not about financial discipline; it's about adding ease and joy to your future plans. Similar to your comfort fund, buckets dedicated to future spending help you live the life you want without money dictating your choices. In this case, big spending funds let you name what matters to you, so you can make sure the money is there when you need it.

You might have big spending funds for specific items you want to buy, like a new couch, or dedicated to areas of life that matter most to you, like travel or gifts. These goals will change throughout your life as your priorities and interests change. For example, you might be in a season of being invited to a lot of weddings, baby showers, graduations, or retirement parties. Creating an open-ended "events" fund for one or each of those purposes ensures those expenses don't compete with your regular commitments or strain your Yes Fund when they pop up. If it's accessible to you, use the reverse budgeting technique we discussed in chapter 3 to fill these funds automatically.

Unlike your Yes Fund (everyday spending) and your comfort fund (urgent or chance spending), the money in your big spending funds should have a specific purpose. As Erik Noren demonstrated in chapter 8, too much savings can be as much of a burden as too little. Giving this money a purpose makes it easier, psychologically, to spend when the opportunity comes. Giving yourself permission to spend from these funds is an important and overlooked aspect of short-term savings plans. In the same way budget culture moralizes debt as obviously bad, it moralizes savings as obviously good—even if those savings serve no short- or long-term purpose. It's too easy to get caught up in saving for saving's sake, with no plan for how you'll use the money, but setting aside money endlessly without a purpose is just hoarding. Big spending funds give your savings efforts a context: you're holding it for now because you have a specific use for it in mind. Planning for big spending alongside other commitments reminds you that you can and should spend money on things that add ease and joy to your life and the lives of the people around you.

The typical advice for short-term savings is to pick a target amount and target date, and set aside money regularly to meet those goals. But those constraints don't always make sense, aren't always possible to hit, and don't let you enjoy big spending in flexible ways that fit your life. This stringent type of budgeted savings reeks of perfectionism: either you make the perfect plan and save the right amount of money to buy something at the right time, or you've failed.

Instead, you can plan for big spending in all the ways that allow for the realities of your experience. Big spending funds can include a target date, like an upcoming wedding or holiday, or a target amount to buy a specific item, but they don't have to. Your big spending plans could also be open-ended, like putting money into a fund for fashion, travel, or birthdays. Avoid arbitrary time or price targets that add unnecessary stress to money management, and focus instead on naming a purpose for your money so your efforts are driven by joy instead of discipline.

Types of big spending goals include:

- **Open-ended:** Set money aside with a purpose, but without a price tag or date. This strategy is a fit for things that come up without a planned date or price tag, like home or car maintenance, pricey fashion items, travel, or kids' birthday parties.
- **Time-targeted:** Set money aside with a date in mind to spend it. The date is your constraint, so the amount you

set aside is based on what's available in that time frame. You could use this for vacation, holidays, or weddings.

- **Price-targeted:** Set money aside for a specific item with a price. The price is your constraint, so you'll make the purchase, like a big-ticket item or medical procedure, whenever you have that amount saved.
- **Time- and price-targeted:** Set aside a specific amount of money by a specific date. Most of the time, you don't need this many constraints on your funds, but this strategy could come in handy if you need a particular item by a hard deadline, like a new grill before Memorial Day weekend.

This planning keeps big spending from feeling like a splurge, so you feel less shame and less like you need to restrict in response. You don't have to be the kind of person who plans your life six months in advance to feel prepared for every big spending opportunity that comes along. Prepare instead by naming what matters to you and putting money toward it in any way that makes sense for your financial situation. Creating big spending goals without strict target amounts or dates lets you absorb out-of-the-ordinary purchases without the budget culture pressure of planning exactly what you'll do with every dollar.

Spend Joyfully

When you give up budgeting and incorporate conscious spending into your life, you might experience a period of what feels like out-of-control spending. That's in line with the restrict-and-splurge cycle people experience while attempting to maintain a budget, and it's a natural response to the time you've spent following budget culture's restrictive rules.

Give yourself space to experiment with less restricted spending, based on what you know about your finances through your money map. As you get more comfortable with a conscious approach to spending and planning for future big spending, the pendulum should slow, so you find yourself closer and closer to balance and don't feel the urge to splurge to stave off the scarcity your brain has been trained to expect.

Reflection: Align Your Values with Your Goals

Before naming spending goals, name the values that drive you toward your goals. Make a list of personal values you hold, and build out your goals from there. (For example, if "family ties" are a personal value, a financial goal might be a vacation or holiday fund that lets you spend time with your extended family.) For each list item, answer these questions:

- What is a personal value you hold? (Consider things that support your head, heart, and health.)
- In what ways do you already spend money to support that value?
- What are some other ways you'd like to spend money to better support that value?
- What kind of big spending fund(s) would help you achieve those additional goals?

CHAPTER 11

You Can Give Money Away

The advice about money we tend to receive throughout our lives focuses on how to get more and give away less of it. Budget culture treats money as the end goal itself, so all of the available information and advice is focused on having money in the end. That misses the point of using money to live a life.

As we've seen throughout this book, money is just one piece of the whole of your life. It's one tool available to support the life and world you want. Yielding to your inner voice and using money in a satisfying and joyful way means listening to any decisions that align with your head, heart, and health—and that can include giving money away in big or small ways. In fact, if you're truly tapping into your intuition and understanding your place in a community of humans, generosity with money is a must.

Unfortunately, in our culture, thinking about giving money away can raise feelings of fear and scarcity. And budget culture messaging amplifies those feelings and reinforces them through budgeting habits and an individualistic mindset.

Budget Culture Makes Generosity Feel Foolish

Budget culture guides our financial decisions from a place of greed, rather than generosity. Most of us aren't *greedy people*, but the way budget culture teaches us to think about money is rooted in greed. Every conventional rule about money management is biased toward the fantasy of being rich, so financial advice is designed to teach us to hoard money and feel like a chump giving it away.

I didn't realize I'd been steeped in this lesson until I started earning enough money to give a lot of it away. When I was growing up, my parents ran our household paycheck-to-paycheck and diligently saved any extra to climb their way out of the working class. I don't remember any giving, except for the weekly contribution to the church collection basket. There were no alumni foundations or charitable organizations knocking on our door for donations. Our last name wasn't going to show up on a bench anywhere.

But my sisters and I had benefited from our parents' efforts, and we faced much different financial circumstances as young adults than they had. By the time the pandemic took over the United States in early 2020, I was running my own business and earning more money than I'd made in my last full-time job. I'd just returned to Wisconsin after living in Florida for four years, and the lower cost of living plus reduced spending under safe-at-home orders meant I had an ever-growing surplus of money at a time when twenty-one million Americans were unexpectedly out of work and stranded in an evaporated job market.[1]

I was excited to discover online tip jars, charity networks for workers in industries like theater, retail, and food service. They were a way to keep contributing money to workers who relied largely on tips and had no way to earn an income with their places of employment shut down or empty of customers. I donated regularly and dumped around a thousand dollars across several accounts when my stimulus check arrived from the federal government. I also shared the link in my family text thread for anyone who wanted to do the same—I knew at least a couple of my sisters would be happy for a way to contribute, too.

But my mom was worried. I assured her my income had held strong, and my household didn't need help from the stimulus check. But she warned the group, "Hold on to that in case your family needs it in the future!"

She wasn't alone in that mindset. Around 30 percent of the $1,200 stimulus checks doled out to households that year under the CARES Act went straight into savings. Another 30 percent went toward another common financial goal, debt repayment, so households only spent about 40 percent of the funds on average. Even those households with resource constraints—those who couldn't cover an unexpected bill equal to their monthly income—were no more likely to spend the money than those without constraints. They were the most likely to pay down debt. Younger, more educated households, like mine, whose members more likely had access to income during the shutdown, were the most likely to put the money into savings.[2]

My sisters and I (and our respective families) were comfortable, healthy, and financially secure amid the crisis. We certainly hadn't been raised to be selfish or uncaring, but a scarcity mindset runs deep. My parents' experiences of growing up in poverty and raising kids on working-class incomes, combined with budget culture messaging that taught them their hard work, frugality, and discipline were to credit for their current comfort, undergirded a fear of letting any money slip away.

What You Own Isn't Truly Yours

With a scarcity mindset, you see lack and competition, instead of the enoughness of abundance. With everything, but money in particular, our culture trains us to believe we never have what we need, and there's not enough to go around. Our culture's focus on individuality and individual responsibility makes it hard to be generous and easy to ignore someone else's need. Advice for "responsible" money management is focused on hoarding what you can, worrying about finding the next dollar, and taking precautions to avoid losing everything you have.

There's no room for generosity in that mindset, because it convinces you that you inevitably get less when someone else gets more. You can begin to break down that belief by first understanding that nothing is truly yours to begin with.

The difference between seeing scarcity in the world and seeing abundance is understanding that whatever you own isn't truly yours; it's just in your care for now. A lot of religious traditions define money in this way—not as something for you to acquire and own but as something available for you to steward through the world temporarily. Various dogmas have various ideas about the "right" ways to be a good steward of money, but generosity is a common thread.

Giving is an important part of financial stewardship. Money is a tool to shape the life and world around you. When you hold it in your hands, you hold the responsibility to contribute to that world in a life-giving way. That money was placed in your hands precisely so you could contribute to your world. As we talked about in chapter 4, the resources you have access to aren't a reflection of your worthiness. Knowing that is important for your self-esteem, but it also means you have no more right to ownership over those resources than anyone else. When you see money as a communal and transient resource, you don't have to fear scarcity when you give it away or use it to benefit someone else. Their gain isn't your loss, because there was never a difference between "your" money and "their" money in the first place.

That also means generosity isn't about being a savior. When you have more resources than others in your community, it's not your job to save poor people by choosing to share. Giving is an expression of human connection and an acknowledgment of your role as a conduit for, rather than an owner of, resources.

I encourage you to examine your mindset for feelings of fear and scarcity when you think about giving money away. Where do you feel resistance? What's at the root of that resistance? Where do you feel ownership? How can you let go of that mindset so you feel secure while giving money away?

Humans Are Designed to Share

It's easy to discount giving as your last priority in money management—which, inevitably, means you never quite get around to it. Laura Leavitt and her husband found that their weekly meeting about money and other planning helped to bring into focus not only their relationship and life goals but also their financial priorities. Having the conversation created space to decide charitable giving would outrank other spending.

"I loved the moment when, over enchiladas at our favorite Mexican place, my husband and I first committed to doubling our monthly donations to charity and figuring out how to live without those extra dollars," she writes. "Little things added up for the years after that, and we've now donated over $10,000! We're glad we've been building this charitable giving habit."

Humans' tendency toward a scarcity mindset and greedy behavior might feel like our nature, but those are responses to capitalism, not human nature, which instead favors collectivism. In fact, humans get primal pleasure from acts of charity, just like Laura and her husband did.

When neuroscientists at the National Institutes of Health scanned the brains of volunteers and asked them to imagine a scenario where they would either donate a sum of money to charity or keep it for themselves, they were surprised to find generosity caused great pleasure. When volunteers imagined donating the money to charity—placing others' interests above their own—it lit up a part of their brain that's usually activated by food or sex. That means deciding to use your resources to benefit someone else isn't an act of overcoming a natural instinct for self-preservation, but actually one that fulfills a need hardwired in your brain.[3]

Giving money or being a community resource for others through acts of service fulfills your natural need to connect with others. You might have heard that "humans are social creatures," wired to get along with our tribes to stay safe, but did you know there's an actual biological drive toward community regardless of self-preservation?

"We tend to assume that people's behavior is narrowly self-interested, focused on getting more material benefits for themselves and avoiding physical threats and the exertion of effort," scientist Matthew Lieberman tells *Scientific American*. "But because of how social pain and pleasure are wired into our operating system, these are motivational ends in and of themselves."[4]

Giving isn't just a way to preserve your social status and safety within a community. It's a natural, life-giving need of its own, like food.

Opportunities for Giving

Opportunities for generosity show up in our lives and culture in many ways. I consider them in three categories: charity, gifts, and taxes (yes, taxes!). These are all important ways to share your resources to benefit others, but the mindset and culture around each is quite different.

CHARITY

Charity is an opportunity to give money, time, services, goods, or other resources to an organization with a mission to help people or society. In the United States, charitable organizations are defined through our tax code, but you could apply the term more broadly to any giving that reaches individuals in need through an organized effort or enterprise.

Charity might be the first thing that comes to mind when you think of giving. Giving through charitable organizations is a common way to organize your generosity; it lets you offer service through your resources and lets professionals figure out how to allocate the money to serve whatever cause you want to support. Giving to charities also usually comes with an income tax deduction, so it's the most agreeable with budget culture: you can be generous, but you get rewarded, too.

Any organization can be "charitable"—i.e., take donations to provide pro bono services—but most charities you'll encounter are nonprofit organizations. That means they don't distribute profits to shareholders the way for-profit companies do; they have to use all of their resources to provide services. Different types of nonprofits get tax benefits based on their status. As a donor, you can claim a donation as a tax deduction on your income tax return if you donate money to a 501(c)(3) organization (named after the section that governs it in the Internal Revenue Code). Those are charitable organizations, religious organizations, private foundations, and some other nonprofits. Other types of nonprofits solicit donations but don't qualify you for a tax deduction, including political campaigns and advocacy organizations.

The tax-exempt status of nonprofits is a way to support organizations that serve their communities and a way to encourage people to give those organizations money. But nonprofits are a creation of capitalism: well-meaning organizations often use their nonprofit status to justify exploiting workers through low-paid or free labor; less-well-meaning organizations and donors might explicitly use tax exemptions as a tool to benefit their balance sheets. "Nonprofit" and "charitable" are broad categories, so give at least a cursory glance at an operation and its services before you give money. A source like Charity Navigator can help you quickly see a rating for charities based on their governance, service impact, and financials.

GIFTS

Gifts, in contrast to giving through the government or a charitable organization, are a way to give directly to an individual. Opportunities for gift-giving are abundant in our culture. They might be tied to a financial need, like giving cash to a stranger who needs bus fare or giving to a GoFundMe to pay a friend's hospital bills. They might be tied to community, like taking turns delivering groceries to a disabled neighbor. They might be tied to cultural traditions, like holiday gifts. Or they might be tied to relationship building, like picking up a memento that lets a family member know you were thinking of them while you were traveling. In any case, gifts are voluntary and don't yield a direct financial reward; they're a type of giving born of simple generosity.

TAXES

Finally, taxes are legally required giving that reaches individuals in need through government spending and services. As a society, we determine priorities for these resources by voting on policies and representatives in elections. Support for taxation and government spending that serves our communities is an opportunity for generosity that often gets obscured by a scarcity mindset that's propagated for political benefit.

The American attitude toward taxes tends to be one of a necessary evil smart people avoid as much as possible, but I prefer Anne

Helen Petersen's reframe of taxes as "paying for civilization." Just like charitable giving and direct gift giving, paying taxes is a way to give to your community and society.

Petersen writes, "I'm not dumb, and I take deductions like everyone else. But I've also made a conscious decision to think of paying taxes not as a burden to get out of, but as a willingly performed obligation, a way of being a citizen in my community."[5]

If civic duty doesn't speak to you, think of taxes instead as a form of tithing, the Judeo-Christian term for a tradition of providing mutual aid to support those in economic need. Some organizations have taken advantage of the concept to obligate members to support the institution itself. But the biblical stories of tithing instead describe the social practice of giving according to your ability to others according to their need, whether those are citizens without means to care for themselves or people who have dedicated their lives in service of the community (such as priests or other workers in the church).

I appreciate that we can't take a Pollyanna view of taxes and simply hand over money to our governments without holding them accountable. Our tax dollars do pay for wonderful things like national parks, safe highways, public schools, and libraries that provide life and sustenance for our communities—but also, the way our government allocates money is influenced by corporate interests and often harms people more than it helps them. That's how we get things like military bloat and why we haven't gotten things like free health care for all. But we can ask our lawmakers to change that. If you want your taxes to support health care, childcare, parental leave, and ending childhood poverty—instead of paying for tanks the military didn't ask for—vote for representatives who promise to fight for that change, and stay in touch with them to make sure they do. Holding representatives accountable for how they allocate the taxes we give is as much a part of the generosity of taxes as paying in the first place.

Embrace Generosity

It might feel at first like the idea of generosity is much easier to support than the act. Like my parents during the pandemic, you might feel a responsibility to take care of yourself—and your family—first. Budget culture might convince you of a thousand tiny steps you need to take with your money before you can consider giving any of it away.

But making room for giving is less about moving money around to find a surplus and much more about adopting a mindset of abundance and generosity. You have to believe in the availability and the communal nature of resources. How you think and feel about money dictates how you behave around it, so it's not fair to ask yourself to give money away while you're battling feelings of scarcity. That'll only make giving feel painful, and—as we learned with budgeting—you're not likely to embrace generosity if it always hurts to part with money.

The first step to generous money management is to care for your relationship with money so you can release the many beliefs budget culture has taught you and make giving feel as abundant and joyful as receiving—or even more!

In chapter 12, we'll explore some practices and experiments to help you overcome a scarcity mindset and embrace joy, abundance, and generosity in your relationship with money.

Just like every other aspect of budget-free living, I don't prescribe any "right" amount of giving. You might set a target for yourself based on cultural or religious traditions or expectations. You might set an arbitrary target simply to combat a scarcity mindset and hold yourself accountable for giving. Or you might not rely on setting a target at all. The amount is less important than the mindset. Generosity is about embracing that understanding that you're a steward, not an owner, of resources and learning to use what's available to you to serve your community and your world.

In a healthy relationship with money, generosity is as joyful and life-giving as spending for your own satisfaction or need. But, just as we discussed with spending in general, that doesn't mean you're supposed to see to any other financial needs or commitments before using money this way. As with any other aspect of your finances, you can adjust your financial resources, commitments, and goals to make space for the giving that makes sense for you.

Like other parts of money management, automation is the simplest way to build giving into your financial plan without creating an extra obligation or stressor to add to your ticker. You can automate giving through recurring donations to organizations (which they love!) or by developing a routine of, say, choosing someone in your community once a month to give a gift to. If you earn income, taxation already automates some giving for you. Stay informed about how your local, state, and federal governments use those funds, and hold your representatives accountable to initiatives aligned with your head, heart, and health—and those of the communities around you.

Reflection: Be Generous

What opportunities do you see in your life for giving? How do those support your financial wellness and that of your communities? Reflect on your opportunities for giving through these questions.

Does your stewardship of resources:

- Respect and utilize the strengths of people in your community?
- Support equal opportunities for growth and development?
- Respect the diversity of personal goals and interests?
- Support the causes you care about in the world?
- Serve people you care about?
- Make the positive impact you want to make?
- Avoid or prevent outcomes you'd consider bad?
- Ensure fair pay for those who labor in service?
- Prioritize community health and safety?

CHAPTER 12

Your Budget-Free Life

Divesting from budget culture is more than another strategy to improve your personal financial circumstances; it's a radical step toward a better way of thinking and talking about money in your life.

In his memoir *Born a Crime: Stories from a South African Childhood*, comedian Trevor Noah writes, "People don't want to be rich. They want to be able to choose. The richer you are, the more choices you have. That is the freedom of money."[1]

This is what so-called financial independence means to me, and it has nothing to do with your wealth or income. It's about your relationship with money. It's about releasing the power money has to determine your path in life—this is a budget-free life. Noah shared this truth after he became rich. But anyone can feel it simply by releasing the power a dollar has over you. That dollar isn't more important than your happiness, health, relationships, free time, or comfort. It's not worth your sacrifice. Budget-free living is about diminishing and releasing its power, so you can live the life you want without money weighing in.

Letting go of the fantasy of being rich, instead pursuing what you truly want out of each day of your life, is an act of resistance against budget culture. This inner work might feel like the least effective, because you won't see a direct impact on the community or world around you. But it's the most important step you can take to make any kind of broader change. Without embracing a budget-free approach yourself, you can't fully participate in action to dismantle budget culture for others.

Attempting to resist or revise capitalism while holding on to a budget culture mindset results in the half measures we've come to expect in our society. That approach has gotten us charitable organizations that underpay workers, a health insurance marketplace that uses government funds to subsidize overpriced private health care, workplace cultures that substitute comfy couches and beer fridges for job stability and fair pay, and mission-driven business owners who rely on underpriced overseas labor. We can't keep trying to revise capitalism without examining how it's affected our personal relationships with money. Encouraging solidarity and social safety within your community requires you to first recognize and release the posture of restriction, shame, and greed around money that budget culture has taught you to adopt.

What If Money Wasn't the Thing?

Around 2006, my friend Lynn was recently divorced, a new empty nester, and nurturing a new relationship with the person who would become her second husband. She was primed to discover the next transformation in her life.

In the preceding years, Lynn had earned her first master's degree, in humanities, while working full-time as a teacher at an early childhood center for children with developmental disabilities. Still married, she'd been raising five children, and her then husband "wasn't thrilled" with her focusing attention on her studies.

"I felt self-conscious about spending a lot of time reading," Lynn says, "so I would get up very early in the morning, like at four or five, and do my schoolwork, so it wasn't really obvious that I was spending a lot of time focused on that work."

Based on the topic of her first master's thesis, professors had encouraged Lynn to enroll in a second master's program to pursue her interests. She learned about the possibility of earning a stipend and free tuition as a graduate teaching assistant, so she'd be able to quit her full-time job to focus on school. She worked part-time as an itinerant service coordinator with a public program for parents of at-risk children, and she supplemented that income with her graduate assistant stipend and student loans.

Her time teaching as a master's student made it clear to Lynn this was the work she wanted to do; she wanted to be a university professor. Once all her kids were over eighteen and out of the house and her first marriage was behind her, she was ready for the next step.

Lynn was determined to make grad school work, despite the statistical disadvantage of a working-class background she shared with a minority of students in her program. Of just three working-class candidates in the program, two dropped out; Lynn was the only one of her cohort without a middle-class upbringing to complete her doctorate.

Most people in Lynn's position would have seen her financial situation as a barrier to achieving that progress. That's not a mindset problem; it's a real-world problem. A 2012 report found that just 14 percent of people from the lowest socioeconomic backgrounds had a bachelor's degree or higher—compared with 60 percent of people from the highest socioeconomic backgrounds and 29 percent of people in the middle. When the researchers asked high school seniors the level of education they expected to reach, just a quarter of the poorest students expected to earn even a bachelor's degree, while more than half of the richest students expected to earn an advanced degree.[2]

But Lynn wasn't going to let money be the thing to hold her back.

"I wanted my life to change," she says. "I wanted to be doing something different."

She was accepted into a prestigious PhD program at the University of Wisconsin. She sold her house and made the move from Ohio to Madison, Wisconsin, with about $18,000 in hand. She paid for tuition by taking out more federal student loans, covered living expenses with loan refunds and a teaching stipend, and put big-ticket items (like a refrigerator and flights home) on credit cards.

While they lived in Madison, her soon-to-be husband traveled back and forth to Ohio for part-time work, but he focused most of his efforts on tending to their home and reminding Lynn to drink water while she wrote her dissertation, so she could focus one hundred percent on earning her doctorate. This distribution of labor, without the burden of earning a living, let Lynn complete her PhD in five years—this time with total support from her husband.

"He'd be willing to spend hours reading my work, talking to me about it," she says. "He was really completely devoted to supporting me in my schoolwork."

This support also freed some of Lynn's energy to continue to support her kids emotionally through the ups and downs of early adulthood. "If all that would have been happening without [him], that may have done me in," she says. "I may have ended up feeling like I couldn't have finished. Or it may have been that the kids got less support from me."

Budget culture likes to celebrate triumphs like Lynn's when they involve someone working multiple jobs while scrimping and saving to put themselves through college. A personal finance book might feature a character who pulled herself up by her bootstraps, working nights and weekends to put herself through grad school, or one whose husband took on an extra job to cover their expenses while she studied. Lynn and her husband did neither of those. She accepted tens of thousands in student loans and, eventually, $60,000 in credit card debt with intention. She knew her repayment commitments would impact her standard of living when she started working after the program; she jokingly calls her method "planned irresponsibility."

When Lynn finished her program and realized just how high the credit card debt had gotten, she filed and qualified for bankruptcy to eliminate it. A few months later she started a tenure-track position at a public university. After ten years of public service and on-time loan payments, she qualified for the federal government's Public Service Loan Forgiveness program, which canceled around $120,000 in remaining student loan debt. In 2020 she became a homeowner again for the first time since selling her house to go to grad school.

An approach to money that sees only the needs of the head—one that sees money as simple math, the way budget culture teaches it—would have asked Lynn to make compromises. She might have gone to a less prestigious school. She might have worked part-time and taken longer to complete the program. She might have asked her husband to be the breadwinner and gone without his domestic and emotional support. She might have forgone her advanced degrees altogether—stayed in her hometown with her bachelor's degree and continued at her full-time job.

But a budget-free approach to money recognizes not only the needs of the head, but also those of the heart and health. It sees that none of those sacrifices would have been worth making for Lynn, just to have a more balanced budget. None of those compromises would have given Lynn the experience she sought or the chance to make the contribution she could make. By taking advantage of a variety of resources and tending to her debt without shame, Lynn was able to join the tiny minority of working-class people to earn a PhD and a professorship and—as Dave Ramsey likes to say—change the trajectory of her family tree.

Financial educator Hadassah Damien writes at her blog *Ride Free Fearless Money*, "What if money wasn't the thing making problems in your life? . . . You can act in ways where money isn't the thing that forces all your decisions, before you have an heiress-sized bucket of money . . . there are choices we can make to de-center money."[3]

Living a budget-free life is about de-centering money. That can take any form that makes sense for you; there's no perfect formula. This book gives you a lens through which you can see the flaws in budget culture and begin to form an approach that meets your unique needs. The point is to resist the budget culture mindset and stop letting money call the shots.

Coping with Budget Culture

When you recognize everything that's wrong with budget culture, you might experience the same urge I did, which is to never engage with budget culture again. (I felt the same way when I began to recognize diet culture.) Unfortunately, this probably isn't possible.

Dismantling budget culture will be a long journey. We've been aware of diet culture for decades, and—despite significant progress—fatphobia and restrictive diets still dominate our cultural relationship with food and bodies. Even as we learn and grow as a society, capitalism continues to find ways to redirect us toward restriction, shame, and greed. Whatever work you do to change your relationship with money, you'll continue to be surrounded by budget culture attitudes and expectations, including that internalized perfectionism that tries to drown out your inner voice.

"I know, on a rational level, that tracking every dime that passes through my bank account is simply a way of distracting myself from all the ways my finances are out of my control," journalist L.V. Anderson writes for *Slate* of her transition from yo-yo dieting to obsessive budgeting. "I could get fired or laid off, I could get hit by a car or get cancer, I could get sued, the stocks in my retirement accounts could crash and not recover.

"But I'd rather not dwell on these possibilities. I'd rather believe—despite my experience with dieting—that if I keep logging my spending and keeping it in check, someday I'll have enough money, and all my other problems will just go away."[4]

This is the siren call of budget culture. The fantasy of being rich keeps you striving for the right combination of behaviors and rules that'll make every other problem disappear. It feeds on fears capitalism creates (like lack of job stability and health care) and those no one can avoid (like illness or death), and it offers its simplistic maxims as solutions. As Anderson points out, you know rationally that no set of perfectionist habits can address the massive issues that feed your anxiety. But the behaviors offer an illusion of control, and you get constant reassurance from financial coaches, advisors, and educators that you're doing the right thing—and that can be enough to get you through the day.

Because of the deep talons budget culture has in all our lives, it's not realistic to expect yourself to unlearn everything you've learned about money. This is a process, and one you'll work through for—I'm sorry!—the rest of your life.

And regardless of where you are on the journey of your relationship with money, you still live in budget culture. Almost every piece of education and advice about money you'll ever encounter is filtered through budget culture. You'll encounter it in every conversation you have about work, money management, spending, and life decisions forever. You can't protect yourself or the people you care about from budget culture one hundred percent of the time. But you can approach your new relationship with money with awareness and a goal of avoiding as much harm as you reasonably can.

Don't expect perfection of yourself—that's a budget culture mindset! Give yourself grace to learn a new way of thinking and talking about money, and move forward from there. We live in a world where a lot of effort is made to uphold capitalism and wealth inequality, and not a lot of effort is going into changing either of those. This world needs your imperfect efforts, however small, however erratic. Looking at a gigantic problem like budget culture can be overwhelming—there are so many issues, where do you even begin? But the point is to just begin. You're reading the first book to ever name budget culture—there's a long road ahead in this work, and I hope this book gives you the tools you need to take your first steps.

Explore Your Relationship with Money

Shifting your relationship with money is about loving the ways you experience work and money in your life. You could have any number and variety of money beliefs that serve or limit you in a variety of ways. Untangling those, strengthening what serves you and dropping what doesn't, is a long process and a lot of work. No one expects you to change everything overnight.

Instead, experiment with just one small thing right now. Commit to doing it for a week, and see how you feel. If you love it, do another week, then two or three. If it's not working for you, drop it, and try another experiment. Experimenting takes the pressure off that giant project we call "self-improvement." And it eliminates the perfectionism that might keep you from trying anything at all; this is only an experiment, so you can't do it wrong.

Here are a few exercises and experiments you can come back to anytime you're ready to take another step in your relationship with money.

RECOGNIZE WHERE YOUR ACTIONS ARE GUIDING YOU

Your relationship with money is made up of not only your financial circumstances but also a set of beliefs and desires you hold about money, whether you're aware of them or not.

Alfred Adler, an Austrian psychologist and early colleague and supporter of Sigmund Freud, is one of the lesser-known but most enduring founders of modern psychotherapy. Adlerian psychology understands all behavior as having a goal-oriented purpose; everything you do is a step toward something you want to achieve, even if that desire is subconscious.[5]

For example, if you name a desire to become rich, but you continually find reasons to turn down job offers that would increase your income, that might be your inner voice telling you that you want more ease and peace, not more money. Rather than seeing your actions as self-sabotage, listen to their purpose. That can help you understand what you really desire and get a closer look at your relationship with money.

Not listening to that inner voice can keep you grasping at money based on goals budget culture has laid out for you—whether that's making career decisions based on pay, limiting spending, or hoarding money out of fear or greed. Tuning in to the decisions your subconscious makes can help you see what truly matters to you. Adler theorized every person's basic goals are meaningful work, satisfying friendships, and learning to love yourself and others. These aims are much more likely to lead you toward joy and generosity than toward restriction and discipline.

Consider the example of Erik Noren, whose relationship with savings we talked about in chapter 8. The enormous resistance he feels when he tries to spend money on himself is laden with budget culture shame and guilt about his worthiness to care for himself. The enormous savings he's built might reflect a conscious desire to have a financial safety net, or maybe to amass wealth. But if you examine that resistance and see that it comes with questions about worthiness, you might recognize that what Erik's inner voice is seeking isn't more money; it's self-worth. The more he tunes in to this voice, the more his subconscious decisions steer him toward learning to love himself—a purpose that demands much different money moves from those a goal of wealth-building demands.

GIVE YOURSELF REMINDERS

Deep-dive journal exercises feel good—for a moment. You're going to discover a lot about yourself and experience some aha moments by answering the questions throughout this book. But a few thought experiments won't entirely uproot beliefs that are embedded deep in your psyche. (I've written an entire book on the subject, and I still work on my budget culture beliefs *every day*.) Orienting yourself away from scarcity and restriction and toward abundance and generosity requires daily awareness and action.

The same way you make decisions easy by automating money management, you can automate your inner work by setting reminders for yourself.

Giving yourself daily reminders of abundance can quiet the messages of scarcity you encounter through budget culture.

Here are some examples; take anything that works for you, and create your own!

- I'm worthy of everything I have and everything that's coming my way.
- There's always more than enough.
- I know what to do with my money.

- There's always more coming.
- I have the power to change a life.
- There's more than one kind of wealth.
- I'm grateful for what I have and for everything that's coming my way.
- I'm fearless about money.

You could say these out loud to yourself, write them in a journal, hang posters on your walls, or leave Post-it notes around your office—do whatever makes sense for you, and give yourself flexibility to adjust as your needs change. Basic as it sounds, just seeing these affirmations or hearing yourself say them over and over can remind your brain they're true.

PRACTICE GRATITUDE

Through journaling or mantras, raise your awareness to what you're thankful for each day. Don't think about it too long; just jot down what comes up to complete the sentence *Today I'm grateful for . . .* It could be a huge moment, like asking someone to marry you, or something you want to be more aware of each day, like the squirrels in your yard every morning. Doing this simple practice consistently helps you tune in to the abundance of resources, joy, and ease around you.

BE GENEROUS IN TINY WAYS

Give money away every day this week—whether it's your spare change or a few hundred dollars. Keep your eye out for opportunities, whether it's buying lunch for a friend, dropping money in a busker's pot, or sending a check to an organization in your community. Consider how it feels to be generous, regardless of whether you have a lot or a little yourself.

LOOK FOR POSITIVE MODELS

Who already has the relationship with money you want to have? Which messages and stories do you see them sharing? Grab some note cards and jot down some characteristics and strategies that seem to be working for them. Come back to those cards to inspire new experiments in the future.

MAP YOUR MONEY

Anytime your money feels out of balance or unsatisfying, return to your money map to glean information about what's working and what's not.

TALK ABOUT MONEY

Normalize sharing your financial circumstances with friends and strangers to take the stigma and shame out of financial decisions.

As Laura Leavitt said of her family's weekly meeting: "I don't know that every family will get the same financial boon from a family meeting that we have, but a communication boon is likely to be a financial boon in many cases. We all benefit from understanding each other a little better as a family, and there's something really exhilarating about helping each other to achieve big goals, one week at a time."

Use Your Control and Influence

Making adjustments to your financial situation to find a Yes Fund and money management plan that lets you use money in alignment with your head, heart, and health starts with understanding where you have influence and control to make changes to your circumstances. Consider the popular Circle of Control model inspired by author Stephen Covey's *The 7 Habits of Highly Effective People*:

- **No control:** In the outermost circle, which facets of your finances do you have no control over whatsoever? This might include things like the structure of our economy, the job market, and prices at the grocery store. Your individual actions won't change those circumstances immediately, so these are truths you have to live with.

- **Complete control:** In the innermost circle, which facets of your finances do you have complete control over? This might include things like whether you accept a job offer, where you choose to live, and which commitments you prioritize each month. You can change these circumstances with your individual actions and choices alone.

- **Influence:** In between those two circles, in which facets of your finances do you have less than complete control, but you can influence outcomes and how they affect your experience? This might include things like how much money you earn, what you owe each month in debt payments, and how much you spend on groceries.

When you reflect on your circle of control, I suspect you'll discover you have a lot more influence over your circumstances than you might have believed. No, you can't control the structure of the credit scoring system that sets you up with a 23 percent interest rate on a credit card you need to pay your bills. But you can influence how much impact that has on your experience through how you use that resource and how you deal with the debt once you accumulate it. No, you can't control systemic discrimination that impacts your experience in a job. But you can influence how that impacts your financial circumstances by taking advantage of community and debt resources.

Look at your control and influence over your financial circumstances anytime your Yes Fund is less than what you want it to be. Consider how you can use them to make changes to the major parts of your money map to get to the Yes Fund that supports the life you want to live.

What If There's Not Enough?

Regardless of how much you shift your mindset toward a budget-free approach, managing money without stress requires having enough—whatever that means to you. You have to have enough resources to fund your commitments, goals, spending, and giving, whether those resources come from income, assets, community resources, or debt. And sometimes, I know, there just aren't enough resources to cover it all. How do you spend with ease and joy if you're doing everything you can to cover your commitments right now?

In reality, you might not be able to do it all right now. You can't expect to have your money in balance if it takes everything you've got just to provide your basic needs and rightful comforts. Like I said at the beginning of this book, a budget-free approach doesn't promise the fantasy of being rich. Instead, the promise of this radical reimagining is that you can learn to forgive yourself and the people around you for your financial circumstances. You can stop believing you're to blame for your hardship and solely responsible for your salvation.

Instead of homing in on budget culture practices to restrict your spending when there's not enough, look at the whole of your financial circumstances. Understand not just your behaviors but the external forces and circumstances impacting your options. Let go of your responsibility to uphold our economic system, and focus instead on your control and influence over your experience in spite of the ways it wants to hold you back.

Here are a few reminders of practical strategies we've discussed to shift your finances to use money according to your priorities when it feels like there's not enough:

- **Recognize and utilize resources.** Can you change jobs, add a side gig, ask for a raise, sell an asset, use community resources, open a credit card, or take out a loan to expand your resources?
- **Deprioritize and cut commitments.** Can you move, deprioritize debt payments, triage bills, cancel commitments, or switch service providers to reduce your commitments and redirect those funds toward other priorities?
- **Pause on goals.** Can you slow or stop debt payoff, reduce your comfort fund, delay big spending, or

deprioritize long-term saving to make room for something you value more?

- **Reduce your spending.** Examine your needs to find ways to redirect day-to-day spending toward goals that matter more to you.

Deciding what to shuffle when resources are limited is a highly personal decision, so only you can say what makes sense for you. Use your money map to get a clear picture of your financial situation, consequences, and options, and make the decision-making process a little easier.

Regardless of your resources or circumstances, remember that money is just one aspect of your life, not the driving force. Resist the urge to strive only for more money when you feel the strain of limited resources. Instead, tune in to your inner voice to discover what you need in your experience—your big rocks. Go after them, and let the money pebbles follow.

Trust Yourself

The most frustrating part of questioning a dominant paradigm is understanding there's no alternative "right" answer. A budget-free approach means getting comfortable not knowing the right answer to any question you have about money.

Your inner voice will often be at odds with the lessons you've learned about money and the messages you get every day about how to work and what to buy. You're consistently surrounded by budget culture, no matter how well you personally learn to divest from it, and those forces work hard to convince you to question what you know to be true. This is tough.

Our various systems of oppression thrive on our need for an illusion of certainty, and budget culture is no different. I can't offer that certainty, and I challenge you to find comfort without it. Understand that what budget culture promises is a fantasy, and the rules it lays out become irrelevant with the slightest variable. The certainty that budget culture promises isn't real. To resist the forces of budget culture, you have to get out of the comfort zone of those illusory rules and get okay with not knowing. I've offered a lot of ideas and tools to help you do that, but there's one simple thing you can remember: trust yourself.

Trust in your ability to steward money and serve your people. Self-trust is the greatest act of resistance to budget culture, and it's the first step to collective financial freedom—a life free from worrying about money, for everyone.

Reflection: Your Inner Voice

Do you struggle to connect with your inner voice? What's the feeling you get when you know you've trusted your gut? What fears or beliefs keep you from doing that more often?

CHAPTER 13

Toward a Budget-Free Society

After all this, you might wonder, *So what?*

People have been paying lip service to the ills of capitalism forever, but economic insecurity, inequality, and consumerism only seem to be getting worse. You might wonder: What good is it to place a personal budget-free lens on a world so bound up in budget culture?

Divesting from budget culture only begins with your personal relationship with money. That foundational act gives you an opportunity to model a new approach to money that can turn your personal habits into broader advocacy for your community and society.

As many activists will tell you, making change starts at the community level and is about the kinds of conversations you have with the people you see and engage with every day. That's why my discussion about budget culture focuses on your individual relationship with money. It's the key to changing how you talk and teach about money with the people around you.

It's easy to feel small in the face of overwhelming global problems; I certainly do. Budget culture—as a manifestation of capitalism—sits at the center of gigantic issues like poverty and climate change. These aren't issues any individual person can solve, and that fact can make these changes to your own relationship with money feel fruitless. But you don't have to change the whole system this month, this year, or even in your lifetime. Progress is progress, and—as we've learned—there's no such thing as perfection, anyway.

Remember the apocryphal quote often misattributed to the English philosopher G. K. Chesterton: "Anything worth doing is worth doing badly."[1]

Dismantling budget culture is worth doing—even if we can't do it perfectly or all at once. Spreading this information through your community is worth doing. Considering the questions in your money map is worth doing. Investigating your relationship with money is worth doing. Dropping your budget is worth doing. All of this is worth doing—even if your state continues to defund education, you have to stay in a job whose dress code bans dreadlocks, and you can't get your aunt to stop critiquing your cousin's latest purchases in front of the whole family. I still shop on Amazon to find comforts that aren't for sale in my rural community. I own a business in a right-to-work state. I don't disown family members for reading Dave Ramsey books. I cheer on fellow entrepreneurs even when their business relies on multinational corporate clients. This complicated world has complicated us inside. Nothing will untangle that entirely. We can only tune in more deeply to the still, small voice inside of us and see what comes up. Shifting how we think about money away from budget culture norms and toward a more inclusive, budget-free set of shared values and beliefs is about having a new kind of conversation about money. Think of this final chapter as your mini field guide to creating space for that conversation.

Don't Become the Least Fun Person at Every Party

When you learn a new thing that impacts your life, there's a temptation to become an evangelist. Good! It's great to spread the word. But inundating the people around you with arguments that everything they believe is wrong isn't a strong strategy for helping people discover a new paradigm. As an anti-budget advocate, consider yourself instead a guide in helping them discover a truth for themselves.

Remember budget culture is a new concept, so most people you meet haven't been steeped in anti-budget rhetoric—just the opposite. Most people have implicitly or explicitly learned that budgeting and the restriction, shame, and greed associated with budget culture are inevitable in money management. Most people haven't even named capitalism; they simply believe our way of using money is human nature.

As you consider the practices throughout this chapter that'll help you model a budget-free life and lead anti-budget conversations, keep your audience in mind. Approach people with compassion first, and understand that everyone is generally trying to do the best for themselves and the people around them based on what they've been taught. Don't alienate people by turning budget culture's shame and blame back onto them; a budget-free approach requires understanding and grace for everyone's relationship with money—even your miserly neighbor hoarding pennies under his mattress or a billionaire heiress afraid to derail her family's legacy.

No one wants to be cornered at a party by the person who's just experienced a paradigm shift and needs everyone to know it—no matter how important that paradigm shift is. Remember you're always talking to a human on the other side of the conversation, and listen to the needs of their head, heart, and health just as you've learned to listen to yours.

"Some of the best discussions with my grandmother occurred when we could find common ground," Jack Sauter writes for *Barn Raiser* of conversations with his conservative grandmother about his views as a Democratic Socialist.[2]

Sauter offers advice for reaching across the divide when discussing an unfamiliar paradigm: "We don't have to act like our present situation is acceptable. A shared sense of grievance is not sufficient for political agreement, but it can be a useful starting point."

You might have a tough time finding people who already agree budgeting is bad, debt is fine, and saving for retirement is an ethical minefield—but it's not so hard to find people who sense there's *something* wrong with our system. Many people are dissatisfied with their relationships with work and money and know it's somehow not just their problem, but they don't have the language to describe it. Start with that shared understanding of something feeling off, and work toward a shared language to describe how budget culture contributes to their discomfort.

"Even when agreement feels impossible, we shouldn't lose sight that we share in common struggles," Sauter writes. And, in probably the most important piece of advice for discussing any kind of social change, he says: "No matter how much skill or stamina you bring to these conversations, the most useful ability is knowing when to stop the discussion."

Flip the Script

A key step to challenging any dominant paradigm is to recognize it around you. Look for places where you see budget culture influencing your life and society, so you can actively question it.

When you catch yourself turning blame inward and questioning your mindset or willpower to fix what doesn't work about your money, reset your focus to the world around you, and notice what's happening. See how the world is or isn't made for you, based on your financial situation. Where do you feel welcomed, or not? Do you feel comfortable and safe in your home? Do you feel comfortable in your clothing, on your furniture, using your devices? Are you satisfied with your food? Do you have reliable and safe transportation? Are you living where you want to be and doing what you want to do with your days? Do you feel empowered with choice? Can you care for your children, parents, or other loved ones the way you'd like to? Can you attend to your physical and mental health as much as you want to?

Notice how your comfort, dignity, and choices in life are affected by your financial situation, and consider how those would be different for someone in a different situation. Do coworkers with more access to resources seem to be more rested and less stressed throughout the day? Do neighbors with lower income find it harder to spend quality time with their kids? Observe how you perceive and treat people based on their financial circumstances and choices. Notice your somatic reactions to certain money moves. Do you feel tight when your partner buys something without consulting you? Instead of turning that response into a reaction against them, sit with it and ask yourself why.

Advocacy doesn't mean turning each of these moments into an opportunity to lecture the people around you about budget culture and budget-free living. You can make an impact simply by taking care not to reinforce budget culture with language and messages that play into its toxic beliefs. Consider the language shifts you've learned throughout this book:

- Income → Resources
- Fixed expenses → Commitments
- Emergency fund → Comfort fund
- Wants vs. needs → Alignment with head, heart, and health
- Afford → Access

Like many damaging social issues and cultish trends, budget culture lives as much in our language as in our actions and explicit teachings. Using budget culture's language can inadvertently perpetuate its messages. Changing your language and questioning those messages can be a regular reminder to yourself and the people around you of the beliefs you want to dismantle.

Model Budget-Free Behavior

Sometimes the best way to lead social change is to live out the new paradigm in your life. This doesn't require you to be a teacher, a preacher, or even an active advocate. Just living a budget-free approach can show the people around you that a different approach to money is possible. That change in perspective could spark their own questions and conversations about the effects of budget culture (even if they don't have the language to describe it yet).

Pay attention as you go through your day to judgments of how you use money. Are you frequently praised for avoiding an "unnecessary" purchase? Do you get criticized for credit card use? Do your friends respond with jealousy after you buy an expensive item? Does your family react with fear when you give money away? Whether judgment is intended as positive or negative is irrelevant; casually judging money moves as good or bad is a symptom of budget culture. These moments give you opportunities to challenge that thinking.

For example:

- When someone praises you for financial restraint, you could mention your conscious spending practice or Yes Fund explicitly, or simply say, "I don't believe in restriction; that purchase just wasn't for me today."
- If friends are jealous over expensive purchases, avoid crediting your hard work or savings habits, and focus on the joy the item brings you.
- When you hear someone judge their own or someone else's purchases, let them know, "I try not to think of any spending as 'good' or 'bad.' "
- When conversations about work turn into one-upmanship about busyness, keep your focus on how much you love your work or your gratitude for the life your work supports.

Embracing conscious spending and a mindful approach to money management adds ease to your own relationship with money. Modeling them is a natural way to advocate for others to adopt them, too.

Seek out Financial Solidarity

For the 5.9 million unbanked households in the United States, traditional financial resources are out of reach. These folks don't have access to or don't rely on formal financial institutions for financial needs like saving and borrowing. Americans are unbanked or underbanked for all kinds of reasons: insufficient documentation, language differences, barriers to trust, lack of representation in the institution, challenges with transportation, location of banks. These barriers leave underserved communities to rely on alternative ways to access the resources they need, innovations we could all learn from.

Lending circles are one example of an innovative financial resource—one that has deep historical roots around the world. Formally dubbed by researchers as Rotating Savings and Credit Associations (ROSCAs), lending circles are a group of people who make regular contributions to a fund that's given to each contributor in rotation.[3] This is a type of unofficial debt resource communities around the world have relied on for centuries.

"In financial education things tend to be taken for granted; everyone just assumes that these values or these ways to do things are the way to go," says Miguel Quiñones, a PhD student at the University of Minnesota whose research interests are situated at the intersection of culture and family financial socialization. "But our families, they don't really adhere to those certain values."

Miguel is a first-generation Mexican American, the son of parents who emigrated from Mexico to the Chicago area, where Miguel grew up in what he called "a bubble" of an immigrant community.

Lending circles, called *tandas* in many parts of Mexico and among Mexican immigrants in the United States, were commonplace for Miguel's family and community. He didn't recognize this and other informal financial practices as specific to his community until he left the bubble to attend college at the University of Illinois in Champaign and experienced a bit of culture shock.

"I realized that the way that I learned to do things and the way that I grew up to think about things regarding money and finance from my immigrant community were actually, from a purely financial and American individualist perspective, not ideal," he says.

Yet the community approach to finance Miguel learned growing up presents a model with great benefits that our capitalist approach to money doesn't recognize. Typical financial advice doesn't consider a *tanda* an "ideal" financial service, because your borrowing and repayment aren't reported to credit bureaus like they would be if you borrowed from a financial institution—even though *tandas* do support the development of savings habits and represent a history of reliable debt use and repayment. Looking outside of our ingrained systems toward ways to use money in solidarity with your community can help you see viable alternatives that are hard to imagine if you're just swimming in the waters of budget culture.

Support Access to Financial Education

You can do good by supporting access to financial education for everyone—even while we're still working to make the content of that education inclusive and budget-free.

"I approach financial education as if it were the social justice issue of our time because I believe it is," says Yanely Espinal, a director of educational outreach for Next Gen Personal Finance (NGPF), a nonprofit advocating for access to personal finance education. "Keeping in mind that I can't single-handedly tackle or solve major systemic issues trapping families in poverty, I know that I can channel my efforts into creating systemic change that'll positively affect not only your children's access to financial education and mine, but also their children and their children's children and so on—for generations to come."[4]

Through NGPF, Yanely champions state-level legislation that makes a semester of financial education a requirement for public high school graduation. The organization also provides lesson plans, materials, resources, professional development, and community to make sure educators have everything they need to teach personal finance. This kind of legislation is growing in popularity, and the requirement is passing in more and more states. But most of these mandates are unfunded, leaving teachers scrambling to put together a curriculum they aren't trained to teach.[5] Organizations like NGPF back up their advocacy by filling that gap with resources to help teachers provide financial education with confidence.

Find out whether your state requires financial education and whether your legislature has introduced a bill on the subject—many have. Write, email, and call your representatives to ask them to support—and fund!—access to financial education in your state. If there's no legislation on the table, you can instead contact the school board for your district to ask them to support financial education in the curriculum. If you've got the knowledge and time, you could even offer to teach personal finance yourself. Volunteer with organizations that serve kids and teens in your community or pitch a course to a local community college. At youdontneedabudget.com, you can find more resources like NGPF that'll help you lead conversations about money, even if you've never taught personal finance before.

Change Workplace Culture

You might or might not have a lot of influence over the decisions your company makes, so don't consider this a scolding if you're not able to immediately change the rules at your workplace. Instead, I'm including suggestions here to get you thinking about practices that can support a more equitable workplace, encourage workers to claim ownership and autonomy in work, and help everyone around you do good work.

You might be the main decision maker and be able to implement new policies straightaway. Or you might be an entry-level worker on your first day, just trying to figure out where the bathroom is or how to log in to a video call without disturbing too many people. Using your influence at work depends on what kind of influence you have to wield. As an executive, it might mean overhauling policies and hiring people who care about equity and change. As a newbie, it might mean simply asking questions when a boss or HR rep gives you space: How does this company support caretakers? What efforts do hiring managers make to reach diverse candidates? Why does the company use the compensation structure it uses?

Look for opportunities to support, implement, or bargain for some of these big or small policies in your workplace that improve your personal and collective relationships with money:

- Benefits like paid family leave, unlimited sick leave, paid vacation and personal days, work-from-home options, and flextime, which make work more accessible and inclusive for anyone who doesn't fit the white, male standard paid work has traditionally been designed for.
- Fair-chance hiring of folks who've been involved in the justice system.
- Unionization, coop ownership, and democratic decision-making.
- Camera-off virtual job interviews and meetings, which eliminate fatigue as well as stress about someone's appearance and the condition of their home or workspace.
- A stipend for anything required to do the job, including computers and phones, as well as wardrobe and home office supplies.
- Clearly defined start and end times for the workday, including official social activities like holiday parties.
- Ongoing comprehensive and plain-language education about finances related to work, including retirement plans, health care benefits, and payroll taxes.

- Ongoing professional development that includes transitioning employees into their next jobs, even if those are outside of the company.

Put Your Vote to Work

Many of the issues that impact your finances can't be addressed through individual actions or mindset changes. You can't end poverty through insightful conversations in your community (though you can absolutely start or contribute to a movement this way). Some of budget culture's biggest problems require coordinated, collective action—but your role in that action can be a simple, single step: use your vote.

The most powerful individual thing you can do to have a significant impact on your society is to vote. I'm sure this isn't the first time you've heard that, and it's worth repeating over and over again. Show up to vote, not only every four years for presidential elections but every year, sometimes multiple times in a year, for whatever's on the ballot: partisan primaries; US Senate and House representatives; state legislators, governors, and Supreme Court judges; mayors, city council members, and county board members; county clerks, sheriffs, and coroners; school board members; referenda, constitutional amendments, and local ordinances.

It's easy to feel like your vote doesn't make a difference, because government moves at a slow pace and politicians are bad at highlighting the long-term impacts of policies. But we had one incredible opportunity to see how a straightforward policy can have an enormous—and immediate—economic impact on millions of lives when Congress passed the American Rescue Plan Act (ARPA) in 2021 that included significant changes to the child tax credit for low- to moderate-income families.

For one year, ARPA increased the tax credit amount, added monthly payments to the existing annual one, and let families claim the credit even if they had no earnings. The plan played a role in the largest drop in child poverty on record in our country.[6] Data from the Census Bureau estimates the measure lifted 2.9 million American children out of poverty in 2021, disproportionately helping Black and Latine families. After the expanded credit expired at the end of the year, the child poverty rate more than doubled in 2022, returning to 2019 levels.[7]

"Giving people cash works," says Joanna Ain, associate director of policy at Prosperity Now, an advocacy organization focused on racial and economic justice.

In addition to advocating for a return of the expanded child tax credit, one of Prosperity Now's top priorities is a complementary policy called "baby bonds." A policy once proposed by Thomas Paine and championed in the modern era by the economist Derek Hamilton, baby bonds provide every kid when they're born with an investment account they can access when they turn eighteen. The government makes ongoing investments into the account, with higher amounts going to kids from the lowest-income families. Eighteen-year-olds can use the funds toward wealth-building activities, including homeownership, small business, retirement savings, or higher education. The American Opportunity Accounts Act that's been introduced several times in Congress would provide about $46,000 to the lowest-income kids when they turn eighteen.[8]

"This is really a game changing amount," says Ain.

In 2019, researcher Naomi Zewde estimated the difference a baby bond policy that had started in the mid-1990s could have made for young people today. In Zewde's simulation, the wealth gap between white and Black households would drop dramatically. If they'd gotten baby bonds starting at birth, the median net worth of a white person age eighteen to twenty-five would have been about 1.4 times that of a Black person the same age. The existence of that gap is problematic, but it pales in comparison to our reality. Brace yourself: in 2015, the actual ratio of white to Black net worth was 15.9 to one—an average white eighteen-to-twenty-five-year-old had nearly sixteen times the wealth of their Black counterpart.

Ain notes the phenomenal impact of simply giving cash to people in need through simple—and relatively low-cost[9]—policies like monthly income through the child tax credit and wealth-building resources through baby bond accounts. And she, like so many others, says the most important thing each of us can do to support this kind of change is to vote.

"People should be voting, and as they're voting, they should think about . . . the values of the person they're voting for and make sure they align to their own," says Ain. "Once folks are in office, as much as folks feel comfortable: advocating, making phone calls, writing letters, writing emails, and standing up for children and families and these policies that are so important for them."

And if you don't feel like your single vote can make a difference? "Then bring five of your friends when you vote," Ain says. "To make it bigger than you, bring your pals."

Beyond obvious welfare policies, consider the economic implications of other types of policies as you decide who and what to support or oppose. For example:

- US Supreme Court justices (nominated by the president and subject to approval by our elected senators) regularly decide on cases that affect federal agencies, which oversee everything from environmental regulations to labor rights to consumer protections. Historically, conservative presidents tend to nominate judges who go on to oppose regulations that protect the environment, consumers, and workers.
- Congress writes our tax code, which determines a lot about how we invest in this country—including rules for retirement accounts and tax breaks on investment income.
- State legislators tend to hold the power over your local workplace experience. They have a ton of leeway in creating antidiscrimination laws, minimum wages, and union requirements, for example.
- Local governments, including your county and city representatives and executives, and school boards, determine a lot of the funding that affects your everyday life—schools, police departments, parks, public services, and local business development.
- State-level policies allowing undocumented immigrants to get driver's licenses can make the difference between someone having access to a job or not.

- State-funded free school meals for all students not only address food insecurity but also reduce stigma for children living in poverty.

Keep an eye on your local paper or a national resource like Ballotpedia ahead of an election to see who and what will be on the ballot in your area. Check USA.gov, a website run by the US government, for information on how to register to vote in your state and where and how you can cast a vote (e.g., early voting, at the polls, or by mail).

Know the Role You Play

People fall into different roles in movements for change. You might get easily overwhelmed, lost, or burned out by the sheer magnitude of budget culture and every other way capitalism erodes our society. You might be propelled to frantic action by the crisis it represents in our world. Or you might appreciate clear marching orders so you know exactly which issues to focus on and how to make an impact.

Social change movement leader Deepa Iyer has created the Social Change Ecosystem Map to help different types of individuals and organizations engage effectively in social change efforts. The ecosystem concept suggests that we're more effective and more sustainable in our social change work when we build connections with others, and it lets us see beyond our titles toward how we can contribute to a movement.[10]

"I encourage you to ask: 'How can I bring my wisest self forward to collaborate with others in order to bring about systemic societal transformation?'" Iyer writes in her workbook *Social Change Now: A Guide for Reflection and Connection.*[11]

Iyer's Social Change Ecosystem Map includes a center circle listing shared values: equity, liberation, justice, and solidarity. Surrounding the center circle are ten ways people and organizations might show up in social change movements to support these values:

- **Frontline Responders:** Assembling and organizing resources, networks, and messages.
- **Visionaries:** Imagining the boldest possibilities.
- **Builders:** Developing and implementing ideas, practices, people, and resources.
- **Disrupters:** Taking risks to shake up the status quo, raise awareness, and build power.
- **Caregivers:** Nurturing people and community.
- **Experimenters:** Innovating and pioneering new ideas.
- **Weavers:** Seeing connections among people, places, organizations, ideas, and movements.
- **Storytellers:** Sharing community stories and experiences through art and media.
- **Healers:** Tending to traumas caused by systems of oppression.
- **Guides:** Teaching and advising others.

"Often, when we face a social crisis, we feel catalyzed and motivated to play as many roles as possible," Iyer writes. "However, this is not sustainable for the long run. . . . When we recognize that we are part of a larger and durable ecosystem, we can move forward with the confidence that others are playing their own roles effectively."

Where do you have influence and play influential roles in thinking, teaching, and talking about money? Use Iyer's map to understand your role in advocating for an inclusive, budget-free approach to money. If you're a builder, for example, you might start a lending circle among friends and family. If you're a caregiver, you might volunteer at your local food pantry. If you're a frontline responder, you might knock on doors to get out the vote for candidates who advocate for stronger workplace protections in your state. If you work for a "guide" organization, like a high school, you might help vet financial education resources to avoid reinforcing budget culture for your students.

Individual Lives Made Better

It might be intimidating to imagine incorporating any one of these ideas into your life. Seeing them all laid out here together is almost certainly overwhelming. It's important to remember as you take in all of this—the change in your own relationship with money, the new ways to talk about money, the changes you want to see in our culture—that no one can ever do everything. That's not at all what you're aiming for.

The disabled journalist and disability activist Lucy Webster writes about the exhaustion you can feel when you're part of a movement for change—and the reminder that helps her get through: "I try to remember that activism is a hike up [Mount] Everest, not an ascent of a gym climbing wall. That all progress is incremental, and almost never linear. That when we are tired, there's an army of people ready to take some of the strain. That success . . . lies in the individual lives made better, in the hands outstretched in solidarity."[12]

It's exhausting to learn, change, and work every day toward a better version of yourself and then look out at the world around you and see the same old problems persisting. But keep perspective and know that every step you take against budget culture in the ways you think, teach, or talk about money makes someone's life that much better—by moving us a bit deeper into this new kind of conversation about money.

Your Money Map

The following exercises are designed to help you apply what you've learned throughout this book to get a clear picture of your personal financial situation—to understand where your money comes from, where it's going, and what (if any) changes you want to make. Return to them anytime you need to learn more about your relationship with money.

The money map isn't a budget or spending plan. It's not a measure of whether you're doing "good enough" with money. Its purpose isn't to set a rule about whether you can spend money or how much. Forgive yourself if you feel drawn to using it this way, and recognize the internalized budget culture shaping that habit. Release the structures and expectations of budget culture, and use this tool as space to reflect on and more deeply understand the money in your life. With that space, you can make decisions that serve your whole head, heart, and health.

Grab a notebook to answer the questions below, or visit youdont needabudget.com for printable and fillable money map worksheets.

1. Recognize Your Resources

Start your financial inventory with what you have so you can recognize the resources around you.

- **Income:** How much do you earn each month? (Note: If your income is inconsistent from month to month, check your pay stubs or bank account for the amount deposited for each of the past six months, then divide by six for an average.)
- **Assets:** What do you own? No need to do a full inventory here; just think of a few high-ticket items you might own, like a home/property, vehicles, jewelry, or electronics.
- **Community support:** Where can you get help? List resources available in your community or from the government to cover specific needs, like SNAP, food banks, rental assistance, housing vouchers, shelters, childcare from family/neighbors, etc. If you know it, note the amount of the monthly cost covered.
- **Debt resources:** What can you borrow to extend your resources when you need to?

2. Name Your Commitments

List the amounts of your monthly commitments, including any regular payments you make toward life costs and debt payments. Next to each of these commitments, make a note of what happens if you don't pay. Some items that might be on your list:

Life costs	Debt payments
Mortgage/rent	Student loan
Cable/internet	Auto loan/lease

Electricity	Credit card or line of credit
Gas	Phone (lease)
Phone (service)	Other product lease/financing
Other utilities	
Health insurance	
Life insurance	
Home/renters insurance	
Auto insurance	
Other insurance	
Streaming services	
App subscriptions	
Software	
Household services	
Gym membership	
Therapy	
Medicine	

3. Name Your Goals

DEBT REPAYMENT GOALS

Get a handle on your full debt picture by listing all your outstanding debts here. Look back at the debt payment commitments you listed in step 2 to understand the consequences of missed payments and the impact holding or repaying a debt might have on your financial wellness. With that information, map out any goals you have for your debt.

For each debt you want to pay off, note the following:

- What type of debt is it (student loans, auto loans, credit card debt, product financing, etc.)?
- Who do you owe it to?
- What is the outstanding amount?
- What is your minimum monthly payment (from commitments, in step 2)?
- What (if any) extra payment do you want to make each month?
- At that payment rate, how long will it be before this debt goes away?

Note: If you're not sure how much you owe or which company you owe it to, use a free service to get an easy-to-read report. Find suggested apps at youdontneedabudget.com.

COMFORT FUND GOALS

List your comfort fund goals and plan for how you'll contribute to it. Start by noting the target you want to reach and any savings you already have. Then, figure out monthly(ish) contributions you want to make to hit your comfort fund target.

LONG-TERM SAVINGS GOALS

List your long-term savings goals, a plan for how you'll contribute to them, and what kind of account you'll hold the money in. You might note the target amount you want to reach, the monthly contribution that fits into your plan, your target year for retirement (or another time to start drawing money from the account), or all three. Add up your total monthly contributions to see how your savings plan fits into your overall money map.

BIG SPENDING FUNDS

List your current big spending funds, and for each, include:

- A purpose (how you'll use the money).
- A target date if it has one (it's okay if it doesn't!).
- A target amount if it has one (it's okay if it doesn't!).
- A plan for contributing to the fund (e.g., how often you want to set aside money and how much, or that you'll throw in extra when you get a tax refund or earn over a certain amount of tips in a shift at work). Add up your total monthly contributions to see how your big spending plans fit into your overall money map.

If you can't name a purpose for a savings fund, rethink your savings plan and notice where budget culture beliefs might be influencing you. Consider that you might be hoarding money out of fear or greed, or using savings as a justification for restricted spending. Try to give it a purpose and a plan here, or find a different way to use that money (like spending it or giving it away).

4. Set Up Your Yes Fund

Find your Yes Fund through the information you've gathered in your money map using this formula:

(Resources) minus (Commitments) minus (Goals) = Yes Fund estimate

There's no right number for your Yes Fund. On your first run-through, it might be bigger than you expected or smaller—it might even be negative. That's okay. Approach this with neutrality and without judgment. The number you find in your Yes Fund doesn't set a rule about whether you can spend money or give it away; it just helps you better understand the consequences of those money moves.

Acknowledgments

I wouldn't be thinking or writing about money right now if I hadn't faithfully followed my unwitting mentor into a job in personal finance media. Thank you to Alexis Grant for your guiding hand for so many writers, and for being so great to work with that I was willing to move across the country and dive into an industry I was sure I'd hate just to be your employee. Thank you for giving me the freedom and support I needed to learn and grow and claim expertise in this space.

The theory of budget culture wouldn't exist without the anti-diet journalists and educators who've given me the framework not only to heal from diet culture but also to name and begin divesting from the same cultural patterns in money. Virginia Sole-Smith, Aubrey Gordon, Michael Hobbes, Christy Harrison, Sonya Renee Taylor, Virgie Tovar—the message of this book and this movement was born in the moments I spent laughing and learning with your groundbreaking work.

To my agent, Justin Brouckaert and the team at Aevitas, for changing my life with an email. Thank you for helping to massage this theory into something I'm unbelievably proud to share. Another early champion, Marisa Vigilante, was the first person to call my ideas "anticapitalist," and I'll be forever grateful to her for helping me find my lane.

Talia Krohn, Karina Leon, Katherine Akey, Lauren Ortiz, Julianna Lee, Miranda Ottewell, Arik Hardin, and the whole team at Little, Brown Spark ushered this book into being with astonishing grace and efficiency. Thank you for your incredible respect for an idea that felt so vulnerable, and for knowing all the right levers to pull to make it the best it can be for every reader.

Heather van der Hoop and Jessica Lawlor edited the first pieces I ever wrote on budget culture. Their sharp questions and gentle challenges molded my vague concept into a conversation worth having—and, oh my goodness, do these editors make me a stronger writer!

Thank you to Anne Helen Petersen for being "obsessed" with budget culture and lending me your platform to validate the idea with your generous and gentle audience.

I owe the bulk of this book to the sources who make up its bones, for the generosity they've shown in sharing their stories through interviews, essays, podcast conversations, Q&As, books, and more. To interviewees whose stories didn't make it in, know the book carries the spirit of your experience and everything it taught me. The movement toward a budget-free society rests on the foundation set by countless thinkers and teachers before me, and I'm honored to build on their wisdom.

A warm shout-out to the crew on the "healthy remote" Slack, who were at my side through my journey into personal finance and personal development, who kept me sane working solo throughout the pandemic, and who stayed in my corner while I took on the absurd twin challenges of writing a book and buying a business.

My beta readers and author buddies—Marian, Carson, Jacque, Kathy, Wade, and Heather—have been so generous with their time and experiences. Their companionship and input kept me from feeling the loneliness so many authors talk about as inevitable.

To my partner, Stefan. Thank you for being there during the "sort of a freelance writer" years, for enduring Florida while I found my calling in personal finance, for letting me info-dump whenever I needed to process my theories out loud, and for sitting quietly with me whenever I needed to turn them over inside my head. Thank you for jumping on board with calling our savings a "comfort fund" before I even asked you to. Thank you for reading every *Healthy Rich* post even after I've told you all about it. Thank you for reading the first pages of *You Don't Need a Budget* and assuring me they were good—I needed that to get to the end.

Thank you to my mom for having the grit to build a life, against all odds, that gave me the luxury to think this deeply about the kind of life I want to build.

Finally, my deepest gratitude goes out to every *Healthy Rich* reader who has subscribed, read, commented on, shared, and paid for my work over the years. I continue to learn and be challenged, to search for answers to new questions, and to discover new perspectives on work and money with every new connection. This work could be just ideas in a void; you all make it a conversation, and with your help it will be a movement that changes the way people think and talk about money.

Notes

Introduction

1. Anne Helen Petersen, *Can't Even: How Millennials Became the Burnout Generation* (New York: HarperCollins, 2020).
2. Emily Badger, "Why the Poor Pay More for Toilet Paper—and Almost Everything Else," *Washington Post*, March 8, 2016, https://www.washingtonpost.com/news/wonk/wp/2016/03/08/why-the-poor-pay-more-for-toilet-paper-and-just-about-everything-else/. For the original study, see A. Yesim Orhun and Mike Palazzolo, "Frugality Is Hard to Afford," *Journal of Marketing Research* 56, no. 1: 1–17.
3. Office of the State Auditor, *Utah's General Financial Literacy Graduation Requirement: A Program Review*, October 5, 2018, https://reporting.auditor.utah.gov/servlet/servlet.FileDownload?file=015410000038ypZAAQ.
4. Yoosoon Chang et al., "A Trajectories-Based Approach to Measuring Intergenerational Mobility" (BFI Working Paper 2023-36, Becker Friedman Institute for Economics, University of Chicago, March 2023), https://bfi.uchicago.edu/wp-content/uploads/2023/03/BFI_WP_2023-36.pdf.
5. Helaine Olen, *Pound Foolish: Exposing the Dark Side of the Personal Finance Industry* (New York: Penguin, 2012), 51–53.
6. Audre Lorde, "There Is No Hierarchy of Oppressions," in *Homophobia and Education* (New York: Council on Interracial Books for Children, 1983).

Chapter 1

1. Dana Miranda, "A Friend in Our Group Said, 'This Feels Like a Cult,'" *Healthy Rich*, September 18, 2023, https://www.healthyrich.co/p/kel-schulze-dave-ramsey.
2. Michel Foucault, *Discipline and Punish: The Birth of the Prison* (New York: Vintage, 2012).
3. Gilles Deleuze, "Postscript on the Societies of Control," Anarchist Library, May 1990, https://theanarchistlibrary.org/library/gilles-deleuze-postscript-on-the-societies-of-control.

4. Tara McMullin, "Self-Control, Surveillance, and the Body at Work," *What Works,* July 20, 2023, https://www.whatworks.fyi/p/body-at-work-why-self-control-1 -rule-of-the-21st-century-economy.

5. Tema Okun, "White Supremacy Culture," https://www.whitesupremacyculture .info/uploads/4/3/5/7/43579015/okun_-_white_sup_culture.pdf.

6. Jacob S. Hacker, *The Great Risk Shift: The New Economic Insecurity and the Decline of the American Dream,* 2nd ed. (New York: Oxford University Press, 2019), xiv.

7. Hacker, *The Great Risk Shift,* xvi.

8. Kate Harding, "The Fantasy of Being Thin," *Kate Harding's Shapely Prose* (blog), November 27, 2007, https://web.archive.org/web/20071213040522 /https://kateharding.net/2007/11/27/the-fantasy-of-being-thin/.

9. Willis Towers Watson, "Despite Improvement in Their Financial Wellbeing, U.S. Workers Remain Worried," WTW, February 11, 2020, https://www.wtwco .com/en-us/news/2020/02/despite-improvement-in-their-financial-wellbeing -us-workers-remain-worried.

10. Amanda Montell, *Cultish: The Language of Fanaticism* (New York: Harper Wave, 2021), 12.

Chapter 2

1. *Merriam-Webster,* s.v. "budget," accessed March 30, 2024, https://www.merriam -webster.com/dictionary/budget.

2. Edward Shepard, "The Fascinating Meaning of 'Budget,'" Tiller, April 7, 2023, https://www.tillerhq.com/the-fascinating-meanings-hidden-in-the-word-budget/.

3. Whitney Pulteney and Robert Earl, *The Budget Opened; Or, an Answer to a Pamphlet Intitled a Letter from a Member of Parliament to His Friends in the Country Concerning the Duties on Wine and Tobacco* (Sacramento, CA: Hardpress, 2018), https://books.google.com/books/about/The_Budget_Opened_Or_an_Answer _to_a_Pamp.html?id=NksStwEACAAJ.

4. "Holidays in Paris," *New York Daily Herald,* January 15, 1874, https://www .newspapers.com/image/329391349/?terms=%22household%20budget%22 %20&match=1.

5. Mary B. Welch, *Mrs. Welch's Cook Book* (Des Moines: Mills, 1884), 51, https:// digitalcollections.lib.iastate.edu/islandora/object/isu%3ACookbooks_492.

6. Kate B. Vaughn, "Mrs. Vaughn Tells How to Be Saving to Give Talk on Cooking Economy," *Oakland (CA) Tribune,* February 9, 1915, https://www.newspapers .com/image/80737503/.

7. Helaine Olen, *Pound Foolish: Exposing the Dark Side of the Personal Finance Industry* (New York: Penguin, 2012), 14–15.

8. "Smart Girl Budgets Her Bonnets," *Boston Globe,* January 1, 1950, Newspapers .com, https://www.newspapers.com/image/433408422/?terms=budgeting&match =1 (subscription required).

9. Historical graph for search on "budgeting," start date 1901, end date 2000, Newspapers.com, https://www.newspapers.com/search/?country=us&date-end =2000&date-start=1900&keyword=budgeting (subscription required).

10. Olen, *Pound Foolish*, 20.

11. Sarah Foster, "Survey: More Than Half of Americans Couldn't Cover Three Months of Expenses with an Emergency Fund," Bankrate, July 20, 2021, https:// www.bankrate.com/banking/savings/emergency-savings-survey-july-2021/.

12. Mike Winters, "Americans Say They're on Track for Retirement—but Many Probably Aren't Saving Enough," *CNBC Make It,* December 9, 2021, https://www .cnbc.com/2021/12/09/americans-say-theyre-on-track-for-retirement.html.

13. Zack Friedman, "Student Loan Debt Statistics in 2022: A Record $1.7 Trillion," *Forbes*, May 16, 2022, https://www.forbes.com/sites/zackfriedman/2022/05/16 /student-loan-debt-statistics-in-2022-a-record-17-trillion/?sh=4b7d2cd94d5a.

14. "Infographic: Money, Inflation a Source of Stress for Many U.S. Adults," American Psychological Association, 2022, https://www.apa.org/news/press/releases /stress/2022/infographics/infographic-money-inflation.

15. For the relationship between financial stress and psychological stress, see Soomin Ryu and Lu Fan, "The Relationship between Financial Worries and Psychological Distress Among U.S. Adults," *Journal of Family and Economic Issues* 44, no. 1 (2023): 16–33, https://www.ncbi.nlm.nih.gov/pmc/articles/PMC8806009/; for financial stress and insomnia, see Jacqueline Warth et al., "Over-Indebtedness and Its Association with Sleep and Sleep Medication Use," *BMC Public Health* 19, no. 957 (2019), https://bmcpublichealth.biomedcentral.com/articles/10.1186/s12889 -019-7231-1; and for financial stress and coronary heart disease, see Kaitlyn E. Moran et al., "Financial Stress and Risk of Coronary Heart Disease in the Jackson Heart Study," *American Journal of Preventative Medicine* 56, no. 2 (February 2019), https://pubmed.ncbi.nlm.nih.gov/30661571/.

16. Carol Graham, "The High Costs of Being Poor in America: Stress, Pain, and Worry," Brookings Institution, February 19, 2015, https://www.brookings.edu /articles/the-high-costs-of-being-poor-in-america-stress-pain-and-worry/.

17. Christina Kan, Philip Fernbach, and John Lynch, "Personal Budgeting: Does It Work?," *NA—Advances in Consumer Research* 46 (2018): 298–302.

18. Dennis Jacobe, "One in Three Americans Prepare a Detailed Household Budget," *Gallop News,* June 3, 2013, https://news.gallup.com/poll/162872/one-three -americans-prepare-detailed-household-budget.aspx.

19. Google Trends, s.v. "how to budget," accessed March 26, 2024, https://trends .google.com/trends/explore?date=all&geo=US&q=how%20to%20budget.

20. Google Trends, s.v. "best budgeting apps," accessed March 26, 2024, https:// trends.google.com/trends/explore?date=all&geo=US&q=best%20budgeting %20app.

21. Financial Consumer Agency of Canada, "Sustained Behaviour Change through Financial Education: A Budgeting Longitudinal Study Using Mobile Technology," June 2019, https://www.canada.ca/en/financial-consumer-agency/programs/research/financial-education-budgeting-mobile-technology-follow-up-study.html.

22. Robert H. Shmerling, "When Dieting Doesn't Work," *Harvard Health Blog*, May 26, 2020, https://www.health.harvard.edu/blog/when-dieting-doesnt-work-2020052519889.

23. Christy Harrison, *Anti-Diet: Reclaim Your Time, Money, Well-Being, and Happiness Through Intuitive Eating* (Boston: Little, Brown Spark, 2019), 85–90.

24. Harrison, *Anti-Diet*, 97–98.

25. Carolyn Becker et al., "Food Insecurity and Eating Disorder Pathology," *International Journal of Eating Disorders* 50, no. 9 (September 2017): 1031–40.

26. Roberto A. Abreu-Mendoza et al., "The Contributions of Executive Functions to Mathematical Learning Difficulties and Mathematical Talent during Adolescence," *PLOS One* 13, no. 12 (2018), https://www.ncbi.nlm.nih.gov/pmc/articles/PMC6292664/.

27. Harrison, *Anti-Diet*, 197.

Chapter 3

1. Stephen Covey, A. Roger Merrill, and Rebecca R. Merrill, *First Things First* (New York: Simon & Schuster, 1995), 88.

2. American Psychological Association, "Stress in America 2022," October 2022, https://www.apa.org/news/press/releases/stress/2022/concerned-future-inflation.

3. Gemma Hartley, "Women Aren't Nags—We're Just Fed Up," *Harper's Bazaar*, September 27, 2017, https://www.harpersbazaar.com/culture/features/a12063822/emotional-labor-gender-equality/.

4. Richard Fry et al., "In a Growing Share of U.S. Marriages, Husbands and Wives Earn about the Same," Pew Research Center, April 13, 2023, https://www.pewresearch.org/social-trends/2023/04/13/in-a-growing-share-of-u-s-marriages-husbands-and-wives-earn-about-the-same/.

5. Claire Cain Miller, "How Same-Sex Couples Divide Chores, and What It Reveals About Modern Parenting," *New York Times*, May 16, 2018, https://www.nytimes.com/2018/05/16/upshot/same-sex-couples-divide-chores-much-more-evenly-until-they-become-parents.html.

6. Glennon Doyle and Amanda Doyle, "Overwhelm: Is Our Exhaustion a Sign That We're CareTicking Time Bombs?," episode 6, June 15, 2021, in *We Can Do Hard Things*, podcast, transcript at https://momastery.com/blog/episode-06/.

7. Laura Leavitt, "How Our Weekly Family Meeting Helps Us Tend to Our Time, Money, Relationship and Goals," *Healthy Rich*, October 17, 2022, https://www.healthyrich.co/p/planning-family-meetings.

Chapter 4

1. Mark Fisher, *Capitalist Realism: Is There No Alternative?* (Winchester, UK: Zero Books, 2010), 2.
2. "SNAP Participation Rates by State, All Eligible People (FY 2018)," USDA Food and Nutrition Service, https://www.fns.usda.gov/usamap.
3. Matthew Notowidigdo, "Low-Income Americans Are Missing Out on the Public Benefits They're Eligible For. Simple Interventions Can Help," *J-PAL* (blog), July 24, 2018, https://www.povertyactionlab.org/blog/7-24-18/low-income -americans-are-missing-out-public-benefits-theyre-eligible-simple.

Chapter 5

1. Leora Klapper, Annamaria Lusardi, and Peter van Oudheusden, *Financial Literacy around the World: Insights from the Standard & Poor's Ratings Services Global Financial Literacy Survey*, 2015, https://gflec.org/wp-content/uploads /2015/11/3313-Finlit_Report_FINAL-5.11.16.pdf.
2. "Weber, Calvinism and the Spirit of Modern Capitalism," Tutor2u, updated July 17, 2018, https://www.tutor2u.net/sociology/reference/sociology-weber- calvinism-and-spirit-of-modern-capitalism.
3. Charles Ward, "Protestant Work Ethic That Took Root in Faith Is Now Ingrained in Our Culture," *Houston Chronicle*, September 1, 2017, https://www.chron.com /life/houston-belief/article/Protestant-work-ethic-that-took-root-in-faith-is -1834963.php.
4. Tara McMullin, "All Parasites Have Value," *What Works*, April 5, 2023, https:// taramcmullin.substack.com/p/all-parasites-have-value.
5. Sonya Renee Taylor, "What If You Loved Your Body?," interview by Glennon Doyle, Amanda Doyle, and Abby Wambach, *We Can Do Hard Things* (podcast), episode168, transcript at https://momastery.com/blog/we-can-do-hard-things -ep-168/.
6. Martha Weinman Lear, "The Second Feminist Wave," *New York Times*, March 10, 1968, https://timesmachine.nytimes.com/timesmachine/1968/03 /10/90032407.html?zoom=15.07&pageNumber=323.
7. Jenny Blake, *Free Time: Lose the Busywork, Love Your Business* (London: Swift Press, 2022), 70.
8. Blake, *Free Time*, 69.
9. *American Time Use Survey — 2022 Results*, Bureau of Labor Statistics, June 22, 2023, https://www.bls.gov/news.release/pdf/atus.pdf.
10. Tricia Hersey, *Rest Is Resistance: A Manifesto* (Boston: Little, Brown, 2022), 3.
11. Hersey, *Rest Is Resistance,* 96.
12. Hersey, *Rest Is Resistance,* 60.
13. Simone Stolzoff, "Please Don't Call My Job a Calling," *New York Times,* June 5, 2023, https://www.nytimes.com/2023/06/05/opinion/employment-exploitation -unions.html.

14. Sarah Prager, "How Freelancing Let Me Stop Worrying Whether Jobs Would Accept Me as a Queer Woman," *Healthy Rich*, March 13, 2023, https://www.healthy rich.co/p/queer-freelancing.

15. Daniella Flores, "We Doubled Our Cost of Living to Move to a State That Respects LGBTQ+ Rights," *Healthy Rich*, August 2, 2022, https://www.healthyrich.co /p/lgbtq-friendly-move.

16. *I Like to Dabble*, https://iliketodabble.com/about/.

17. DisCo Ball Wiki, "DisCO Governance," accessed April 13, 2024, https://ball .disco.coop/DisCO_Governance.

18. "National Labor Relations Act," National Labor Relations Board, https://www .nlrb.gov/guidance/key-reference-materials/national-labor-relations-act.

19. Bureau of Labor Statistics, *Union Members—2023*, news release, January 23, 2024, https://www.bls.gov/news.release/pdf/union2.pdf.

20. Hamilton Nolan, "Everything We're Doing Is Not Enough," *How Things Work*, https://www.hamiltonnolan.com/p/everything-were-doing-is-not-enough.

Chapter 6

1. Chris Arnold, "Rents across U.S. Rise above $2,000 a Month for the First Time Ever," NPR, June 9, 2022, https://www.npr.org/2022/06/09/1103919413/rents -across-u-s-rise-above-2-000-a-month-for-the-first-time-ever.

Chapter 7

1. Dana Miranda, "My Student Loan Balance Has Ballooned by Over $30,000 since College, but I'll Never Be Shamed into Refinancing," *Business Insider*, June 9, 2022, https://www.businessinsider.com/personal-finance/never-refinancing -student-loan-debt-shamed-2023-1.

2. Anchor Down VU (@furtweng), "Debt is not a shameful moral failing, but not fulfilling the obligation made when signing is," Twitter, January 26, 2023, 8:48 p.m., https://twitter.com/furtweng/status/1618712507463634945.

3. Carson Kohler, "From Dave Ramsey to Modern Frugality with Jen Smith," *Healthy Rich*, August 29, 2022, https://www.healthyrich.co/p/dave-ramsey-modern -frugality#details.

4. *The Complex Story of American Debt: Liabilities in Family Balance Sheets,* a report from the Pew Charitable Trusts, July 2015, https://www.pewtrusts.org/~/media /assets/2015/07/reach-of-debt-report_artfinal.pdf.

5. Sharada Dharmasankar and Bhash Mazumder, "Have Borrowers Recovered from Foreclosures during the Great Recession?," *Chicago Fed Letter*, no. 370 (2016), https://www.chicagofed.org/publications/chicago-fed-letter/2016/370#ftn1.

6. "Fact Sheet: President Biden Announces Student Loan Relief for Borrowers Who Need It Most," statement, White House Briefing Room, August 24, 2022, https://www.whitehouse.gov/briefing-room/statements-releases/2022/08/24/fact

-sheet-president-biden-announces-student-loan-relief-for-borrowers-who-need-it
-most/.

7. Cory Turner and Sequoia Carrillo, "Americans Support Student Loan Forgiveness, but Would Rather Rein In College Costs," *Morning Edition*, NPR,
June 17, 2022, https://www.npr.org/2022/06/17/1104920545/poll-student-loan
-forgiveness.

8. Erica Sandberg, Barri Segal, and Claire Dickey, "Poll: 60% Who Have Credit
Card Debt Have Owed Their Creditors for at Least 12 Months," Creditcards
.com, September 19, 2022, https://www.creditcards.com/statistics/credit-card
-debt-poll/.

9. Shameek Rakshit et al., "The Burden of Medical Debt in the United States,"
Health System Tracker, February 12, 2024, https://www.healthsystemtracker.org
/brief/the-burden-of-medical-debt-in-the-united-states/.

10. Board of the Governors of the Federal Reserve System, "Consumer Credit—
G19," March 7, 2024, https://www.federalreserve.gov/releases/g19/current/.

11. "What Is an Unfair, Deceptive or Abusive Practice by a Debt Collector?,"
Consumer Financial Protection Bureau, last revised August 2, 2023, https://
www.consumerfinance.gov/ask-cfpb/what-is-an-unfair-practice-by-a-debt
-collector-en-1401/.

12. Dana Miranda, "How to Be a Better Ally to the People the Personal Finance
Industry Ignores," *Healthy Rich*, September 12, 2022, https://www.healthyrich
.co/p/money-conversation-panel-recap.

13. Hacker, *The Great Risk Shift*, 3.

14. "Bankruptcy," US Courts, https://www.uscourts.gov/services-forms/bankruptcy.

15. Zack Friedman, "Can You Discharge Your Student Loans in Bankruptcy?," *Forbes*,
January 9, 2019, https://www.forbes.com/sites/zackfriedman/2019/01/09/student
-loans-bankruptcy-discharge/?sh=4f5620d66d56.

16. "What's in My FICO® Scores?," MiFico, https://www.myfico.com/credit-education
/whats-in-your-credit-score.

Chapter 8

1. Ramat Oyetunji, *One Year after F.I.R.E.: Stories and Lessons Learned from a
Whirlwind Year Filled with Self-Discovery* (Tinu, 2022), 23.

2. Jessica, "Coast FI vs. Slow FI: What's the Difference?," *The Fioneers* (blog), May
9, 2022, https://thefioneers.com/coast-fi-vs-slow-fi/.

3. Judy L. Postmus et al., "Understanding Economic Abuse in the Lives of Survivors," *Journal of Interpersonal Violence* 27, no. 3 (2012): 411–30, https://journals
.sagepub.com/doi/abs/10.1177/0886260511421669.

4. Dana Miranda, "12 Steps to Protect Your Finances When Leaving an Abusive Relationship," *Penny Hoarder*, 2016, https://www.thepennyhoarder.com
/save-money/leaving-an-abusive-relationship/.

5. Anastasia McRae, comment, January 23, 2023, *Healthy Rich*, https://www
.healthyrich.co/p/easy-money-save/comment/12144302.

Chapter 9

1. Kim Parker and Richard Fry, "More Than Half of U.S. Households Have
   Some Investment in the Stock Market," Pew Research Center, March 25, 2020,
   https://www.pewresearch.org/short-reads/2020/03/25/more-than-half-of-u-s
   -households-have-some-investment-in-the-stock-market/.
2. Board of the Governors of the Federal Reserve System, "Distribution of Household
   Wealth in the U.S. since 1989," https://www.federalreserve.gov/releases/z1
   /dataviz/dfa/distribute/chart/.
3. Alexis Grant, Laura Boach, and Jessica Sager, "How a 7-Hour Workweek Led
   to Anna Maste's 7-Figure Sale," *They Got Acquired*, April 25, 2002, https://they
   gotacquired.com/podcast/anna-maste-boondockers-welcome/.
4. "If Index Funds Perform Better, Why Are Actively Managed Funds More Popular?," *Knowledge at Wharton*, February 2, 2011, https://knowledge.wharton
   .upenn.edu/article/if-index-funds-perform-better-why-are-actively-managed
   -funds-more-popular/.
5. Karsten Walker, presentation for the Financial Education Innovation & Impact
   Summit, 2022.

Chapter 10

1. Penny, "Why I'm Fine with Failing a No Spend Month," *She Picks Up Pennies*,
   January 27, 2023, https://shepicksuppennies.com/why-im-fine-with-failing-a
   -no-spend-month/.
2. Karl Marx, *Economic and Philosophic Manuscripts of 1844*, translated by Mark
   Milligan (Moscow: Progress, 1959), https://www.marxists.org/archive/marx
   /works/1844/manuscripts/preface.htm.
3. Susan Biali Haas, *The Resilient Life: Manage Stress, Prevent Burnout, and Strengthen
   Your Mental and Physical Health* (New York: Beaufort Books, 2022), 191.
4. Dana Miranda, "Running a Business While Menstruating," *Healthy Rich*, July
   22, 2022, https://www.healthyrich.co/p/business-menstruating.
5. Stephanie C. Lazzaro et al., "The Impact of Menstrual Cycle Phase on Economic
   Choice and Rationality," *PLoS One* 11, no. 1 (2016), https://www.ncbi.nlm
   .nih.gov/pmc/articles/PMC4732761/.
6. Karen J. Pine and Ben C. Fletcher, "Women's Spending Behaviour Is Menstrual-
   Cycle Sensitive," *Personality and Individual Differences*, 50, no. 1 (January 2011):
   74–78, https://www.sciencedirect.com/science/article/abs/pii/S0191886910004289.
7. Alex Kasprak, "Did You Know That Men Also Have Hormonal Cycles?," *Buzz-
   Feed News*, June 26, 2015, https://www.buzzfeednews.com/article/alexkasprak
   /that-time-of-the-day-bro.

8. Dana Miranda, "What Does Your Body Have to Tell You about Money?," *Healthy Rich*, September 26, 2023, https://www.healthyrich.co/p/somatics-of-money.

9. Tricia Hersey, *Rest Is Resistance: Free Yourself from Grind Culture and Reclaim Your Life* (London: Octopus, 2022), 97.

10. Kiana Blaylock, "Money and Prayer: How Prayer Became a Financial Habit," *Healthy Rich*, August 15, 2022, https://www.healthyrich.co/p/money-and-prayer.

Chapter 11

1. "Unemployment Rises in 2020, as the Country Battles the COVID-19 Pandemic," *Monthly Labor Review*, June 2021, https://www.bls.gov/opub/mlr/2021/article/unemployment-rises-in-2020-as-the-country-battles-the-covid-19-pandemic.htm.

2. "Most Stimulus Payments Were Saved or Applied to Debt," *Digest* (National Bureau of American Health), October 1, 2020, https://www.nber.org/digest/oct20/most-stimulus-payments-were-saved-or-applied-debt.

3. Shankar Vedantam, "If It Feels Good to Be Good, It Might Be Only Natural," *Washington Post*, May 28, 2007, https://www.washingtonpost.com/wp-dyn/content/article/2007/05/27/AR2007052701056.html.

4. Gareth Cook, "Why We Are Wired to Connect," *Scientific American*, October 22, 2013, https://www.scientificamerican.com/article/why-we-are-wired-to-connect/.

5. Anne Helen Petersen, "Paying for Civilization," *Culture Study*, November 17, 2019, https://annehelen.substack.com/p/paying-for-civilization.

Chapter 12

1. Trevor Noah, *Born a Crime: Stories From a South African Childhood* (New York: One World, 2016), 188.

2. *Postsecondary Attainment: Differences by Socioeconomic Status*, National Center for Education Statistics, 2012, https://nces.ed.gov/programs/coe/pdf/coe_tva.pdf.

3. Hadassah Damien, "Financial Freedom > Financial Independence," *Ride Free Fearless Money* (blog), https://www.ridefreefearlessmoney.com/blog/2023/01/financial-freedom-financial-independence/.

4. L. V. Anderson, "I Stopped Dieting and Started Budgeting," *Slate*, June 30, 2016, https://slate.com/human-interest/2016/06/dieting-and-budgeting-does-not-work-how-the-need-to-control-food-and-money-is-unhealthy.html.

5. Jon Carlson and Matt Englar-Carlson, *Adlerian Psychotherapy* (Washington, DC: American Psychological Association, 2017).

Chapter 13

1. "Familiar (Mis)Quotations," *Inside Higher Ed*, April 7, 2011, https://www.insidehighered.com/views/2011/04/08/familiar-misquotations.

2. Jack Sauter, "How to Tell Your Grandmother You Are a Socialist," *Barn Raiser*, December 24, 2022, https://barnraisingmedia.com/how-to-tell-your-grand mother-you-are-a-socialist/.

3. Antonieta Castro-Cosío, "'Informal' Financial Practices in the South Bronx: Family, *Compadres*, and Acquaintances," *Journal of Family and Economic Issues*, June 19, 2023, https://doi.org/10.1007/s10834-023-09912-0.

4. Yanely Espinal, "I Approach Financial Education as the Social Justice Issue of Our Time," interview by Dana Miranda, *Healthy Rich*, July 4, 2023, https://www .healthyrich.co/p/yanely-espinal.

5. Dana Miranda, "As a Personal Finance Writer, I Have Mixed Feelings about Financial Literacy," *Business Insider*, April 2023, updated February 1, 2024, https://www.businessinsider.com/personal-finance/personal-finance-writer -mixed-feelings-financial-literacy-2023-4.

6. Priya Pandey et al., *Historic 2021 Decline in Child Poverty Proves Effectiveness of Federal Investments*, CLASP, September 2022, https://www.clasp.org/wp-content /uploads/2022/09/2022.9.14_Historic-2021-Decline-in-Child-Poverty -Proves-Effectiveness-of-Federal-Investments.pdf.

7. Emily A. Shrider and John Creamer, *Poverty in the United States: 2022*, US Department of Commerce report no. P60-280, September 12, 2023, https:// www.census.gov/library/publications/2023/demo/p60-280.html.

8. "Booker, Pressley Reintroduce Bicameral 'Baby Bonds' Legislation to Tackle Wealth Inequality," Cory Booker (official website), February 15, 2023, https:// www.booker.senate.gov/news/press/booker-pressley-reintroduce-bicameral -baby-bonds-legislation-to-tackle-wealth-inequality.

9. Annie Lowrey, "A Cheap, Race-Neutral Way to Close the Racial Wealth Gap," *Atlantic*, June 29, 2020, https://www.theatlantic.com/ideas/archive/2020/06 /close-racial-wealth-gap-baby-bonds/613525/.

10. "Social Change Ecosystem Map," Building Movement Project, https://building movement.org/our-work/movement-building/social-change-ecosystem-map/.

11. Deepa Iyer, *Social Change Now: A Guide for Reflection and Connection* (Washing-ton, DC: Thick Press, 2022), 12.

12. Lucy Webster, "Exhausted," *The View from Down Here* (blog), September 28, 2023, https://lucywebster.substack.com/p/exhausted.

Index

Index

Index

About the Author

Dana Miranda is a Certified Educator in Personal Finance (CEPF) and a personal finance journalist. After leaving a leadership position with a popular financial media start-up and spending two years as a freelance writer, she created *Healthy Rich*, a newsletter about how capitalism impacts the ways we think, teach, and talk about money.

Dana has shared her expertise as a contributor to *Forbes*, *Business Insider*, the *New York Times*, CNBC, NextAdvisor, *Culture Study*, The Motley Fool, *Money* magazine, The Penny Hoarder, and *Inc.* magazine. *Healthy Rich* has been featured in publications including *Bankrate*, *Real Simple*, and *Forbes*, where it was named a safe resource for LGBTQ+ financial education in 2022.

She lives in central Wisconsin with her partner.